CHRISTOPHER ABBOTT g
Ph.D. from the University of
Manchester.

Studies in Medieval Mysticism

Volume 2

JULIAN OF NORWICH
AUTOBIOGRAPHY AND THEOLOGY

Studies in Medieval Mysticism

ISSN 1465–5683

GENERAL EDITORS
Anne Clark Bartlett
Rosalynn Voaden

Volume 1: St Birgitta of Sweden
Bridget Morris

Studies in Medieval Mysticism offers a forum for works exploring the textures and traditions of western European mystical and visionary literature, from late Antiquity to the Reformation, including both well- and lesser-known mystics and their texts. The series particularly welcomes publications which combine textual and manuscript study with current critical theories, to offer innovative approaches to medieval mystical literature.

Proposals or queries may be sent directly to the editors or publisher at the addresses given below; all submissions will receive prompt and informed consideration.

Professor Anne Clark Bartlett, Department of English, DePaul University, 802 West Belden Avenue, Chicago, IL 60614, USA

Professor Rosalynn Voaden, Department of English, Arizona State University, PO Box 870302, Tempe, AZ 85287, USA

Caroline Palmer, Boydell & Brewer Limited, PO Box 9, Woodbridge, Suffolk, IP12 3DF, UK

JULIAN OF NORWICH
AUTOBIOGRAPHY AND THEOLOGY

Christopher Abbott

D. S. BREWER

First published 1999
D. S. Brewer, Cambridge

ISBN 0 85991 548 4

D. S. Brewer is an imprint of Boydell & Brewer Ltd
PO Box 9, Woodbridge, Suffolk IP12 3DF, UK
and of Boydell & Brewer Inc.
PO Box 41026, Rochester, NY 14604–4126, USA
website: http://www.boydell.co.uk

A catalogue record for this book is available
from the British Library

Library of Congress Cataloging-in-Publication Data
Abbott, Christopher, 1966–
    Julian of Norwich: autobiography and theology / Christopher
Abbott.
        p.   cm. – (Studies in medieval mysticism; v. 2)
    Includes bibliographical references and index.
    ISBN 0–85991–548–4 (alk. paper)
    1. Julian, of Norwich, b. 1343. Revelations of divine love.
I. Title. II. Series.
BV4832.2.J853A23   1999
248.2′2′092–dc21
[B]   98–56168

This publication is printed on acid-free paper

Printed in Great Britain by
St Edmundsbury Press Ltd, Bury St Edmunds, Suffolk

CONTENTS

CONTENTS

TO MY PARENTS

ACKNOWLEDGEMENTS

This book has its origins in a doctoral thesis submitted to the University of Manchester. I am hugely indebted to my former supervisor, Dr John Anderson, for his generous and constructive response to my efforts; and for his availability, encouragement and good-humoured, tactful support since I began work on Julian of Norwich in October 1991. I must also thank very warmly my doctoral examiners, Professor S. S. Hussey and Dr W. Collier, for their mercy.

The English Benedictine Congregation, both monks and nuns, have had a crucial role for hundreds of years in the preservation and transmission of Julian's legacy. I wish to thank the Abbess of Stanbrook Abbey, Worcester, and more particularly the Librarian, Dame Gertrude Brown, for allowing me, over a paradisal few days in June 1994, to consult at leisure their cherished copy of Serenus Cressy's 1670 edition of Julian's Long Text. Still with the EBC, in 1996–7 *The Downside Review*, under the editorship of Dom Daniel Rees, published the substance of Chapter 2 in the form of two articles (see Bibliography). I appreciate very much their interest and encouragement.

Without the self-effacing professionalism of good librarians the would-be scholar would remain precisely that. I record my thanks to staff at the Bibliothèque Nationale, Paris; the Bodleian Library, Oxford; the British Library, London; and the John Rylands University Library of Manchester.

I am also immensely grateful to the following for help of various kinds: in Cambridge, Ms Sylvia Adamson, Professor Sir Henry Chadwick and Ms Anne Henry; in Durham, Dr Peter Phillips; in London, Mr Jonathan Pacey and Mr John Coughlin; in Manchester, Mrs Joanne Millington, Mr and Mrs S. Ollieuz, Mr Barney Quinn and Ms Clare Suthers; at Mount St Bernard Abbey, Dom John Moakler, Fr Justin Barr and Fr Rufus Pound; in New York, Mr Martin Rowe; and in Oxford, Dr Vincent Gillespie and Dr Robert Smith.

Great and special thanks must go to my long-suffering family: to my parents, Terence and Lillian Abbott, who saw the worst moments; to my brothers and sisters, especially Joan (for all kinds of things) and John (for help with the computer); and finally, to 'the beloved Auntie Peggy' whose particular generosity got me off the starting-block.

Finally, a particular word of thanks to Caroline Palmer and Pru Harrison of Boydell & Brewer for their ready support and guidance.

ABBREVIATIONS

Manuscripts

A	MS British Library Additional 33790 [Short text]
P	MS Bibliothèque Nationale Fonds anglais 40 [Long Text]
S1	MS British Library Sloane 2499 [Long Text]
S2	MS British Library Sloane 3705
SS	S1 and S2 in substantial agreement.

Other Abbreviations

CW	*A Book of Showings to the Anchoress Julian of Norwich*, ed. Edmund Colledge and James Walsh, 2 volumes (Toronto, 1978)
EETS, o.s.	Early English Text Society, original series
G	Julian of Norwich, *A Revelation of Love*, ed. Marion Glasscoe, revised edition (Exeter, 1993)
LT	The Long Text of Julian's *Revelation*
MMTE	*The Medieval Mystical Tradition in England*, ed. Marion Glasscoe (Exeter, 1980 and 1982; and Cambridge, 1992)
RSV	The Revised Standard Version of the Bible
ST	The Short Text of Julian's *Revelation*

PREFACE

Most full-length studies of Julian of Norwich produced during the past twenty or thirty years have started by providing the reader with basic information about Julian and her writing, and perhaps broader information about her social and historical context. These days such an introduction no longer seems necessary, at least within the field of Middle English religious and literary studies, and even beyond it, since Julian has achieved unusual fame among medieval writers. Unlike most of her contemporaries she is now to be found – in some form or other – on the shelves of general bookshops and even of quite small local libraries. On a recent visit to a fairly large bookshop in a fairly large English city I located three copies of Clifton Wolters' Penguin Classics translation of Julian, but no Chaucer. An anomalous situation, I suppose, but perhaps it does point to something. In its own way, Julian's *Revelation* has taken off.

And yet, alas, it is not so simple. My reference to 'Julian's *Revelation*' demands immediate qualification. While umpteen versions of Julian's Long Text are available – editions in (more or less) Middle English, and also the many modernized versions which have been appearing since the mid-nineteenth century – the primary sources on which all of these versions ultimately depend are few, late and dialectally at odds. Accounts of the manuscript problems associated with Julian are given in numerous editions and studies, and need not be rehearsed pedantically here;[1] but there is something that does need saying in this regard. The combination of the lateness and paucity of the manuscript evidence, and of the startling differences between the few recensions we have (notably between P and S1 – see 'Abbreviations'), means that all critical judgements about what Julian actually *wrote*, and therefore about what she *meant*, are inevitably provisional in character. However, my general feeling is that the Julian scholar does have enough to go on, despite the obvious problems; that although we might be very far from establishing a single, true and authoritative version of the Long Text, the major extant manuscripts are in sufficient agreement with one another to provide a

---

[1] Accounts of the manuscripts, and of the associated problems, can be found in the introductions to the Middle English editions: CW pp. 1–33; G pp. vii–xxi; and also in Georgina Ronan Crampton's more recent edition of LT, *The Shewings of Julian of Norwich* (Kalamazoo, Michigan, 1993), especially pp. 19–23. See also Alexandra Barratt, 'How many children had Julian of Norwich? Editions, translations and versions of her revelations', in *Vox Mystica: Essays for Valerie M. Lagorio*, ed. A. C. Bartlett et al. (Cambridge, 1995), pp. 27–39.

credible basis for academic discussion. So I decide to see the glass as half full rather than half empty: by which I mean to imply a certain optimism, but also an awareness of the perils of this venture and an openness to correction. In a very timely article, Alexandra Barratt is quite rightly (and very wittily) scathing about the tendency of writers on Julian, and editors/modernizers of Julian, precisely to repress any real sense of both the poverty and the ambiguity of the manuscript evidence; a repression which frees them to invent a Julian suspiciously after their own likeness.[2] When I first read Barratt's article I laughed with recognition, but also trembled for my own work. Have I committed the very sins against Julian which Barratt identifies? I hope not, but the reader will have to decide.

My book focuses on the Long Text rather than the Short Text. I entirely accept that ST is well worthy of discussion in its own right; and I also share Nicholas Watson's view that ST was probably not, as has often been assumed, scribbled down the minute Julian had got her breath back after the visions.[3] It is not a collection of naïve jottings, but a substantial, sophisticated and significant piece of writing, and highly coherent. What is more, it exists in a unique fifteenth century manuscript, which might have made life simpler. But the LT is such a peculiar and astonishing work: in its thematic range and ambition, in its organization and coherence, in its intellectual and linguistic precision, in its variety of tone, in its emotional depth; and above all in the implicit claim it makes for the religious authority of its non-clerical, female author. So I focus on LT as Julian's 'last word', though without entirely neglecting ST which I take to be a *fairly* early draft of the last version. Unless otherwise stated, all my references are to LT (which I habitually refer to as 'the text').

Many writers on Julian, even at quite an academic level, opt to cite her work in modernized form. Given Julian's wide and cross-disciplinary appeal this is perfectly understandable; but also, of course, intrinsically unsatisfactory. As a policy, it effectively precludes discussion about Julian's distinctive linguistic achievement, but more importantly about the way language itself might be regarded as a constituent of meaning in Julian's case. This is particularly serious because Julian's writing, lexically and syntactically, is highly-wrought, highly coherent, but also quite strange and peculiar. Its linguistic qualities, including also its poetical compression and self-allusiveness, are not easily replicated in modern English. In translations, much that is of the essence is simply lost; and this not only semantically (which is regrettable enough), but in terms of

---

[2] Barratt, 'How many children had Julian of Norwich?' See n. 1, above.

[3] See Nicholas Watson, 'The Composition of Julian of Norwich's *Revelation of Love'*, *Speculum*, 68 (1993), pp. 637–683. Note especially Sections 2 and 3 of this article.

textual architecture, of light and space, of internal acoustic resonance. And yet, such loss seems unnecessary. With time and space, and with resort to the glossaries available in all of the Middle English editions, any educated English-speaking reader will be able to manage Julian's own language (to the extent that we have that), and it is worth the effort. Furthermore, her text itself, if attended to with sufficient diligence, can educate readers in its own language since most of the key terms accumulate peculiar resonances as the work proceeds. For all these reasons, Julian is quoted in Middle English throughout this book.

I do not wish, however, to denigrate those modernized versions of Julian which are currently in use. My own interest in Julian was ignited by one of them, and I have kept two or three versions on hand throughout my work on this book. Clearly not everyone does have the leisure to grapple with Middle English, and especially with the Middle English of a text which, despite its fame somewhat to the contrary, is by no means an easy read in respect of its subject-matter. Julian does not, after all, 'belong' to scholars.

Note on Texts

Unless otherwise stated, all quotations of the Long Text [LT] of Julian's *Revelation* are cited from ed. Marion Glasscoe, *A Revelation of Love*, revised edition (Exeter, 1993) [G]. This edition is based on British Library MS Sloane 2499 [S1]. I agree broadly with Glasscoe's view that the language of S1 'is much closer to fourteenth-century English than that of P' (for P, see below). All references to G are given thus: chapter number/page number.

For LT I have also drawn frequently on the version based on MS Bibliothèque Nationale Fonds anglais 40 [P, for Paris] in ed. Edmund Colledge and James Walsh, *A Book of Showings to the Anchoress Julian of Norwich*, 2 volumes (Toronto, 1978) [CW] – the P manuscript of LT remains an indispensable corrective and supplement to S1, and really rather more than that. I have also used CW's version of the Short Text [ST] edited from MS British Library Additional 33790 [A]. References to CW, whether ST or LT, are given thus: CW page number/line number.

Textual references are not normally repeated consecutively within the same paragraph, though I have occasionally broken this rule in paragraphs of unusual length. Where a quotation is given without a textual reference, please see the reference immediately prior.

Textual Interpolations

Some of my quotations from G contain textual interpolations either from CW, or from P as given in the notes to G, pp. 138–43. To identify such interpolations, qualified square brackets are used thus:

[CW: . . .] – denotes interpolation from corresponding point in CW;
[P: . . .] – denotes interpolation from P as given in the notes to G;
[G: . . .] – denotes editorial square brackets as given in the text of G.

Brackets (square or otherwise) enclosing parts of words are proper to the edition being cited.

1

Julian of Norwich and Autobiography

A Voice

IT SEEMS LIKELY that, as a writer, Julian of Norwich did not have much of a following in her own lifetime. The sad lack of early manuscripts suggests as much. That she had some kind of local fame as a wise spiritual counsellor is clear from the documented visit of Margery Kempe, but this seems to be the unique evidence for such fame.[1] In any case, *The Book of Margery Kempe* makes no reference to Julian's writing, and the absence of such comment is telling given Margery's evident interest in availing herself of whatever pious literature was around in East Anglia at the time, and also in setting down her own religious experiences. It suggests she was quite ignorant of Julian's status as a fellow medieval woman religious writer.

It is obviously impossible to say with certainty why Julian's work did not take off quite the way, for example, that Walter Hilton's writings did, or the works of the *Cloud*-author. Clearly someone like Hilton was helped by his clerical status, and the broadly traditional and schematic nature of his writing. Such work from such a figure would have had a ready and appreciative audience, well-versed in scripture and in the vigorous contemplative spirituality of the age. Julian, on the other hand, might well have had cause to feel cagey about her own writing, which is much more speculative and idiosyncratic; and is also, needless to say, the work of a woman and a non-cleric. Or perhaps her spiritual mentor was cagey about it and advised against its circulation. There may have been concerns about its theological content, or about how Julian herself might suffer on account of it. But whatever the unattainable answers to these questions, Julian's writing must initially, and indeed for many subsequent years, have had a quite limited circulation. The process of preservation and transmission must have been precarious, and there is almost a *samizdat* feel to those versions of the Long Text which finally pop up in the seventeenth and eighteenth centuries, apparently copied out by

[1] *The Book of Margery Kempe*, ed. Sanford Brown Meech with prefatory note by Hope Emily Allen, EETS, o.s., 212 (London, 1940), pp. 42–3.

recusant English Benedictine nuns in their French exile. Although a fifteenth century version of the Short Text does exist, the backward trail for an early and reliable version of the Long Text disappears into the forest at around 1650.

Like the so-far unfound early manuscripts of her writings, Julian herself has a certain 'disappeared' quality. We do not know where she originally came from, and the dialectal characteristics of the manuscripts of both Long Text and Short Text are little help, since they quite possibly employ the preferred and native dialectal forms of the early copyists rather than Julian's own. Apart from what she herself tells us, and even that little is more implied than stated, we know nothing of her early life, her family, her upbringing, her social status, and nothing specific about what it was that landed her finally in an anchoress's cell. Neither do we have any firm death date, the evidence from Norwich wills being inconclusive.[2] Those who speculate, on the basis of her motherhood-of-God theme, that Julian may have borne children are on pretty shaky ground.[3] Most human beings have some idea of what a mother is, and we ought to bear in mind that Julian's description of God's motherliness is written, as it were, from the *child's* side.

Yet, despite this chronic lack of detail about Julian's life, few medieval personalities have been adopted quite so enthusiastically by such a variety of interest-groups. Few other such figures have found themselves gathered to so many twentieth century bosoms with such apparent personal affection. It is as though, far from being a more or less unknown quantity, Julian's own person is so transparent, so available, even more than half a millenium after her death, that anybody might claim her and freely presume on her. Perhaps the very scarcity of reliable biographical data makes Julian all the more susceptible to such treatment. Agendas of one kind or another now seem wound around her absence like so many winding-cloths around the phantom mummy, so that one may justifiably speak of a Julian myth; or better, of various mythic Julians. There is Julian the Anglican saint, Julian the feminist, Julian the eco-theologian, Julian the New Age 'oceanic' mystic, Julian the proto-liberal Christian ('no wrath in God' and all that). There are Julian-groups, in the United States and elsewhere, and there is a religious order named for her. She has even entered the soundbite age: few medieval religious writers are quoted as widely and as often, and as briefly.

Of course it ill behoves a writer introducing yet another book on Julian

---

[2] See introduction to CW, pp. 33–5 where the editors quite clearly fail to establish a secure identification of Julian of Norwich as beneficiary of a number of early fifteenth century wills.

[3] For just one example, see Sr Benedicta, 'Julian the Solitary', in Kenneth Leech and Sr Benedicta, *Julian Reconsidered* (Fairacres, Oxford, 1988), esp. pp. 24–5.

to insult others who have made some kind of running out of her, whatever their style. Bandwagons, after all, are for jumping on. The important question here is not so much about what degree of truth there might be said to be in the various mythic Julians, or in the relative merits of the interpretations made of her life and work, but of why she exerts such a fascination. Why is it that so many who have encountered Julian's work, in any of the available forms, have seemed to feel the magnetism of a distinct personality, a substantial and sympathetic personality which they have variously sought to claim as their own, to emulate, or otherwise to engage? The answer must lie in the writings themselves, and specifically in the way they project Julian's own voice. Because, despite its transmission through the medium of linguistically discordant late manuscripts (at least in the case of LT), a real voice does come crackling down to us from the fifteenth century. A voice with a distinct timbre. The voice of a restless, intelligent, vital human being who possesses an overwhelming urge to communicate. A voice that can be by turns magisterial, self-effacing, humorous, oracular. This voice, while it is experienced by us at certain removes, is in its way a reliable witness to the living reality of the author, to her unique humanity. In Julian's case, the intellectual and imaginative power, the tonal subtlety and variety, and the ultimate coherence of her writing makes the witness particularly credible and engaging. It is no wonder that anyone should respond to these strong traces of a strong personality, and want Julian on side.

Julian writes in the first person about her own experiences, and directly out of her reflection on those experiences comes a remarkably bold theological vision. It is a central claim of this book that, in Julian's case, the personal and the theological are best taken together, and we will call upon a certain broad concept of autobiography in order to explore the relationship between Julian's personal experience as she records it and the incarnational theology which she develops out of it. The intention is finally to show that the witness Julian's writing gives of a life lived is inextricable from, and in a sense illustrative of, her mature theological vision. It can only be hoped that in laying the emphasis on Julian's own engagement with interlocking problems of identity, faith, religious authority and writing, we will avoid at least the worst excesses of mythologization and projection.

Genre

Before any attempt is made to link Julian's *Revelation* with as complex and elusive a generic category as autobiography it is necessary to sound a brief note of caution on the question of genre as such. A critical interest in the generic identity of a particular text can be compared with the power to bind and loose invested in the keys of the Kingdom. On the one hand, the sense of a particular work's uniqueness can be virtually sacrificed to an impulse to prove that the work is a greater or lesser example of a type. Such an enterprise would tend to soft-pedal troubling questions about the purity of a given genre (indeed, of the very possibility of generic purity) and the complex relations between a literary production and the antecedents proposed for it, or which it might seem to propose for itself. Although, fortunately, it is rarely encountered in such an extreme form, this is a picture of interpretation at its most claustrophobic and uncreative, binding the critic by means of an over-determined hermeneutical framework. On the other hand, even texts such as Julian's do not drop down from heaven. There is a certain generic determination in any use of language, which implies that there is always scope for trying to get closer to a text by means of a sensitive appraisal of the various changes it rings upon generic and rhetorical possibility. In any case, there is the easily underestimated consideration that to approach a text with a particular genre in mind – however loosely one defines such a genre – has the overriding merit of getting discussion off the ground, of liberating the critic from the sheer panic which, in darker moments, can be inspired by the otherness of the text.

In the wide and fertile field of medieval religious writing in English, understood for present purposes to include texts ranging from *Ancrene Wisse* to *The Book of Margery Kempe*, Julian's *Revelation* stands out as distinctly *sui generis*. Any literary taxonomist attempting to account for this text in terms of genre would be advised to borrow the methodology of the apophatic theologian, buying affirmation with denial (albeit at a pretty disadvantageous rate of exchange), bearing in mind also that generic categories themselves hardly form a stable currency. The *Revelation* is not a book of spiritual instruction in the formal, didactic manner of *The Cloud of Unknowing* and other works ascribed to the *Cloud*-author, or of Walter Hilton's systematic treatment of the spiritual life, *The Scale of Perfection*, although it has significant points of contact with writings of their kind. It cannot be adequately defined as a work of theological explication or speculation, or of scriptural exegesis, although it is clearly the product of a cultivated mind and sensibility. It is not a rule of life like *Ancrene Wisse*, but it presents its theological conclusions as being of genuine, practical import for Christian living. It is not to be yoked too easily with prose meditations on the passion in the manner of Richard Rolle, though the crucified Christ is evoked as the dynamic centre of Julian's textual universe. The *Revelation* cannot be classed with homiletic literature, but it has a message and, on its own evidence, seeks an audience. Even more emphatically, it clearly has no official status as a document of the Church, but its presentation does exude a peculiar confidence, even a sense of authority, despite protestations on the part

4

of the author that she is (or was at the time of her visionary experience?) 'a simple creature that cowde no letter' (2.2) and nothing more than a 'wretch' (8.13).

In this apophatic mood, in which there is no positive that is not wrested from a prior negative, the concept of autobiography is introduced as a hermeneutical tool rather than as a self-evident, straightforwardly knowable genre into which Julian's text will be ingeniously persuaded, the door slamming behind it with a resounding QED. This is to say that the book does not set out to prove the *Revelation* is an autobiography as such. An unqualified designation of that sort would be misleading, and indeed somewhat anachronistic, to the extent that it might appear to assign a distinct and self-consciously *literary* purpose to Julian's generically 'wild' text. Autobiographies as we tend to understand them today were not being written in the fifteenth century, and we ought to bear in mind that Julian does not begin her Long Text, 'This is an autobiography', but 'This is a revelation of love' (1.1). On a slightly different note, the term 'autobiographical elements' has been deliberately avoided and there will be no attempt to raid the text for details of Julian's life which might then be considered in isolation as part of an autobiography that never quite got written. Rather, the intention is to map the terrain of Julian's text – that is, the text as a whole – with a generous concept of the autobiographical that will provide us with somewhere to start from, a definite point of convergence, as it were, between geometrical co-ordinates.[4] This will enable us to locate aspects of the text and bring them into a comprehensible relation to each other and with the larger picture as it emerges.

Whilst it is true – and perhaps it is even a little absurd to point this out – that such a mapping of the text, together with the particular perspectives this permits, belongs to a stratagem of reading that is self-consciously constructed rather than inevitable or self-evident, it will surely be readily granted that there is at least a strong *prima facie* case for considering the text in this way. The choice of stratagem is not arbitrary. Julian writes in the first person and the text is presented as a true record of events in her own life. Even though we are not given anything like the narrative life-story that the term 'autobiography' has come to designate, a text overtly dedicated to the representation of personal experience, however narrowly focused at the anecdotal level, invites some kind of analysis in terms we can call autobiographical. The term 'autobiography' itself might be understood here as referring less to the text's precise genre than to certain of its qualities, and to certain extrinsic and intrinsic conditions of its production. We are not asking whether or how far Julian's text shapes up

---

[4] I have borrowed this image from Leigh Gilmore, *Autobiographics: A Feminist Theory of Women's Self-Representation* (Ithaca and London, 1994), *passim*.

as an autobiography; but (dropping the indefinite article) in what ways, and with what implications, we might speak of the text as autobiography, where 'autobiography' has a philosophical-theoretical as well as a literary resonance.

In fact, recent theoretical work on autobiography has opened up a world of philosophical and literary questions. It has problematized the relation between the autobiographical 'I' and the author, putting in doubt the myth of tranquil self-presence that has been inherent in the writing both of autobiography itself and of academic discussion of the subject. Critics would now want to question not only the rhetorical implications of autobiographical self-construction, but whether any apparently integrated literary self held between the pages of a book is not so much a representation of a real person 'out there' but a fantasy of integrated selfhood. Something impossible in life is achievable in the fiction of autobiography. In addition there is the urgent feminist question: what can a woman make of herself in a man's language? And taking an even broader perspective, how does any autobiographer, or indeed any writer, male or female, enter into negotiation with authoritative cultural institutions in order to establish the legitimacy of their point of view, of their own story, and thus claim a platform from which to speak?[5] This last question has a special pertinence in Julian's case because her autobiographical project cannot be divorced from a search for personal authority within the context of late medieval Catholicism, as we shall see.

More broadly, it is as well to bear in mind that no piece of writing, even if it has pretensions to philosophical or scientific or theological objectivity and thus addresses itself to us in the garb (respectively) of pure reason, empirical fact or divine revelation, actually transcends the contingencies of its production. There is a sense in which the humanly singular writer, with his or her personal quirks, culture, preferences and loyalties, is necessarily disclosed through the work, if obliquely. As though my text bears my DNA (cultural as well as biological). Such oblique self-disclosure – and there is oblique self-disclosure, of course, even when a writer attempts deliberate and direct self-disclosure – is an essential condition of writing. We might say that a certain principle of autobiography is always operative (which is, of course, not at all the same as proposing a simple identification of 'author' and 'text' – both realities are too tricky for that manoeuvre). This is true of Julian's writings in the way that it is true of writing in general. But with Julian there is a further resonance since she is directly concerned with her own

[5] A theme considered in sophisticated detail in Leigh Gilmore, *Autobiographics*, which has clearly influenced me. See especially Chapters 3 and 4 for comment on Julian.

status, identity and authority vis-à-vis God and her fellow Christians, both as a person and as a writer.

But this is not the place to attempt a full survey of autobiographical theory, something that others have done with thoroughness and sophistication, rather to give some indication of the generous possibilities that an interest in 'autobgraphy' might provide. It is hoped that the wisdom of mapping the terrain of Julian's *Revelation* in this way will become apparent, given that such an approach enables us not only to focus on a range of significant questions – rhetorical, theological, anecdotal, historical – but, as indicated earlier, to bring them into a relation with one another and so give us some bearings as we explore the text.

Principally, I hope to demonstrate that Julian's attempt to make public theological sense of her private visionary experience necessarily implies a certain defence of that experience itself, and obliges her to find a theologically and ecclesiologically credible way of affirming the intrinsic value of personal experience as such. The early part of the book (Chapters 1 and 2) deals explicitly with the question of autobiography in relation to Julian's reconstruction of her own experience, whilst the later chapters (3, 4 and 5) interpret her mature theology, and also the crucially-important pastoral dimension of her text, in terms of a certain affirmation of the personal.

The rest of this chapter will fall into three sections. The first will examine the way in which the text as a whole has an intrinsic character of autobiography in that it is predicated on Julian's self-distancing from, and rhetorical reconstruction of, her own past experience. This is true even when, as is quite frequently the case, Julian is not directly reporting past events. If this section considers what we can call the *intrinsic* autobiographicality of the text, the second section will narrow its focus down to the anecdotal, to Julian's use of a first-person narrative as the formal means by which the showings are represented. Here the autobiographicality of the text is at its most overt. By focusing on a number of climactic episodes it is hoped to show that Julian self-consciously implicates the text's would-be revelatory function in the particularity of anecdote. For convenience this can be called the *formal* autobiographicality of the text. The third section will identify certain rhetorical and theological questions related to the autobiographical nature of the text, questions which the rest of the book will subsequently address.

Perspectives: Intrinsic Autobiographicality

Julian's visionary experience is shown to be related to three requests she makes of God with the stated intention of deepening her commitment to him. These requests, described in Julian's Chapter 2, are that she should be given 'mende of his passion', 'bodily sekenesse' to the point of death, and, as a single request, the three wounds of 'very contrition', 'kinde compassion' and 'willfull longing to God' (2.2–3). Whilst acknowledging that her prayer for these special favours has been given a retrospectively enhanced significance in the light of the showings, Julian clearly points to a devotional context prior to the showings in saying that she had 'desired *afore* iii gifts of God' (2.2, my emphasis). This sense of the past is slightly better preserved in P than in SS. In a line missing from SS but found in virtually identical form in A (CW 204.45–6), P reads, 'This sicknes I desyred in my jowth, that I might haue it when I ware xxxth yeare olde' (CW 288.38–9). We could justifiably render this, 'It was during my youth that I experienced a desire for this sickness, and wanted to have it at the age of thirty.' It is questionable whether, at thirty years of age, Julian could still regard herself as being 'in my jowth', though this seems to be implied in SS: 'the ii [desired gift] was bodily sekenesse in youth at xxx yeeres of age' (2.2). What we particularly derive from reading P here is a sense that there was life for Julian before the showings, a period for the incubation of religious desire. This is made all the clearer by her remark, found substantially in SS as well as in P, that the first two requests passed from her mind whilst that for the three wounds 'dwelled with me continually' (2.3).

This sketching-in of the background has its significance. Julian presents the showings as marking a climactic point in her personal history of devotion to Christ. She does not go into detail about the way in which this history unfolded during the period leading up to the visionary experience, but touches upon it lightly so that the reader is given a sense of that perspective.

Just as, in writing about her three-fold prayer, Julian allows us a glimpse back into her past, so at the end of the text she looks forward to the eschatological consummation of all her desire, and the desire of all who will be saved. It is striking that she admits a new, transformative perspective on the past as integral to that fulfilment. The complete meaning of the present is hidden in the future:

> And therfor whan the dome is goven and we ben all browte up above, than we cleerly se in God the privities which be now hidde to us. Than shall non of us be stirid to sey in ony wise 'Lord, if it had ben thus, than it had bene fulle wele'; but we shall seyn al [P: with one] voice: 'Lord, blissid mot thou ben! For it is thus, it is wele. And now se we verily that all thing is done as it was then ordeynd beforn that onything was made.'
> (85.134)

In reconstructing her experience for the spiritual profit of others, Julian is concerned to place her own religious development within both a temporal and an eternal perspective. This is evident from the passages we have been looking at. Her procedure reflects the kind of truth she understands herself to be dealing with, truth that is eternal and universal in its divine aspect, but inalienably personal and particular in its human focus. This double perspective sustains and reinforces a crucial sense of Julian's personal history, so that we can view the details of her experience on the one hand as part of the whole that is her own life; and on the other hand, as part of the larger whole that is the unfinished story of humanity's journey towards its eternal destiny, a journey in which Julian presumes her audience to be likewise engaged.

Julian's orchestration of these perspectives within the text necessarily points to another kind of perspective: that of the maker, the self-conscious writer/artist. Her very act of narration implies a self-distancing movement from the events in question. She reports what she saw, felt and did, and a naïve reader could simply take her narrative at face-value as a record of 'what actually happened'. But the presentation of ostensibly objective truth is inevitably a subjective production, from which we can infer the point of view – the personal *perspective* – of the one who is here making a claim to have undergone all that is described in the text, and to have achieved mastery over past events so as to fashion them into a literary whole. Both the remembering of personal experience, and the conversion of that experience into a literary artefact which is at the same time an interpretation of it, present themselves inevitably as the functions of a subject whose developed perspectives – intellectual, emotional, spiritual – are disclosed in precisely these activities of remembering and interpreting.[6] This is not to ignore the more philosophical problem of whether this remembering, interpreting subject is as stable an entity as might seem to be implied here. For us, the important point is that the existence of what we might call a sovereign autobiographical subject – that is, a subject in control of her own story – is verifiable not from the point of view of essentialist philosophy, but tropologically. It is a function of rhetoric.

This sovereign autobiographical subjectivity is presented as being mediated to Julian through a conscious relation to God, and in this we meet the classic notion of the indivisibility of self-knowledge and the knowledge of God. It is a theme taken up explicitly in Chapter 56, and with an apparent indecision over which of these forms of knowledge has priority:

[6] A. V. C. Schmidt sees an illuminating correspondence between Julian's text and the gospel of John. In each case the author reconstructs past events with a degree of hindsight about their theological significance that influences the particular mode of presentation – this implies an achieved process of understanding. See Schmidt, 'Langland and the Mystical Tradition', in *MMTE* (Exeter, 1980), esp. pp. 21–4.

And thuss I saw full sekirly that it is ridier to us to cum to the knowyng of God than to knowen our owne soule; for our soule is so deepe groundid in God, and so endlesly tresorid, that we may not cum to the knowing therof till we have first knowing of God, which is the maker to whom it is onyd. (56.89)
And notwithstondyng al this, we may never come to full knowyng of God till we know first clerely our owne soule. (56.90)

This theme of the indivisibility of self-knowledge and knowledge of God, particularly strong in medieval monastic tradition, is nevertheless especially associated with St Augustine and brought into sharp focus in his autobiographical *Confessions*. Julian's text, given that it is substantially concerned to reconstruct personal experience in terms of a governing theological rationale, is analogous to *Confessions*. It will be helpful to consider Augustine's influential paradigm and so gain some purchase on a notion of the autobiographical that can be applied to Julian.

Although at least one critic of her theology has described Julian as 'deeply Augustinian',[7] it would be virtually impossible to establish whether she is directly influenced by Augustine through personal study of his work or whether she uses concepts of common theological currency, more or less traceable to Augustine, without being conscious of their exact provenance. More to the point, no suggestion is made here that she deliberately takes *Confessions* as a generic model in the construction of her own text. Anyone searching in Julian for the kind of intense and lyrically-expressed self-scrutiny that is the hallmark of Augustine's work will be disappointed. His text is much more 'egocentric' than Julian's, substantially comprising a drama in which his former self is presented unambiguously as the protagonist. Whilst bearing these provisos in mind, there does remain a correspondence between the two texts which can shed a particular light on the question of authorial perspective – or sovereign autobiographical subjectivity – in the reconstruction of a personal history. Similarly to Augustine, Julian evokes her own passage through a process of spiritual education. The presentation of such a process is predicated on a disjunction between the *remembered* and the *remembering* self,[8] the latter understood to have a certain spiritual under-

---

[7] Grace Jantzen, *Julian of Norwich: Mystic and Theologian* (London, 1987), p. 128. Augustinian echoes in Julian are also noted in Denise Nowakowski Baker, *Julian of Norwich's Showings: From Vision to Book* (Princeton, New Jersey, 1994), especially Chapter 5, 'Reconceiving the *Imago Dei*: the Motherhood of Jesus and the Ideology of the Self'; and in Joan M. Nuth, *Wisdom's Daughter* (New York, 1991).

[8] I owe this distinction between the *remembered* and the *remembering* self to Sylvia Adamson of Cambridge University, and also owe her an apology for making very much my own (no doubt inferior) kind of running out of it. I am particularly grateful to Ms Adamson for sending me an off-print of the

standing which enables it to discern patterns of meaning, a grace of interpretation which the remembered self did not have, or not equally.

The precise form *Confessions* takes as autobiography is derived, as Augustine would have us understand it, from an illuminating faith in God which enables Augustine to make a unity of the disparate elements of events, thoughts, feelings and aspirations experienced over time. We can think of George Eliot's candleflame held against a scratched surface so that the random marks seem arranged in 'a fine series of concentric circles around that little sun'.[9] Writing about *Confessions*, Rowan Williams affirms the indivisibility of the text's theocentric and autobiographical character:

> Augustine is never merely remembering; he is searching for significant patterns, *making* a biography . . . Identity is ultimately in the hand of God; but this does not mean that it is a non-temporal thing. It is to be found, and in some sense *made*, by the infinitely painstaking attention to the contingent strangeness of remembered experience in conscious reference to God . . . The light of God can make a story, a continuous reality, out of the chaos of unhappiness, 'homeless' wandering, hurt and sin.[10]

For Augustine, the true interpretation of a life is discerned according to the measure of one's faith in God. He sees God as the origin and end of all things – above all, of the restless human heart – a person only knowing himself in truth when he grasps, and willingly consents to, his own reality as creature in relation to the creator. This fundamental orientation towards God, the genesis and intensification of which the text sets out to record in respect of its protagonist, is presented as an orientation towards that light which reveals Augustine to himself, though incompletely in this life:

> confitear ergo quid de me sciam, confitear et quid de me nesciam, quoniam et quod de me scio, te mihi lucente scio, et quod de me nescio, tamdiu nescio, donec fiant tenebrae meae sicut meridies in vultu tuo.
>
> (X.5)[11]

fascinating and very substantial article in which she introduces her distinction between the remembered and the remembering self as part of an investigation into the historical origins of 'empathetic narrative'. See Sylvia Adamson, 'From empathetic deixis to empathetic nattative: stylisation and (de-)subjectivisation as processes of language change', *Transactions of the Philological Society*, vol. 92:1 (1994), pp. 55–88.

[9] George Eliot, *Middlemarch*, ed. W. J. Harvey (Harmondsworth, 1965), Chapter 27, p. 297.

[10] Rowan Williams, *The Wound of Knowledge*, second edition (London, 1990), pp. 71–2.

[11] Augustinus, *Confessiones*, ed. Martin Skutella (Stuttgart, 1981), p. 214, lines 8–12.

[Accordingly, let me confess what I know of myself. Let me confess too what I do not know of myself. For what I know of myself I know because you grant me light, and what I do not know of myself, I do not know until such time as my darkness becomes 'like noonday' before your face.[12]]

Augustine presents himself 'scattered in times' (XI.39),[13] his mind afflicted by the 'storms of incoherent events',[14] yet in the light of his conversion he is enabled retrospectively to place both his present and, most especially, his dissipated past self in relation to God who is characterized as a 'solid rock of truth' (IV.14),[15] a source of security[16] and stability,[17] existing in an eternal Today which comprehends past, present and future.[18] The whole text is written as an address to God, this beauty loved so late, who was always *within* but only found after a chastening and often wrong-headed search,[19] a God whose truth imparts form to Augustine.[20] The memorably personal quality of the writing in *Confessions* (notwithstanding its high literary artifice) implies an invisible, attentive divine presence which, rhetorically understood, provides an acoustic boundary within which Augustine's life-story can achieve definition and so resonate with meaning for the benefit both of himself and his audience.

Julian's text, as already indicated, is quite different from *Confessions*.

[12] St Augustine, *Confessions*, trans. Henry Chadwick (Oxford, 1991), pp. 182–3.
[13] XI.xxix (39), Chadwick, p. 244; Skutella, p. 292, lines 20–1: 'at ego in tempora dissilui'.
[14] XI.xxix (39), Chadwick, p. 244; Skutella, p. 292, lines 21–2: 'tumultuosis varietatibus'.
[15] IV.xiv (23), Chadwick, p. 66; Skutella, p. 70, line 28: 'soliditati veritatis'.
[16] II.vi (13), Skutella, p. 33, line 24: 'aut ubi nisi apud te firma securitas?'; 'Where else but with you can reliable security be found' (my translation, after Chadwick, p. 32).
[17] II.x (18), Skutella, p. 36, lines 21–3: 'defluxi abs te ego et erravi, deus meus, nimis devius ab stabilitate tua in adulescentia et factus sum mihi regio egestatis'; Chadwick, p. 34: 'As an adolescent I went astray from you, my God, far from your unmoved stability. I became to myself a region of destitution.'
[18] I.vi (10), Skutella, p. 8, lines 4–6: 'tu autem idem ipse es et omnia crastina atque ultra omniaque hesterna et retro hodie facies, hodie fecisti'; Chadwick, p. 8: '"But you are the same'"; and all tomorrow and hereafter, and indeed all yesterday and further back, you will make a Today, you have made a Today.'
[19] X.xxvii (38), Skutella, p. 237, lines 15–18: 'Sero te amavi, pulchritudo tam antiqua et tam nova, sero te amavi! et ecce intus eras et ego foris et ibi te quaerebam et in ista formosa, quae fecisti, deformis inruebam'; Chadwick, p. 201: 'Late have I loved you, beauty so old and so new: late have I loved you. And see, you were within and I was in the external world and sought you there, and in my unlovely state I plunged into those lovely created things which you made.'
[20] XI.xxx (40), Skutella, p. 292, lines 25–6: 'Et stabo atque solidabor in te, in forma mea, veritate tua'; Chadwick, p. 244: 'Then shall I find stability and solidity in you, in your truth which imparts form to me.'

Her ostensible focus on a specific set of events within the narrow time-span of a few days means that she is not writing a life-story as such (the paucity of biographical information can be contrasted, for example, with the rich detail of Margery Kempe's rumbustious self-portrayal). Nevertheless, the reconstruction of past events is a profoundly autobiographical exercise for Julian in that she, like Augustine, seeks an imparting of form through a conscious relation to divine truth.

There is a suggestive, polyvalent idiom of *vision* running through Julian's text, one which is important both structurally and thematically. In the first place the idiom conveys Julian's perception of the showings themselves, and that at two levels: 'bodily sight' (9.14), referring to the sensory registering of those showings which are visual in character rather than aural; and 'gostly sight' (9.14), paraphraseable (arguably) as 'intuitive spiritual understanding'. But this idiom of vision can also figure for us the seeing and understanding implicit in what Julian presents as an achieved, mature perspective on her personal experience. This is the seeing and understanding, the authorial self-transcendence though self-awareness, to which the text asks to be taken as a witness.

Before pursuing the question of the text's idiom of vision in relation to Julian's interpretative appropriation of her own experience, we should first note that, complementing the language of vision, images of blindness, whether complete or partial, are used in the text to evoke the chief disabling factor in humanity's relationship with God. Human beings have a real difficulty in *receiving* that divine light which would enable them to make a 'true' interpretation of their own condition:

> I understode this man is chongeable in this lif, and be frelte and overcummyng fallith into synne; he is onmytye and onwise of hymself, and also his wil is overleyd; and in this tyme he is in tempest and in sorow and wo, and the cause is blindhede, for he seith not God; for if he sey God continuly he shuld have no mischevous felyng, ne no manner steryng the yernyng that servyth to synne. (47.66)

Later in this chapter Julian says that 'we shal never have ful rest til we sen hym verily and clerly in hevyn' (47.67), and the sight/blindness theme is concretely expressed in the debility of the servant in Chapter 51 who, having fallen 'in a slade' (51.72), is unable to 'turne his face to loke upon his loving lord, which was to hym ful nere' (51.72). The consequence of this lack of vision is that the servant is 'onwise for the tyme' (51.72) and acts in a way that is inappropriate, concentrating on the pain of his fall rather than on the lord's unchanging, loving disposition towards him.

It is *faith* that reorients the fallen person towards God, and in doing so bestows a power of true interpretation. As Julian seems to understand it, faith is not, strictly speaking, something that people exercise in a discrete manner as they would their other physical and mental faculties. Rather, it is the mode of God's self-disclosure within the experience of human subjects and their task is to surrender to it:

> Our feith is a light, kindly command of our endles day, that is our fader, God; in which light our moder, Criste, and our good lord the Holy Gost, ledith us in this passand life. This light is mesurid discretly, nedefully standand to us in the night. (83.132)[21]

Faith, therefore, is not part of the natural equipment of the creature but a source of light that belongs to, and flows from, God himself. During this transient life it inserts believers – though more or less obscurely so far as perception goes – into the mutual coinherence of the persons of the Trinity in their supereminently paradigmatic family life (Father, Mother, Holy Ghost); and it anticipates the final dissolution in the world-to-come, when faith will give way to 'real' sight, of the subject/object dichotomy that characterizes the temporal, pre-eschatological human/divine relationship.

The believer's journey towards the fulness of that relationship is a difficult, testing process of gradual illumination and Julian's use of the imagery of light and vision, in the evocation of both the process and its end, results in some of her most self-consciously 'sublime' writing, which can be read as bringing to a climax the shifting idiom of vision that permeates the text:

> And at the end of wo, sodenly our eye shall ben openyd, and in clerte of light our sight shall be full; which light is God our maker and Holy Gost in Criste Ihesus our savior. Thus I saw and vnderstode that our feith is our light in our night; which light is God our endless day. (83.132)

---

[21] Julian's language in this part of the text is strikingly reminiscent of a passage towards the end of the *Dialogues* of Catherine of Siena (1347–1380), here as rendered in a fifteenth century English translation: 'For I haue tastid & seen wiþ þe liȝt of intellecte, wiþ þi liȝt, þe depþe of þin eendeles trinite [. . .] wiþ þi liȝt þou hast maad me knowe þi truþe. þou art þat verri liȝt aboue nature, in so greet habundaunce & perfeccioun þat þou makist cleer þe liȝt of feiþ. In þe which feiþ I se þat my soule haþ liif, & in þat liȝt it receyueþ þe þat art verri liȝt. In þe liȝt of feiþ it haþ wonne wisdom, þat is, þe wisdom of þin oonli sone' – *The Orcherd of Syon*, ed. Phyllis Hodgson and Gabriel M. Liegey, EETS, o.s., 258 (London, 1966), p. 149, lines 14–15, 25–30. It is, of course, quite possible that there is no direct link between the two authors; and also possible that they have been drinking from the same theological source(s) though at different points of access. But in view of Nicholas Watson's suggestion that Julian could well still have been writing LT 'as late as 1410 or 1415', it is not out of the question that she had access to religious writings from the continent, including writings of women visionaries such as Catherine of Siena and Bridget of Sweden. This is an area that begs for further exploration, but for an appetizing starter see Watson, 'Composition', especially pp. 673–83.

If distance from God can be measured in degrees of blindness, closeness to him can be measured by that clarity of vision which is received through a lesser or greater indundation of divine light, and only received in full after death. In this world, faith is the form which that illumination takes. Bringing this to bear on Julian's reconstruction of her experience, we can see that this light of faith is understood not only as revealing God to Julian, but, in a divine perspective, revealing Julian to herself. Her text is presented as an act of interpretation derived from an achieved (if not definitive) theological awareness of the meaning of her experience.

It is especially in the massive progression from Short Text to Long Text that we can discern Julian's self-consciously artistic and interpretative engagement with the matter of her experience. The rhetorical and religious developments implied and evinced in this progression allow us to infer a subliminal autobiographicality: the story of a living, developing human being whose processes of change are registered precisely by the sheer incommensurability of the two texts. It is worth giving a representative example at this point of the way one passage from the Short Text has been theologically and rhetorically expanded in the Long Text, suggesting that subsequent reflection has enabled Julian to find scope for her mature thinking and feeling within a field of experience which appears initially to have had somewhat narrow dimensions.

Julian's Short Text narration of the actual showings begins several lines into Chapter iii. It relates how, with her eyes fixed on the crucifix (in obedience to the priest who is attending her supposed death-bed[22]) she experiences an intense renewal of her desire for the 'wonnde of compassyoun' (CW 206.52) for the suffering Christ, and then it goes on:

> And in this sodeynly I sawe the rede blode trekylle downe fro vndyr the garlande, alle hate, freschlye, plentefully and lyvelye, ryght as me thought that it was in that tyme that the garlonde of thornys was thyrstede on his blessede heede. Ryght so, both god and man, the same sufferde for me. I conseyvede treulye and myghtyllye that itt was hym selfe that schewyd it me with owtyn any meen; and than I sayde: Benedicite dominus. (CW 210–11.11–17)

The Long Text account of the beginning of the first revelation replicates this passage almost exactly, though with a very significant interpolation. Between the phrases 'with owtyn any meen' and 'and than I sayde: Benedicite dominus', the later version includes the following passage:

[22] 'My curate was sent for to be at my endeing, and by than he cam I had sett my eyen and might not speke. He sett the cross before my face and seid: 'I have browte thee the image of thy maker and saviour. Louke thereupon and comfort thee therewith', 3.4.

And in the same sheweing sodenly the Trinite fulfilled the herte most of ioy. And so I understood it shall be in hevyn withoute end to all that shall come there. For the Trinite is God, God is the Trinite; the Trinite is our maker and keeper, the Trinite is our everlasting lover, everlasting ioy and blisse, be our lord Iesus Christ. And this was shewed in the first and in all; for where Iesus appeireth the blissid Trinite is understond, as to my sight. And I said: 'Benedicite domine!' (4.5–6)

This passage from the Long Text has a clear structural importance. In reconstituting her original text (or what we must *assume* to be her original text), Julian decides to announce the beginning of the divine revelation by drawing the attention of her audience to a sudden and overwhelming experience of joy, one that makes her exclaim, 'Benedicite domine!' It seems strange that this experience is not mentioned in the Short Text, although the Latin exclamation is there[23] (and we may note, by the by, that her Latin seems to have improved, unless a scribe has been tweaking). We can reasonably suggest, therefore, that in the later version, all that Julian feels herself to have received through the revelation as a whole, and through living with it over a period of years, is strategically brought to bear upon her reappraisal of that first gasp of astonishment. In the perspective of maturity, the moment she saw Christ's head start to bleed is understood to have coincided with the 'big bang' of her spiritual life, all future developments being contained potentially in that first explosion of vision. We can see this presentation supported by Julian's statements here about the Trinity and its relation to humanity through the mediation of Christ. These lines condense the text's major concern to explicate the relation between God and humanity as perceived by Julian through the prism of the showings. The theological contours of the world we are about to enter are flashed before us, notwithstanding that, in the time-sequence of Julian's narrative, the showings have only just begun. The self Julian remembers here could not have had the benefit of such a perspective.

Although the basic narrative details pertaining to the revelation as a whole are retained in the progression from the Short to the Long Text, we gain a sense from comparing these corresponding passages that a certain vitality, rhetorical and theological, has expanded the dimensions of Julian's work from within. *The Rule of St Benedict*, an incalculably influential text of the western Church, speaks of the monk's heart being progressively dilated by the deepening experience of the love of God which faithfulness to the monastic life brings him.[24] We might see in the

---

[23] CW 211.17

[24] 'Processu vero conversationis et fidei, dilatato corde inerrabili dilectionis dulcedine curritur via mandatorum Dei', *The Rule of St Benedict*, ed. Timothy Fry et al. (Collegeville, Minnesota, 1980), pp. 164–6; 'But making progress in this

dilation of the heart an image of Julian's widening religious perspective and the rhetorical expansion that goes with it.[25] These two developments, working together, inform the Long Text; and we can read in them Julian's oblique story of herself as both religious subject and author.

This section has considered the achieved authorial perspective which can be read in Julian's very act of writing/revising, and which makes of the Long Text a kind of compressed spiritual, emotional and intellectual autobiography, predicated on a self-conscious disjunction between the remembered and the remembering self. We have called this *intrinsic* autobiographicality. It is a condition of the text's production. The next section will examine Julian's *formal* use of autobiographical anecdote as rhetorical stratagem.

Telling the Tale: Formal Autobiographicality

Although the text announces itself as 'a revelation of love that Iesus Christ, our endless blisse, made in xvi sheweings' (1.1), seeming to imply that what follows is a serenely uncomplicated expression of divine truth, much of the text consists of a first-person narrative with Julian as its subject. The showings are set in the context of her personal history; she portrays herself receiving them and reacting to them; and we are not offered the divine revelation in anything approximating to an abstracted, 'celestial' form (whatever that could be!) which might make a claim to bypass such fleshly contamination. We almost certainly misread that opening statement, 'This is a revelation of love', if we take it to express Julian's opinion that the text gives us untrammelled access to an essence of divine truth. Revelation and narrative are not here independent, extrapolable threads; rather, the text emerges in the necessary relation between the two. Just as we could say that there is no original, immediate truth for Julian to convey that is not itself conditioned by the nature of her perception, so we might also say that there is nothing for her to offer the reader that is not constructed out of the intrinsic tensions of that predicament, even as she seeks, as it were, to float above it through the

way of life and in faith, we shall run along the path of God's commandments, our hearts expanded [*dilatato*] by an indescribable sweetness of love' (my translation, after Fry, p. 165).

[25] B. A. Windeatt writes: 'The developing structure of the text itself becomes self-revealing of the developing spirituality of the author, and the movement between the two levels of the text, shewing and interpretative meditation, crystallizes in literary form – and so carries the reader through – a change in plane of perception that has become itself artistically expressive of the attainment of contemplative understanding', 'The Art of Mystical Loving: Julian of Norwich', in *MMTE* (Exeter, 1980), pp. 68–9.

act of writing. However much she might conceive of her work as giving the reader access to a sphere of transcendent, revealed meanings, and despite the fact that she instructs us to 'levyn the beholding of a wretch it was shewid to, and mightily, wisely and mekely behold God' (8.13), the text gives us no way of engaging with the showings which is not mediated through the narration of Julian's own relation to them. Whether the narrative invites us to observe Julian or to observe *with* her (and it does both of these at different points), she cannot be avoided. Julian's anecdotal self-representation is, in fact, demonstrably implicated in the momentum of the text's avowedly revelatory function.[26]

The showings are presented as belonging to a transcendent order of reality, inaccessible to human beings other than through divine intervention, whilst at the same time no special degree of sanctity is claimed for Julian as recipient. She insists that her experiences do not give her a superior moral or spiritual status to her fellow Christians, who must rely on the ordinary means of grace available to them in the Church's sacraments; and for us to interpret such modesty as being merely conventional – a nod and a wink to the audience, so to speak – would represent a serious misreading of Julian's cultural position and religious

---

[26] For stimulating argument about the degree of rhetorical and intellectual self-consciousness evinced in LT, see Lynn Staley Johnson, 'The Trope of the Scribe and the Question of Literary Authority in the Works of Julian of Norwich and Margery Kempe', *Speculum*, 66 (1991), pp. 820–38. According to Johnson, in the search for religious authority Julian 'depersonalized the [later] text' and 'adopted the persona of the author who inscribes a text, not of the saint whose life is inscribed upon a text' (p. 833). I would agree with Johnson's general perception that LT is the product of a self-conscious, rhetorically-sophisticated author. But I am not entirely convinced by Johnson's arguments about depersonalization since LT does preserve a great deal of anecdotal detail. And we have to acknowledge that, whatever rehtorical strategems are employed to deflect accusations of presumption (and they *are* employed, certainly), the rootedness of the text in the contingencies of Julian's experience is an absolute condition of the text's production. This circle is not, and could not be, squared. Furthermore, Johnson seems to depend too much on it being the case that Julian herself wrote the table of contents in LT Chapter 1, as Colledge and Walsh admittedly do believe (CW 284, note to line 51). Johnson deduces from this that LT looks like 'a book designed for serious thought' (p. 831) since such tables of contents 'emerged from the university world of the thirteenth century'. Yet, quite apart from the fact that Julian is writing in the fifteenth and not the thirteenth century, the Colledge and Walsh argument in favour of Julian's authorship of LT Chapter 1 is itself weak, being based solely on the criterion that the chapter employs rhetorical figures, as Julian does elsewhere. Obviously, a scribe could have used rhetorical constructions of his own; or he could have been borrowing from Julian herself. Either way, the authorship of this chapter is not definitively decided, and is probably undecideable. There are, therefore, insufficient grounds here for important arguments about the text as a whole.

sensibility. The littleness of the human being in the presence of God – indeed, the littleness of the entire creation – is, for Julian, theologically axiomatic.[27] Nevertheless, her visionary claims do place her in an awkward position. The showings inevitably set her apart from others by virtue of their extraordinariness, while her perception of a message for her 'even cristen' (6.10) within the showings means that this very separateness is itself a necessary function of her relationship with them. But the exigencies of *communication* require her at the same time to overcome that separateness, and to exploit the common ground between herself and her audience. She goes some way towards doing this by adducing her own ordinary humanity:

> For the shewing I am not goode but if I love God the better; and in as much as ye love God the better it is more to you than to me. I sey not this to hem that be wise, for thei wote it wele; but I sey it to yow that be simple for ese and comfort; for sothly it was not shewid me that God lovid me better than the lest soule that is in grace, for I am sekir that there be many that never had shewing ner sight, but of the comon techyng of holy church, that loven God better than I . . . (9.13)

Julian has to engage with the problem that her extraordinary experiences seek expression within the ordinary human context inhabited by her audience, and that she herself has to straddle both spheres of experience in the creation of the text. The problem is focused with particular sharpness in the movement between Chapter 3, in which she describes the progress of her near-mortal illness,[28] and Chapter 4, which contains her narration of the first showing. Julian's solution is to lure the reader into her visionary world by recreating her own passage from the mundane to the mystical.

In Chapter 3 Julian depicts herself in the throes of extreme sickness,

---

[27] See Julian's vision of the 'littil thing, the quantitye of an hesil nutt in the palme of my hand', 5.7.

[28] On Julian's near-mortal illness, see James T. McIlwain, 'The "bodelye syeknes" of Julian of Norwich', *Journal of Medieval History*, 10 (1984), pp. 167–80. For a feminist perspective on Julian's illness and related themes, see Elizabeth Robertson, 'Medieval Medical Views of Women and Female Spirituality in the *Ancrene Wisse* and Julian of Norwich's *Showings*', in ed. Linda Lomperis and Sarah Stanbury, *Feminist Approaches to the Body in Medieval Literature* (Philadelphia, 1993), pp. 142–67. Robertson argues persuasively that Julian's detailed presentation of her own bodily suffering 'not only reflects her sense of herself as rooted in the body but accentuates her work as distinctively feminine' (p. 154). She also makes the important point that Julian's configuration of her own suffering with that of Christ enables a reimagining of Christ himself in terms of a 'feminized body' which, as it were, 'redeems the sensual' (p. 156). This modulates into Julian's image of Christ the mother which represents a distinctive, 'feminized' soteriology (see especially pp. 156–7).

apparently so close to death that, having received the 'rites of holy church' she 'weened not a levyd till day' (3.4). Her condition deteriorates over the next couple of days so that death seems to be taking a gradual hold, first below the level of the waist and then in the upper part of her body:

> Thus I durid till day, and be than my body was dede fro the middis downewarde as to my feleing . . . After this the other party of my body began to dyen so ferforth that onethys I had ony feleing, with shortnes of onde. And then I went sothly to have passid. (3.4–5)

Whether or not Colledge and Walsh are correct in noting 'a clinical exactness'[29] of detail in this chapter, Julian's narration of her progressive incapacity also serves a rhetorical purpose in that it creates a dramatic tension eventually resolved by the words:

> And, in this, sodenly all my peyne was taken fro me and I was as hele, and namely in the other party of my body, as ever I was aforn. I mervalid at this soden change for methought it was a privy workeing of God and not of kinde. (3.5)

Although Julian says that she still believed herself to be at the point of death ('I trusted nevyr the more to levyn', 3.5), and in fact wished to die ('I had lever a be deliveryd of this world', 3.5), the procedure of the narrative constitutes an interpretative deployment of the matter of personal experience. The illness is presented as the instrument of a transformation of perception, preparing Julian to rise to a higher plane of cognition, and so it signifies a kind of dying in respect of an exclusively mundane level of consciousness rather than actual physical dying.[30] The sudden recovery, effected through what she understands to be 'a privy workeing of God and not of kinde' (3.5) does not simply restore her to a previous state of bodily health but marks the successful completion of a rite of passage into a visionary state. Julian recalls the three requests which she had earlier made of God, especially that for 'minde and felyng' (3.5) of Christ's

---

[29] CW 3, note to line 34.

[30] For a suggestive psychological interpretation of Julian's desire for a near-mortal illness, see Bernadette Lorenzo, 'The Mystical Experience of Julian of Norwich with reference to the Epistle to the Hebrews ch.ix: Semiotic and Psychoanalytic Analysis', trans. Yvette Le Guillou, in *MMTE* (Exeter, 1982), pp. 161–81. The article is very speculative, and rather brutally pins Julian down within a taken-for-granted post-Freudian conceptual framework. But it is full of interesting, if unprovable, perceptions – for example: 'The subjects that bear excessive marks of primitive stages, either foetal or oral, have a deep urgent need for strong and extreme sensations, imperatively they have to feel they have a skin, a limit, but this is unreachable, extremely distant, it can only be got at through excessiveness. That is why Julian will [make] this most unusual request to God: that he should send her a severe illness that would lead her to the border of death, which she would not however cross', p. 163.

passion, and then the first showing begins with the animation of the crucifix:

> In this sodenly I sawe the rede blode trekelyn downe fro under the garlande, hote and freisly and ryth plenteously, as it were in the time of his passion that the garlande of thornys was pressid on his blissid hede . . . (4.5)

In the introductory Chapter 1 Julian announces the first showing to be of Christ's 'pretious coroning with thornys' (1.1), yet there are two whole chapters between the outline of the showings given at the start of the text and the narration of the first of them. The story of Julian's illness as related in Chapter 3 focuses and completes an introductory section which, whilst depicting Julian as unusually pious and as having loftier aspirations than most, stresses her bodily nature by locating her precisely in space and time as the subject of the narrative (these particular points will be considered more closely in the next chapter). The illness takes her to an extremity of bodily experience, but an extremity which, however close it seems to bring her (at least in her own estimate) to a transcendent, spiritual reality, remains by definition earthbound and corporeal. This emphasis on Julian's bodiliness and her relation to an ordinary human context stands in contrast to the supernatural character of the showings themselves.

Julian's experience is shown to be constituted of natural and supernatural elements, and it is a major part of her task to represent the relation between these levels of experience in a way that is sympathetic to the reader. The showings are presented as attending upon a dramatic, supernaturally-induced shift of consciousness which underlines the qualitative difference between a natural and a supernatural mode of perception, and the narrative procedure in this section attempts to involve the reader in that shift. In Chapters 2 and 3 Julian recreates her previsionary self. Before the showings started Julian was in a similar situation to the one she must presume to be that of her readers, having received no direct mystical revelation. Like them, her only source of revelation at that time was 'the comon techyng of holy church' (9.13). She takes her readers' non-mystical state as the starting-point by locating it firmly in the text as also her own. Readers are then invited to mirror that vicarious insertion of their non-mystical point of view into the text by making an imaginative insertion into their own mind of what Julian recreates of her mystical awareness. As she makes what is in one sense a presumptive contract with the sensual, unenlightened predicament of her readers, she requires at the same time that those readers, through an ingenuous engagement with the text, should enter into a presumptive contract with her 'spiritualized' condition. The mutual substitution implied in this movement would enable Julian's relation to the showings to become the means of her relation to the audience; and the audience's relation to the text, specifically by identification with the figure of Julian within the text, to become the means of its relation to the showings.

Julian's own relation to the showings is foregrounded throughout the text as something problematical. She is involved in a continual effort of attention, assimilation and interpretation, not simply resting passively in the contemplation of divine mysteries but discerning in the showings an invitation to seek further into those mysteries:

> This [i.e. the face of Christ, disfigured by suffering] saw I bodily, swemely and derkely, and I desired more bodily sight to have sene more clerely. And I was answered in my reason: 'If God wil shew thee more, he shal be thy light. Thee nedith none but him.' For I saw him [G: and sought him]; for we arn now so blynd and so onwise that we never sekyn God til he of his godenes shewith him to us; and we ought se of him graciously, than arn we sterid by the same grace to sekyn with gret desire to se him more blisfully; and thus I saw him and sowte him, and I had him and I wantid him. And this is, and should be, our comon werkyng [P: in this life], as to my sight. (10.15)

God is a playful lover, teasing Julian by alternating revelation and concealment in a game of hide-and-seek which, deferring resolution, continually renews itself and lures her deeper into his world. Julian identifies 'sekyng' and 'fyndyng' (10.16) as basic constituents of the Christian life in general, and we shall see that she presents her own relation to the showings as offering a paradigm of the way seeking and finding are experienced in creative tension by all devout believers. Seeking aspires to finding and finding stimulates further seeking.

The term 'beholdyng' (10.16–17), a probable vernacular equivalent of *contemplatio*,[31] is employed in Chapter 10 interchangeably with 'fyndyng', and in fact comes to be Julian's preferred term for that to which religious seeking aspires. The tension between seeking and beholding can be read in the contrast between the language she uses in order to convey the

---

[31] In his treatise entitled variously *Scala Claustralium, Scala Paradisi* and *Scala Caeli*, Guigo II, a twelfth century Prior of the Grande Chartreuse, distils monastic devotional theory into a paradigmatic image of a four-runged ladder, the four rungs representing: *lectio* (reading of scripture); *meditatio* (rumination and digestion of scriptural reading, with emphasis more on emotional response than analysis); *oratio* (affective prayer); *contemplatio* (mystical union, which comes and goes). A late-fourteenth/early-fifteenth century translation of this treatise, possibly by the *Cloud*-author, can be found in Appendix B of *Deonise Hid Diuinte*, ed. Phyllis Hodgson, EETS, o.s., 231 (London, 1955). Guigo's influence is evident in *The Cloud of Unknowing* itself, notably Chapter 35. See *The Cloud of Unknowing and related treatises*, ed. Phyllis Hodgson (Salzburg, 1982), pp. 39–40.

passive dimension of her reception of enlightenment during the course of the showings, and that by which conveys her sustained, active mental application to what is revealed. The notion of enlightenment is carried by a particular modulation of the idiom of vision mentioned earlier, an idiom rooted in the phrase, 'I saw . . .' This phrase itself indicates, as we have seen, two levels of perception: 'bodily sight' and 'gostly sight' (9.14). Despite the qualitative difference between these modes of perception, they both imply a certain passivity on the part of the subject. The language of passive vision pervades the text, directing the reader to what is seen, physically or intellectually – 'I saw the rede blode' (4.5), I saw God in a poynte' (11.17), 'I sawe and vnderstode that our feith is our light' (88.132) – rather than to the act of seeing. By contrast, the language Julian employs to communicate the intensity of her mental application to the showings puts her own activity as viewing subject at the centre of the picture. The key words here are 'avisement' (11.17) and 'diligens' (22.33), evoking concentration and careful inner deliberation, a precise observation, even interrogation, of the data of revelation, as against mere blind submission.[32] Beholding stimulates seeking, as in the following passage from the beginning of the third revelation:

> And after this I saw God in a poynte, that is to sey, in myn vnderstondyng, be which syght I saw that he is in al things. I beheld with avisement, seing and knowing in sight with a softe drede, and thought: 'What is synne?' for I saw truly that God doth althing be it never so litil. (11.17)

Later in the same chapter Julian remarks, 'Thus migtily, wisely and lovinly was the soule examynyd in this vision' (11.19). The 'revelation of love' (1.1) is not just a token of divine predilection offered for her refreshment, it is an intellectual and emotional challenge, a test of her spiritual seriousness, always stretching her to the limit of her capacities:

> And I beheld with gret diligens for to wetyn how often he woulde deyn if he myght, and sotly the noumbre passid myn understondyng and my wittis so fer that my reson myghte not, ne coude, comprehend it. (22.32)

This passage is echoed by a later one in which Julian describes a similar exhaustion of capacity as she responds to the twelfth showing, which is centred on Christ's repeated proclamation, 'I it am' (26.37):

[32] Julian is, as it were, Christ's conscientious pupil. Her presentation of herself in this respect is at least partly strategic, a gesturing towards Christ (and away from herself) as the centre of authority within her experience and text. See Ritamary Bradley, 'Christ the Teacher in Julian's *Showings*: the Biblical and Patristic Traditions', in *MMTE* (Exeter, 1982), pp. 127–42; and also Johnson, 'The Trope of the Scribe'.

The nombre of the words passyth my witte and al my understondyng and al my mights, and it arn the heyest, as to my syte;
for therin is comprehendid – I cannot tellyn; but the ioy that I saw in
the shewyng of them passyth al that herte may willen and soule may
desire. (26.37)

If spiritual understanding is achieved according to the measure of
God's grace at work in the soul, the pushing of Julian to her personal
limits in this respect signifies a continual augmentation of that measure,
so that each point of arrival becomes a point of departure.[33] The
momentum of this process is sustained throughout the narrative of the

---

[33] This process of continual cognitive/spiritual augmentation is reflected in
Julian's ruminative, amplificatory literary style which can seem merely repetitious to readers who expect things to go more or less from A to B in a smooth,
steady line. Brant Pelphrey is one of these: 'Julian's narration is in fact
repetitious and sometimes haphazard. She describes the order of events in
her visions as she remembers them, without seeing them in a logical sequence,
and without attempting to categorize them by subject matter', *Love Was His
Meaning: The Theology and Mysticism of Julian of Norwich* (Salzburg, 1982), p. 9.
The more than faint suggestion of Pelphrey's critique is that Julian jolly well
ought to have had an eye to logical sequence and categorization by subject
matter. In fact, he exaggerates these 'flaws' since there are plenty of traceable
lines of logical progression within the text. The real problem, on the contrary,
may be that sometimes Julian's logic is too intricate and subtle for us, and her
idiosyncratic terminology more rigorously consistent than perhaps we would
like it to be; especially if we are devotees of the myth of Julian as a homely,
accessible, fireside Christian optimist. Pelphrey's problem with Julian's 'repetitious' literary style may also stem from a certain deficiency of context in his
characterization of Julian's work. Perhaps a more sympathetic approach might
be cultivatable in reference to a specifically *medieval* rhetorical/literary theory.
This may take us some way (though clearly only in a general sense). For
example, Geoffrey of Vinsauf suggests the deployment of a range of rhetorical
devices in order to create a 'spacious' literary style in which power of
signification accumulates precisely through delay, linguistic playfulness, peri-
phrasis, amplification. His paradigm is organic: 'a plentiful harvest springs
from a little seed; great rivers draw their source from a tiny spring; from a
slender twig a great tree rises and spreads', *Poetria Nova of Geoffrey of Vinsauf*,
transf. M. F. Nims (Toronto, 1967), p. 40. But see also especially pp. 24–5. I am
greatly indebted to Anne Henry of Cambridge University for provoking my
own thought in this area, and specifically for drawing my attention to relevant
passages of the *Poetria Nova*. Also of interest on the question of style is Edward
Peter Nolan, *Cry Out and Write: A Feminine [sic] Poetics of Revelation* (New York,
1994). See especially Chapter 2 of this book for Nolan's suggestive discussion of
hypertaxis as a 'masculine' discursive habit and *parataxis* as a 'feminine' one. His
discussion of Julian herself (Chapter 4, 'Julian of Norwich and the *Via Negativa*')
is fascinating, but of limited use since the analysis is largely based, somewhat
perversely, on the Westminster manuscript (see CW, intro. pp. 9–10) which is
really only a series of brief extracts of LT. Nolan offers a brave but unconvincing
defence of his decision to focus on W. Clearly this fifteenth century manuscript
is important, but as a supplement.

showings and is particularly in evidence at certain climactic points when some kind of crisis is shown to precipitate a new level of awareness. At these key moments Julian highlights in a dramatic way the gap between her all-too-human self as the focus of a narrative and the transcendent reality of God's self-revelation. The shift from a pre-visionary to a visionary state registered between Chapters 3 and 4 suggests a certain bridging of that gap but does not remove it. Even though her immediate position in respect of the showings is a privileged one, Julian presents herself as still very much subject to the limitations, and indeed temptations, of her sensual condition. We have already noted that Julian depicts herself attending to the showings with an intense degree of concentration, and considered the significance of this in relation to the way she narrates the development of her spiritual understanding through the creative tension between seeking and beholding. It is at the climactic points in question that the dynamics of this creative tension are most in evidence. We shall take these climactic moments in turn, with a view to demonstrating how Julian's foregrounding of her own relation to the showings is rhetorically strategic: an attempt to implicate autobiographical anecdote in the text's revelatory momentum.

In Chapters 27 and 29 respectively, Julian narrates two moments of climax issuing in her deeper spiritual understanding, and both are focused on the problem of sin. Her concern about this question is not only a matter of intellectual curiosity but has a visceral quality which indicates an intensely personal engagement with the problem, as the following passage shows:

> After this the lord browte to my mynd the longyng that I had to hym aforn; and I saw that nothing letted me but synne, and so I beheld generally in us al. And methowte if synne had not a ben, we should al a ben clene and like to our lord as he made us; and thus, in my foly, aforn this tyme often I wondrid whi by the gret forseyng wysdam of God the begynnyng of synne was not lettid; for than, thowte me, al shulde a be wele. This steryng was mikel to forsakyn, and nevertheless mornyng and sorow I made therefor without reason and discretion. But Iesus, that in this vision enformid me of all that me neydyth, answerid by this worde and seyde: 'Synne is behovabil, but al shal be wel, and al shal be wel, and al manner of thyng shal be wele.' (27.38)

Julian's abandonment of 'reason and discretion'[34] indicates the 'foly' that is itself symptomatic of her human susceptibility and sinfulness: in

---

[34] The coupling of reason and discretion here is not casual. According to Richard of St Victor's allegorical exegesis of Genesis 30:23–4 in *Benjamin Minor* [*The Twelve Patriarchs*], Rachel/reason gives birth to Joseph/discretion: 'Therefore, if we understand reason by Rachel, we quickly discover why Joseph can be born

retrospect, she recognizes as 'mikel to forsaken' (more intelligibly expressed in P as 'moch to be forsaken', CW 404.10) her foolish curiosity about why God did not prevent sin in the first place. Nevertheless, her reference to 'the longyng that I had to hym aforn' indicates at the same time the 'willfull longing to God' (2.3) which exists in tension with her sinfulness. The manifestation of that tension in this episode is resolved by the divine locution beginning, 'Synne is behovabil', marking a new development in Julian's perception of the question that has been troubling her. She goes on in this and the following chapter to express her new understanding. Sin, she asserts, has 'no maner of substance' (27.38); it is known only through 'the peyne that it is cause of' (27.38); this pain is salutary because 'it purgith and makyth us to knowen ourselfe and askyn mercy' (27.38–9); Christ lays 'no manner of blame' (27.39) on humanity for sin, but 'hath compassion on us' (28.39) because of it; and in the world to come 'we shal verily see the cause why he suffrid synne to come; in which syte we shall endlesly ioyen in our lord God' (27.39).[35]

The relation of Chapter 29 to the two previous chapters provides an example of how one resolution of tension is not an end in itself but generates further tension. Beholding stimulates further seeking. Although Julian has already received insight into the problem of sin, at the beginning of Chapter 29 we again find her in a state of anxiety. As she contemplates God's compassion for sinners something still niggles:

from Rachel only since in no way do we doubt that discretion is born from reason alone. Such an offspring from such a mother; Joseph from Rachel; discretion from reason', Richard of St Victor, *The Twelve Patriarchs, The Mystical Ark, Book Three of the Trinity*, trans. Grover A. Zinn (New York, 1979), p. 125.

[35] Julian's attitude towards sin is clearly influenced, whether consciously or not, by Augustine's thinking on the problem of evil. Evil is a corruption of being and has no substantial reality. Sin likewise is without substance. It is striking that LT does not contain the eloquent apostrophe to sin of ST chapter xxiii (CW 271. 26–36). Perhaps the reason for this is that the apostrophizing mood rather conveys a sense that sin does have substantial reality; in LT Chapter 27, by contrast, Julian avoids seeming to offer sin that dignity. For Augustine I have consulted G. R. Evans, *Augustine on Evil* (Cambridge, 1982); and have also been helped in this area by the same author's *Philosophy and Theology in the Middle Ages* (London, 1993), especially pp. 80–85. Perhaps the most enlightening and sophisticated discussion of Julian's own thoughts about sin and related topics is to be found in Denise Baker, *Julian of Norwich's Showings*. Whilst noting a broadly Augustinian influence, Baker acutely observes that Julian's interest in sin is teleological rather than aetiological, concerned less about the possible origins of sin than sin's place in the context of soteriology; see especially pp. 63–82. Joan M. Nuth also refers to Augustine, and supplies a competent account of the historical and religious context in which Julian is writing, *Wisdom's Daughter*, pp. 115–35; also, on similar ground, see Jantzen, *Julian of Norwich*, pp. 167–73; and Brad Peters, 'The Reality of Evil within the Mystic Vision of Julian of Norwich', *Mystics Quarterly*, 13 (1987), pp. 195–202.

> But in this I stode beholdyng generally, swemly and mournyng, seyng thus to our lord in my menyng with ful grete drede: 'A! good lord, how myte al ben wele for the grete hurte that is come by synne to the creatures?' (29.40)

It appears from the first clause of the quotation that Julian is in a state of beholding, yet her experience is not restful or delectable but fearful and anxious, until her divine teacher shows her his 'ful lovely chere' (29.40) and gives her the assurance that the act of atonement made in his passion is 'more worshipfull for manys salvation without comparison, than ever was the synne of Adam harmful' (29.41), and that 'sythe I have made wele the most harme, than it is my wil that thou knowe thereby that I shal make wel al that less' (29.41).

We can see Chapters 27 and 29 as part of a cumulative preparation for an even more significant point of climax that comes in Chapter 50 and which resolves itself into the 'example' of the lord and the servant in Chapter 51. As something which has engaged Julian's meditative powers for 'xx yeres after the tyme of the shewing, save iii monethis' (51.74) and to which she has attended with particular care, '[G: seeing] inwardly with avisement al the poynts and propertes that wer shewid in the same tyme, as ferforth as my witt and vnderstondyng wold servyn' (51.74), the example is presented as crucial both personally and textually. In view of this, the build-up of tension in Chapter 50 has an important dramatic function in preparing the reader for what follows, the peculiar intensity of the anxiety corresponding to the special significance of the example.

In fact, before Chapter 50, Chapters 45–9 set the scene in their focus on the disparity between divine judgement and human judgement, between God's refusal to lay blame on humanity for sin and humanity's perception of and belief in its own blameworthiness. God's judgement is unchanging and generous because he 'demyth us upon our kynde substance which is ever kepte on in hym, hoole and save without end' (45.63). Human beings, on the other hand, are hostages to their 'changeabil sensualyte' (45.63) and mark changeable sensual judgements on the basis of changeable sensual data. In Chapter 50 Julian comes to ponder on this disparity with some unease and addresses her misgivings to God:

> Good lord, I se the that art very truth and I know sothly that we synne grevously al day and ben mekyl blameworthy; and I ne may neyther levyn the k[n]owyng of this sothe, ner I ne se the shewyn to us no manner blame. How may this be? (50.71)

Consideration of this problem takes Julian to an extreme pitch of anxiety, and her predicament embodies a dilemma which the example in Chapter 51 is presented as resolving:

And atwix these ii contraries my reason was gretly traveylid by my blyndhede, and cowde have no rest for drede that his blyssid presens shuld passyn from my syte and I to be left in onknowyng how he beholdyth us in our synne; for either behovid me to sen in God that synne were al don away, or ell me behovid to sen in God how he seith it, wherby I myte trewly knowen how it longyth to me to synne and the manner of our blame. My longyn indurid, hym continuly beholding, and yet I cowde have no patience for great awer and perplexitie, thynkand: 'If I take it thus, that we be not synners ne no blameworthy, it semyth as I shuld eryn and faile of knoweing of this soth. And if it be so that we be synners and blameworthy, good lord, how may it than ben that I cannot sen this sothnes in the, which art my God, my maker, in whom I desire to sen al trueths? [. . .] I cryed inwardly with al my myte, sekyng into God for helpe, menand thus: 'A! lord Iesus, king of bliss, how shall I ben esyd? Ho that shal techyn me and tellen me that me nedyth to wetyn, if I may not at this tyme sen it in the?' (50.71–2)

The direct interrogation of God himself conveys the urgency of the problem and the extent of Julian's need. If her 'mornyng and sorow' (27.38) in Chapter 27 are irrational and a sign of deficient spiritual discretion – symptoms, therefore, of her sinful condition – the way she pleads with God to answer her by challenging him on the grounds of his own divinity focuses attention on this condition even more, as do her impatience and 'great awer and perplexitie' (50.71). The rhetorical stakes are deliberately raised to anticipate God's response in the next chapter:

And than our curtes lord answerd in shewing full mystily a wonderful example of a lord that hath a servant, and gave me syte to my vnderstondyng of botyrn, and the syte was shewid double in the lord, and the syte was shewid dowble in the servant . . . (51.72)

The storm has passed. Julian's representation of herself in Chapter 50 as anxious and importunate can now be balanced against her reference to 'our curtes lord', just as the whole troubled tone of the previous chapter is balanced against the serene idiom employed here which foregrounds God's gracious act of revelation and manoeuvres Julian back into a relatively passive role.

Chapter 51 contains the example of the lord and the servant, together with a fairly lengthy exposition of what Julian has come to understand of it; and subsequent chapters (notably Chapters 52–63) develop related themes in a section of the text which shows Julian at her theologically and linguistically most sophisticated; and, one could say, at her most didactic.

The anecdotal re-emerges briefly in Chapter 64 with Julian's desire to be taken from this world, a narratorially undeveloped episode which nevertheless prepares the ground for the debacle which follows, as we shall see.

It is not in fact until Chapter 66 that the anecdotal re-emerges in earnest, and it does so in the form of another climactic moment in which Julian's narrative self-presentation serves the revelatory momentum of the text as a whole. Similarly to that recorded in Chapter 50, the episode in Chapter 66 looks backwards and forwards: it brings certain themes into dramatic focus but its fuller significance is discernible only through what follows it. Chapter 66 sets in motion a narrative train which finally brings to a culmination Julian's account of her problematical relation to the show-ings; that is, a final crisis of faith which, in the paradoxical dispensation of sin and mercy, both threatens and precipitates her inward personal appropriation of the showings in all their spiritual meaning.

Before examining Chapter 66 in some detail it is necessary to look briefly at what precedes it. In one sense, its 'ancestry' within the text goes back (at least) to the chapters already mentioned dealing with sin and divine judgement (Chapters 45–9), but a more immediate parentage can be identified in one aspect of the theme of Christ's motherhood, especially as it continues the exploration of God's attitude to human sinfulness. Although, as we have seen, Julian understands sin to lack substantial reality, the pain of it is real enough and inspires compassion in Christ for those who suffer it. Nevertheless, as a good mother looking to her child's long-term interests, he allows his own children to fall and experience pain as part of a process of spiritual maturation, the ultimate success of which he guarantees. Although the notion of divine motherhood will be considered more fully in a later chapter of this book, the following passage from Chapter 61 expresses the core of this theme in what we can call its *pastoral* modulation, addressing, that is, the practical implica-tions for the sinner of Christ's motherly disposition:

> The moder may suffre the child to fallen sumtyme and be disesid in dyvers manners for the owen profitt, but she may neve[r] suffre that ony maner of peril cum to the child, for love. And thow our erthly moder may suffre hir child to perishen, our hevynly moder Iesus may not suffre us that arn his children to perishen; for he is almyty, all wisdom and al love; and so is non but he. Blissid mot he ben! But oftentymes whan our fallyn and our wretchidnes is shewid us, we arn so sore adred and so gretly ashamid of ourselfe that onethys we wettyn where that we may holden us. But then will not our curtes moder that we fle awey, for him wer nothing lother. But he will than that we usen the condition of a child; for whan it is disesid or dred it rennith hastely to the moder for helpe with al the myte [. . .] And if we fele us not than esyd al swithe, be we sekir that he usith the condition of a wise moder; for if he sen that it be more profitt to us to morne and to wepen, he suffrith it with ruth and pite into the beste tyme, for love. (61.100)

The chapters which follow continue the concern with 'our frelte and our fallyngs' (62.101). Although these are regarded in the light of God's unchanging and generous judgement, the pain is still evident, such that in Chapter 64 Julian relates her 'gret longyng and desire of Goddis gifte to be deliverid of this world and of this lif' (64.104). It seems that she can no longer tolerate the exhausting tension between spiritual desire and personal sinfulness. God consoles her with the words, 'Sodenly thou shal be taken fro al thy peyne, fro al thy sekenes, fro al this disese and fro al the wo' (64.104), but the deliverance is not to be yet and she still faces her sternest test.

In Chapter 66 Julian relates how, between the fifteenth showing and the sixteenth, she was overtaken by her own human nature, by 'febilnes, wretchidnes and blindness' (66.107). This weakness manifests itself first of all in a physical way as she experiences again the pain that was taken from her towards the end of Chapter 3:

> and anon my sekenes cam agen: first in my hed, with a sound and a dynne; and sodenly all my body was fu[l]fillid with sekenes like as it was aforn, and I was as baren and as drye as I never had comfort but litil. And as a wretch I moned and hevyed for felyng of my bodily pey[n]es and for fayling of comfort, gostly and bodily. (66.108)

For Julian, every kind of human suffering is constellated with sin (and sin is constellated with, indeed absorbed into, Christ crucified).[36] If the disappearance of her pain in Chapter 3 signifies her elevation to a higher level of spiritual perception, its return signifies a decisive move downwards, back into a state of unrelieved spiritual blindness which deprives her even of bodily comfort and makes her especially vulnerable to her own sinfulness. The moral fall for which she prepares us comes in the form of a denial of the divine origin of her experience:

> Than cam a religious person to me and askid how I ferid. And I seyd I had ravid today, and he leuhe loud and inderly. And I seyde: 'The cross that stod afor my face, methowte it blode fast.' (66.108)

Julian is chastened by the change in her visitor's reaction: 'with this word . . . [he] waxid al sad and mervelid' (66.108).[37] She consequently ties

---

[36] 'In this nakid word "synne" our lord browte to my mynd generally al that is not good, and the shamfull dispite and the utter nowtyng that he bare for us in this life, and his dyeng', 27.38.

[37] Felicity Riddy suggests that the 'religious person's' response here is instrumental in summoning Julian's private experience into the world of literate discourse which the cleric himself represents: 'The visions first occurred . . . in a realm of experience outside discourse, which Julian herself designates as madness. It is because the "religious person" takes her seriously when she tells him the crucifix appeared to bleed that she learns to re-evaluate what she has seen. That is, his response and the religious guilt it awakens in her stimulate the whole lengthy process whereby non-rational experience is brought into the

herself up in a knot of scruples, a state of confusion represented as a heady mixture of astonishment, grief and self-reproach:

> And anon I was sor ashamid and astonyed for my recleshede, and I thowte: 'This man takith sadly the lest word that I myte seyen than saw I no more therof'. And whan I saw that he toke it sadly and with so gret reverens, I wepid, ful gretly shamid, and wold have ben shrevyn; but at that tyme I cowde tell it no preist, for I thowte: 'How should a preist levyn me? I leve not our lord God. [. . .] A! lo I, wretch. This was a gret synne, gret onkindness, that I for foly, for feling of a litill bodily peyne, so onwisely lost for the time the comfort of all this blissid shewing of our lord God. Here may you sene what I am of myself . . . (66.108)

As she narrates the story, Julian inevitably gauges her fall in relation to the measure of enlightenment she has so far received, and this makes her momentary abandonment of faith in the divine origin of the showings all the more shamefully significant. Not only is her denial of the showings a 'gret synne', it is a 'gret onkindness', a wanton act of (*unnatural*) discourtesy which sets her in contrast to 'our curtes lord' who, despite her ingratitude, 'wold . . . not leve me' (66.108). We have already noted Julian's assertion that 'God demyth us upon our kynde substance' (45.63) and overlooks, or rather, in a beneficent, motherly way, deals wisely with the moral fickleness caused by the rift between human substance and sensuality; it is a theme which informs the presentation of this episode, as it informs the narrative of subsequent chapters in which Julian's weakness is explored further.

Having lacerated herself with remorse, Julian seeks what little comfort she can: 'And [I] lay still till night trosting in his mercy' (66.108). She assumes 'the condition of a child' (61.100), appealing to her mother's unchanging love and kindness: 'My kind moder, my gracious moder, my dereworthy moder, have mercy on me' (61.100).[38] The motherly kindness of Christ does not immediately make itself felt. On the contrary, Julian's situation seems to worsen in the second half of Chapter 66 as she experiences a nightmare-vision of the devil, vividly if not entirely unconventionally evoked:[39]

> And in the slepe, at the begynnyng, methowte the fend set him in my throte, puttand forth a visage ful nere my face like a yong man; and it

realm of language, textualised, meditated over and given meaning', ' "Women talking about the things of God": a late medieval sub-culture', in ed. Carol Meale, *Women and Literature in Britain, 1150–1500* (Cambridge, 1993), p. 114.

[38] She behaves, that is, with discretion (see n. 34, above).

[39] For literary conventions pertaining to the demonic, see especially the notes to CW Chapter 67. Marion Glasscoe makes the point that devils in the mystery plays may well have appeared in similar form to Julian's apparition, *English Medieval Mystics: Games of Faith* (London, 1993), p. 267, n. 53.

was long and wonder lene; I saw never none such. The color was rede like the tilestone whan it is new brent, with blak spots therin like blak steknes, fouler than the tilestone. His here was rode as rust, evisid aforn, with syde lokks hongyng on the thounys. He grynnid on me with a shrewd semelant, shewing white teeth; and so mekil methowte it the more oggley. Body ne hands had he none shaply, but with his pawes he held me in the throte and would have stranglid me, but he myte not.

(66.108–9)

Although, on the face of it, this episode might seem to mark a deterioration of Julian's moral and spiritual condition, there is a crucial, qualitative difference between this demonic vision and her abandonment of faith in the divine origin of the showings. However temporary, and however much stress she is under, her denial of the showings is a matter of choice (at least in her own estimation), as a 'gret synne' (66.108) must be by definition. But in the second half of the chapter Julian is assailed by the devil, something she has no power to stop. There is no sin where the will is not free. Nevertheless, the one appropriate moral choice which is open to her is precisely the one she makes – an act of trust: 'in all this time I trostid to be savid and kepid by the mercy of God' (66.109). Julian turns her alarm into prayer and the narrative is punctuated here by the phrases 'Benedicite domine!' and 'Blissid be God!' (66.109). In the end she realizes that the devil has been sent to tempt her away from faith in the showings, a dramatic re-enactment of the temptation to which she had earlier succumbed, and so she affirms her faith in them and in 'al the feith of holy church', regarding these as 'bothen one' (66.109). This persevering faith in the face of temptation is shown to be immediately rewarded: 'And anon al vanishid away, and I was browte to gret rest and peas withouten sekenes of body or drede of conscience' (66.109). Julian's success in meeting the challenge of this ghoulish visitation neatly opposes her failure in the first part of Chapter 66 to resist her own weakness, or rather the failure of her confidence in God. The attack, it seems, comes by way of a second chance, offering her an opportunity to acquit herself with honour. Having learned her weakness, she places her trust in God, and all is well.

The turbulence caused by Julian's denial of the showings on the one hand and her subjection to demonic attack on the other resolves itself in Chapter 67 into the sixteenth showing which, as she has already pointed out, 'was conclusion and confirmation to all xv' (66.107):

And than our lord opened my gostly eye and shewid me my soule in midds of my herte. I saw the soule so large as it were an endles world and as it were a blisfull kyngdom; and be the conditions I saw therin I understode that it is a worshipful syte [i.e. city]. In the midds of that syte sitts our lord Iesus, God and man, a faire person and of large stature, heyest bishopp, solemnest king, worshipfulliest lord; and I saw him clad solemnly and worshiply. (67.109)

Of the three modes of perception through which Julian receives the showings, 'bodily sight . . . word formyd in my understondyng and . . . gostly sight' (9.14), the third – which she 'cannot ne may not shew . . . as hopinly ne as fully as I wolde' (9.14) – brings the truest, because most spiritual, illumination. The opening of Julian's 'gostly eye' (67.109), attained after she has been 'browte to gret rest and peas' (66.109), has a parallel in Hilton's *Scale of Perfection* which speaks of a person being simultaneously asleep to the world but awake to God:

> I cannot wake to Jesus unless I sleep to the world, and therefore the grace of the Holy Spirit, shutting the carnal eye, makes the soul sleep from worldly vanity; opening the spiritual eye to wake to the sight of God's majesty, covered under the cloud of his precious humanity, as the gospel says of the apostles when they were with our Lord Jesus in his transfiguration. First, they slept, and then *evigilantes viderunt maiestatum*, awakening they saw his majesty.[40]

The sleep-to-the-world which here brings Julian to a climax of divine illumination is set against the sleep (in the ordinary sense of the word) which exposes her to evil dreams of demonic attack;[41] but that nightmare experience has effectively prepared the ground for presenting this final showing in its special significance as 'conclusion and confirmation to all xv' (66.107). Julian's spiritual vision of her soul as the dwelling place of 'our lord Iesus, God and man' (67.109) looks backwards and forwards. It marks a culmination of the showings, presenting an image of the union between God and humanity which has already appeared in the example of the lord and the servant: 'he made mans soule to ben his owen cyte and his dwellyng place' (51.76); and also, in Chapter 56: 'The worshipfull cyte that our lord Iesus sittith in, it is our sensualite in which he is inclosid' (56.90). It is, at the same time, a mystical foretaste of the eternal sabbath,

---

[40] Walter Hilton, *The Scale of Perfection*, ed. and trans. John P. H. Clark and Rosemary Dorward (Mahwah, New Jersey, 1991), Book 2, Ch. 40, p. 284. A critical edition of the Middle English *Scale* is still awaited.

[41] Marion Glasscoe identifies two contrasting awakenings here: the first, Julian's bodily awakening from a 'nightmare fever of sickness' to bodily health and assurance; the second, a spiritual awakening to the dignity of her own soul as the dwelling-place of Christ, *English Medieval Mystics*, p. 258. In slight contrast to Glasscoe, and in view of the spiritual vision that follows in Chapter 67, I read the phrase 'I was browte to gret rest and peas' (66.109) as suggesting an occlusion of outward, physical realities as well as of phantasmagoria – a pacification of body and mind which can be referred to as a kind of sleep in respect of ordinary psychosomatic consciousness.

God's 'endles day' (83.132), when he will at last find rest in all his creatures, as he does already in the purified soul (quoting the fuller CW):[42]

> He syttyth in þe soule evyn ryghte in peas and rest, and he rulyth and ȝe(m)yth hevyn and erth and all that is. The manhode with the godhed syttyth in rest, the godhede rulyth and ȝe(m)eth withoutyn ony instrument or besynesse. (CW 640.9–12)

Julian calls this a 'delectable syte and a restfull shewyng' (68.110) and says that 'the soule that thus beholdyth, it makith it like to him that is beholdyn, and onyth it in rest and peas be his grace' (68.111, punctuation slightly altered in line with CW 644.48). God rests in her; she rests in him. The climactic sixteenth showing discloses the completion of a retrospectively discernible Augustinian paradigm operative within the text: Julian's concern with the passage from knowledge and love of created things 'wherin is no rest' (5.7) to knowledge and love of God who is 'the very rest' (5.7). In this movement the soul discovers its true identity and destiny: 'quia fecisti nos ad te et inquietum est cor nostrum, donec requiescat in te'[43] ['because you have made us for yourself, and our heart is restless until it rests in you'[44]]. Strikingly, Julian's vision of Christ in Chapter 67 is indivisibly a vision of her own soul ('our lord . . . shewid me my soule', 67.109), and the final indivisibility of God and self suggested here is reminiscent of Augustine's conception and anticipation of God's sabbath rest in eternity:

> Etiam tunc enim sic requies in nobis, quemadmodum nunc operaris in nobis, et ita erit illa requies tua per nos, quemadmodum sunt ista opera tua per nos.[45]

---

[42] Theological interpretation of the theme of God's sabbath rest (Genesis 2:2–3) is traceable at least to Augustine's *Confessions* (see n. 45, below) and to his *De Genesi ad litteram*. But in the twelfth century the general sabbath theme (as pertaining to humanity as well as to God himself) was given a developed mystical interpretation in Aelred of Rievaulx's *Speculum Caritatis*. Aelred's exegesis of passages from Leviticus concerning the three kinds of sabbath (of days, weeks and years see Leviticus 23:23; 25:3–4, 8, 10) allegorizes these sabbaths as three forms of love: love of self (in a non-pejorative sense denoting self-discipline and recollection); love of neighbour; and love of God, which subsumes the first two loves. The final love is the 'sabbath of sabbaths', a mystical participation in God's sabbath rest, begun on earth but only reaching its plenitude in eternity. Each of Aelred's sabbaths is preceded by six workdays, standing for moral and spiritual endeavour. See *The Mirror of Charity* [*Speculum Caritatis*], trans. Elizabeth Connor, intro. and notes by Charles Dumont (Kalamazoo, Michigan, 1990).

[43] *Confessions*, I.i (1), Skutella, p. 1, lines 12–13.

[44] Chadwick, p. 3.

[45] *Confessions*, XIII.xxxvii (52), Skutella, p. 370, lines 22–5.

[There also you will rest in us, just as now you work in us. Your rest will be through us, just as now your works are done through us.[46]]

But we are not invited to conclude that Julian has been simply and cleanly untethered from her past so as to enter a new phase of contemplative repose. In particular, her 'gret synne' (66.108) of denial, far from being forgotten in the narration of the final showing, is presented as virtually precipitating this climactic mystical experience. A momentary lapse has, as it were, given Christ a valuable opportunity, not only to offer Julian fresh encouragement but to deepen her faith in the divine authenticity of the showings. A faith which was briefly denied will, on that account, be made all the firmer. The vision of Christ reigning in Julian's soul can be partly interpreted as a token of the assurance of final victory, as expressed in the locution – a 'word formyd in my understondyng' (9.14) – which is presented as integral to the sixteenth showing.

And when I had beholden this with avisement, than shewid our good lord words full mekely withouten voice and withouten openyng of lipps, ryte as he had done, and said full swetely: 'Wete it now wele that it was no raveing that thou saw today, but take it and leve it, and kepe the therin and comfort the therwith and troste thou therto, and thou shalt not be overcom.' (68.111)

Christ's response to Julian's sin (inseparable, of course, from her own sorrow for that sin) brings her a benefit that she might not otherwise have received, and one which outweighs any harm sustained in her fall. This turning sin to good account – *O felix culpa!* – glances back to Chapter 29 and Julian's realization that Christ's atonement for sin 'is more plesyng to God and more worshipfull for manys salvation . . . than ever was the synne of Adam harmfull' (29.41). It also recapitulates in dramatic form the assertion in Chapter 38 that 'ryth as to every synne is answeryng a peyne be trewth, ryth so, for every synne, to the same soule is goven a bliss by love' (38.52), something she sees exemplified in various saints, but especially in St John of Beverly who, despite his sin, is now in heaven enjoying 'manyfold ioyes overpassing that he shuld hav had if he had not fallen' (38.53). Julian's presentation of the sixteenth showing in direct relation to her sin in Chapter 66 – and we should remember that she makes a point of breaking off the straight narrative of the showings in order to tell us about her sin – is informed by and resonates with earlier discussions of God's transmutation of sin into 'worship': 'Also God shewid that synne shal be no shame but worship to man' (38.52). Julian's compunction, amply demonstrated in her response to the demonic nightmare, has won from God a deeper assurance of the truth in all that she has

---

[46] Chadwick, p. 304.

seen, enabling her to make a more secure personal appropriation of that truth.

As noted previously, at the beginning of Chapter 66 Julian proposes to tell us of her 'febilnes, wretchidnes and blindness' (66.107). After her sin of doubt the sixteenth showing re-establishes and strengthens her confidence in God; and in Chapter 69 that confidence is tested by another visit from the devil, who comes again 'with his hete and with his stinke' (69.112). This time Julian has no problem seeing through his wiles: 'And al this was to stirre me to dispeir, as methowte' (69.112). She is given grace to trust in God, but does not eschew the use of practical strategy to reinforce that trust:

> My bodily eye I sett in the same crosse wher I had ben in comfort aforn that tyme, my tonge with speech of Crists passion and rehersing the feith of holy church, and myn hert to festen on God with al the troste and the myte. (69.112)

After the devil has disappeared for the last time, Julian having been 'deliverd of him be the vertue of Christ passion' (69.112), she makes what reads like a formal declaration of her faith in the truth of the whole revelation, as though to emphasize that the appropriate lessons have been learned and that her faith is now firm:

> I beleve that he is our savior that shewid it, and that it is the feith that he shewid. And therfore I leve it enioyand; and therto I am bounden be al his own menyng, with the next words that folowen: 'Kepe the therin and comfort the therewith and trost thou therto.' (70.113)

Such assurance has been hard won. In the process of winning it, Julian has been stretched again and again to the limit of her capacities, and attempts in the narration of that stretching to accommodate the perspective of her readers by locating their need of education in her own textual persona. At the same time, readers are invited, through their experience of the text, to locate themselves imaginatively within Julian's experience of vision. In this way, author and reader are provisionally identified. There is a parallel in St Bernard of Clairvaux's first sermon on the Song of Songs. Bernard identifies himself with his listeners as one seeking instruction (the image of the loaf in the following passage refers to the Song of Songs itself, broken up and shared in the process of homiletic exegesis):

> Sed quis franget? Adest paterfamilias: cognoscite Dominum in fractione panis. Quis enim alter idoneus? Non equidem ego mihi istud temere arrogaverim. Sic spectetis ad me, ut ex me no exspectetis. Nam ego unus sum de exspectantibus, mendicans at ipse vobiscum cibum animae meae, alimoniam spiritus . . . O piissime, frange esurientibus panem tuum, meis quidem, si dignaris, manibus, sed tuis viribus.[47]

[But who is going to divide this loaf? The Master of the house is present, it is the Lord you must see in the breaking of the bread. For who else could more fittingly do it? It is a task that I would not dare arrogate to myself. So look upon me as one from whom you look for nothing. For I myself am one of the seekers, one who begs along with you for the food of my soul, the nourishment of my spirit . . . O God most kind, break your bread for this hungering flock, through my hands if it should please you, but with an efficacy that is all your own.[48]]

This act of breaking the loaf can be adduced as an image for Julian's narrative self-presentation which creates for her readers the possibility of imaginative access to the revelation as though at first hand. The loaf of revelation is provided by the 'paterfamilias', 'Iesus Christ, our endless blisse' (1.1), but is broken through Julian's hands – which is to say that it depends on her reconstruction of contingent personal experience – to feed a hungry flock of which she presents herself to be a member.

We have been concerned to show here that Julian's narrative self-presentation adds up to much more than the throwing in of a few stray bits of anecdote to add a splash of colour or light relief. Julian's foregrounding of her problematical relation to the showings is integral to the text's self-proclaimed revelatory function and operates in a dynamic way, through the narrated rhythm of seeking and beholding, to recreate a momentum of discovery in which the reader can vicariously participate. We have called this 'formal autobiographicality' because it represents a self-conscious artistic decision to use anecdote as a major rhetorical stratagem, not denying it or relegating it to the margins but formalizing it, giving it a certain prestige within the text as a whole. This formal autobiographicality is, of course, dependant on what we have identified as the 'intrinsic autobiographicality' of Julian's text, that assumption of an achieved perspective on past experience which facilitates both the reconstruction of that experience in the form of a more or less coherent narrative; and the drawing of shareable religious conclusions from it. The 'intrinsic' and the 'formal' should not, therefore, be regarded as discrete categories of autobiography operating independently within the text, as though we could switch from one to the other. In fact, these two aspects combine in an integral autobiographical project.[49]

[47] Sermo I.ii.4, *S. Bernardi Opera*, ed. J. Leclercq, C. H. Talbot and H. M. Rochais (Rome, 1957–), *Sermones Super Cantica Canticorum* (henceforward, *Super Cantica*), vol. I, pp. 4–5.

[48] Bernard of Clairvaux *On the Song of Songs I*, trans. Kilian Walsh with intro. by Corneille M. Halflants, Cistercian Fathers Series, 4 (Kalamazoo, Michigan, 1981), p. 3.

[49] I deliberately use the term 'autobiographical project' in order to avoid too glib a designation of Julian's revelation as 'an autobiography'. I have been influenced

The 'formal' is itself a witness to the 'intrinsic' and is conditioned by it. Certain implication of the autobiographicality of Julian's writing will be examined in the final section of this chapter.

Implications of Autobiography

Julian's reconstruction of personal experience as something of value for others is not an uncomplicated act. Of necessity this autobiographical project comes to fruition (but did it ever come to its *final* fruition?) under a cluster of pressures – religious, cultural, political, emotional, intellectual. Some of these pressures, deriving from Julian's historical and geographical location, are applied from without (though inwardly felt); others are more personal and immediate, emerging within Julian's singular consciousness and conscience. This final section of Chapter 1 will seek to identify significant internal and external pressures under which Julian labours in the making of her text, and in this way prepare the ground for a discussion of the text which will see it as achieving form in creative response to those particular exigencies. It is useful to begin with the Short Text where Julian's sense of the inherent difficulty and potentially alienating nature of her task is present in a more urgent, foregrounded form than in the Long Text. The dynamics of her response in the later redaction to precisely this urgency might then become clearer.

Chapter vi of the Short Text comprises what amounts to a relatively lengthy apologia on Julian's part for her undertaking to publicize her own religious experience and reflections, and reveals the complexity of her predicament as a female 'visionary' seeking the confidence of an audience

by Leigh Gilmore's approach. She writes: 'Julian's text emphasizes its autobiographics, those elements of self-representational practices and discourses, rather than its consolidated status as an autobiography . . .', *Autobiographics*, p. 144. Gilmore coins the term 'autobiographics' to denote those strategies of discourse by which women autobiographers negotiate a space for their own stories within a male-dominated ideological-literary field. My own approach to the autobiographical (specifically to Julian's 'autobiographical project') would include what Gilmore means by 'autobiographics'. But I would also want the term 'autobiographical' to denote something philosophically larger: a sense of the necessary, inescapable rootedness of Julian's whole project (however speculatively theological the writing seems to get) in her own contingent personal experience. More generally on Gilmore, while much that she says is extremely valuable, I do find her approach a bit grimly political at times. It may be the case that in discourse as in society, politics, like the head of King Charles I, gets into everything, and it is no doubt right that we should be wise to it. But that does not mean everything is therefore politics. (For the head of King Charles I getting into everything, see Charles Dickens, *David Copperfield*, notably Chapter 14, 'My Aunt makes up her Mind about me.')

within the context of late medieval Catholicism.[50] Some of the component pressures that go to make up this predicament surface very clearly in this chapter and it is useful to try and separate them, whilst bearing in mind that it is the *combined* effect of these pressures that challenges Julian's emotional and intellectual resources.

The chapter opens with a statement of Julian's conviction that the truths to which she is exposed in the showings are not only related to herself but have a general application:

Alle that I sawe of my selfe I meene in the persone of alle myne evynn cristene, for I am lernede in the gastelye schewynge of oure lorde that he meenys so. (CW 219.1–3)

This, as Julian indicates by the words 'he meenys so', is not for her merely a question of personal opinion, a feeling that what she has received might possibly be useful to others. Much more than that, she states and reaffirms in both texts a belief that the general application is intrinsic to the showings themselves, their true raison d'être.[51] The revelation as a whole is given 'in comforthe of vs alle' (CW 219.8) and is, together with the teaching it contains, 'of Jhesu Chryste to edificacion of 30ure saule' (CW 219.9). Two things, then, are clear in Julian's mind: the showings have a divine origin, and God himself intends the teaching they contain to reach a wider audience.

Julian's impulse to publicize her experience is presented in chapter vi as a compelling manifestation of the will of God in the context of her personal relationship with him, a relationship in which obedience is the natural touchstone of faith.[52] We can identify this as the first and most

---

[50] This aspect of Julian's personal and authorial predicament is well summed-up, and contextualized, in Nicholas Watson, *Richard Rolle and the Invention of Authority* (Cambridge, 1991), p. 4.

[51] Felicity Riddy writes: 'Again and again, [Julian] explicitly denies her own singularity', '"Women talking about the things of God"', p. 115. Riddy explores the implications of this in relation to Julian's becoming, through clerical approval, 'a member of a group which enables her to speak in the extraordinarily challenging way she does, to assume her voices of power'. There is much truth in this, but it is important to observe also that one obvious implication of Julian's generalizing from her own experience is that that experience, in its very particularity, is understood as being worth generalizing from.

[52] I differ here from Nicholas Watson who does not see a necessary link between Julian's obedience to God and the making of the text. Watson refers to 'the revealing circumstance that unlike many similar experiences given to Continental women, [Julian's] revelation contained no commission to write', 'Composition', p. 652; and then goes on to deduce from this that while 'she makes much of the *general impression* she had while her vision was in progress that it was meant for everyone . . . *such a feeling is far from providing any justification in itself for writing a book*' (my emphasis). Watson does seem to load

significant of the pressures to which Julian is subject: the pressure of one highly religious individual's sense of a conscientious obligation to her creator. If she is to keep faith with God she can hardly do otherwise than respond wholeheartedly to what he seems to be asking, as she explicitly and provocatively insists in anticipation of an objection to her gender:

> Botte for I am a womann, schulde I therfore leve that I schulde nouȝt telle ȝowe the goodenes of god, syne that I sawe in that same tyme that is his wille, that it be knawenn? (CW 222.46–8)

Julian's acceptance of the task entrusted to her by God 'for the profytte of many oder' (CW 220.17–18) constitutes, therefore, an act of obedience, which means that the performance of that task is bound up inextricably with the question of her faithfulness to him. This is a fundamental principle of Julian's self-understanding as presented in chapter vi. In the following passage her own desire that the showings should be more generally known is expressed with a forthrightness derived from the stated conviction that in this matter her personal desire coincides with the divine will:

> it is goddys wille and my desyre that ȝe take it with als grete ioye and lykynge as Jhesu hadde schewyd it to ȝowe as he dyd to me [. . .] And so ys my desyre that it schulde be to euery ilke manne the same profytte that I desyrede to my self and þerto was styrryd of god in the fyrste tyme when I sawe itte; for yt (ys) comonn and generale as we ar alle ane, and I am sekere I sawe it for the profytte of many oder
> (CW 219–20.9–11,14–18)

Were it not for striking evidence to the contrary, we might be inclined to suspect that Julian's perception of a divine mandate as the compelling and animating power of what might be called her prophetic task ought to be sufficient insurance against feelings of self-doubt in this undertaking. Yet her tone in chapter vi is less than imbued with a sense of confidence in God, tending to slide into defensiveness as she focuses on her vulnerable

his argument somewhat by using the phrase 'general impression' to character-ize Julian's sense of the revelation's being for everyone. What Watson calls a 'general impression' may just as well have been an *exigent pressure*, the intensity of which we might infer precisely from the energy that has gone into the activities of textual production and – especially – of revision. Julian explicitly writes in ST chapter vi of her perception that God wants the revelation to 'be knawenn' (CW 222.48), and it is hard to know what other form than that of a text could answer this demand. The further point ought also to be made that contrasting Julian with Continental visionaries (as Watson does), whilst valid and instructive in some ways, does not produce positive arguments about the specifics of Julian's case.

position in relation to her presumed audience. We can read a considerable degree of anxiety in the piling up of self-deprecatory and apologetic statements which have, in their cumulative effect, an urgency beyond that of a merely conventional modesty. She advises her audience to 'leve the behaldynge of the wrechid wor(m)e, synfulle creature, that it was shewyd vnto' (CW 219.4–6) and to concentrate on God, the true source of revelation. She is especially concerned to stress that her extraordinary visionary experience does not of itself give her any spiritual advantage over the common run of believers:

> For the schewynge I am not goode but ȝif y love god the better . . . For sothly it was nought schewyd vnto me that god loves me bettere thane the leste sawlle that is in grace. For I am sekere thare ys fulle many that nevere hadde schewynge ne syght botte of the common techynge of haly kyrke that loves god better þan I. (CW 220.11–12, 18–21)

It is, however, towards the end of the chapter that the tensions of Julian's predicament are most clearly evident as she asserts her duty to God whilst at the same time struggling to define, and justify, her position in relation to the audience:

> Botte god for bede that ȝe schulde saye or take it so I am a techere, for I meene nouȝt soo, no I mente nevere so; for I am a womann, leued, febille and freylle. Botte I wate wele, this that I saye, I hafe it of the schewynge of hym tha(t) es souerayne techare. Botte sotheleye charyte styrres me to telle ȝowe it, for I wolde god ware knawenn, and mynn evynn crystene spede, as I wolde be my selfe to the mare hatyng of synne and lovynge of god. Botte for I am a womann, schulde I therfore leve that I schulde nouȝt telle ȝowe the goodenes of god, syne that I sawe in that same tyme that is his wille, that it be knawenn? (CW 222.40–8)

Somewhat paradoxically for a chapter in which one of Julian's stated concerns is to impress upon the reader that she herself is of no consequence, 'ryght nought' (CW 220.22) as she puts it, we have here an emotionally-charged, syntactically-contorted passage which brings the raw immediacy of Julian's personal situation startlingly to the surface. To the reader only familiar with the Long Text, the troubled 'egocentricity' of this passage will come as something of a revelation in itself. Julian departs from what has been basically a controlled, formal, even a detached tone in the preceding section of the chapter and seems suddenly to be in need of the sympathy of her audience, appearing to clutch for steadiness at that fourfold, defensive 'Botte'.[53] Her defiant pleading in the final rhetorical

---

[53] Nicholas Watson justly observes that the conjunction of the four 'buts' generates a rhetorical force that 'was less in Middle than in formal Modern English, but was nonetheless real', 'Composition', p. 652.

question; her emphatic protestation, 'for I meene nouȝt soo, no I mente nevere so'; that invocation of her 'souerayne techare' in anticipation of objections to her gender: together these communicate a palpable, complicated anxiety.[54]

We have already noted that Julian's sense of her accountability to God constitutes the first of the pressures under which she has to write. The self-consciousness exhibited so unmistakably in this chapter is itself another pressure, directly consequential upon her obedience to God. In attempting to create a text through which the revelations can be publicized, Julian inevitably exposes herself to the scrutiny of an audience which is entitled to question her truthfulness, her motivation; and, above all in this religious context, the kind of authority she claims for herself. The unavoidable claim to personal enlightenment which is intrinsic to her prophetic task means that at all points, no matter how seemingly speculative or abstract it gets, her writing is rooted in the poor, vulnerable soil of contingent personal experience. This is true whether we are concerned with intrinsic autobiographicality, or with the way Julian grasps the nettle, so to speak, and deploys autobiographical anecdote as part of her rhetorical strategy. The witness of chapter vi is that, at this earlier stage of composition, Julian's exposure to an audience, both as author and as the self-proclaimed subject of extraordinary spiritual experience, is a source of deep embarrassment.

In the first place, the kind of implicit value being set on personal experience here is a factor which immediately queers the pitch of Julian's whole project. Her authorial predicament is that of one who, firmly believing she has received a revelation from God which she is obliged to communicate, must create a text that does justice to her visionary experience whilst at the same time authenticating itself in terms which are credible within the religious and cultural context she shares with her contemporary audience. Put simply, the text's message will stand or fall according to how successful she is in establishing the legitimacy of her self-exposure. Why should her private and subjective experience carry any weight in a public realm where dogmatic truth is dispensed to the faithful through a hierarchical structure which claims an absolute, objective, divine guarantee for its authority?

In addition, the religious institutions in relation to which Julian must negotiate her claims to authoritative experience are not themselves untroubled, nor do they exist in an a-historical vacuum.[55] An unlikely

---

[54] The foregrounding of Julian's anxiety in ST chapter vi is discussed particularly in Watson, 'Composition'; in Johnson, 'Trope of the Scribe'; and the implications of this anxiety, if not quite so much of this particular passage, in Riddy, ' "Women talking about the things of God" ' (though the passage is cited, see p. 111).

[55] Leigh Gilmore writes that 'autobiography is driven by an authorization

and officially unaccredited seafarer in the waters of theological discourse, Julian is obliged to weigh anchor in very stormy weather. Having her visionary experience in 1373 and producing her (at least) two accounts some time between then and the end of the first quarter of the fifteenth century, Julian was most active as a writer at a time of quite definite religious tensions. On the broad canvas, the fact of the Great Schism (1378–1417), when there were always at least two claimants to the papal throne and sometimes three, can only lend a certain poignancy to Julian's express concern for the unity in Christ of all Christians, and to her lament for Holy Church, which she says 'shal be shakyn in sorows and anguis and tribulation in this world as men shakyth a cloth in the wynde' (28.39).[56] Closer to home there is also the problem of John Wycliffe and the Lollards (not to be glibly conflated) who opposed much that was traditional in Catholic belief and practice.[57] Given this background, Julian's claim to charismatic authority for her theological insights, a claim which would be problematical at any time, might even have been potentially dangerous.[58]

complex. Its writers attempt to situate themselves in relation to [the ideologically-prevailing] discourses of "truth" and "identity", *Autobiographics*, p. 124.

[56] For information on the larger religio-political scene I have used Steven Ozment, *The Age of Reform 1250–1550: An Intellectual and Religious History of Late Medieval and Reformation Europe* (New Haven and London, 1980). On the Great Schism, see especially pp. 155–72. Ozment is particularly enlightening on the doctrinal and political ferment of the 1378–1417 period.

[57] On John Wycliffe and the Lollards there is much excellent material, notably: Margaret Aston, *Lollards and Reformers: Images and Literacy in Late Medieval Religion* (London, 1984); Anne Hudson, *Lollards and Their Books* (London, 1985) and *The Premature Reformation: Wycliffite Texts and Lollard History* (Oxford, 1988), also ed. Hudson, *Selections from English Wycliffite Writings* (Cambridge, 1978). In addition, I have been very much helped by: R. N. Swanson, *Church and Society in Late Medieval England*, paperback edition (Oxford, 1993), Chapter 7, 'Nonconformity and Dislocation', especially pp. 312–47; and Malcolm Lambert, *Medieval Heresy: Popular Movements from the Gregorian Reform to the Reformation*, second edition, with new subtitle (Oxford, 1993). Nicholas Watson has an excellent discussion of the question of a possible link between anxieties about Lollardy and the writing of Julian's text, see 'Composition', pp. 657–66. He suggests that her stress on the specifically imagistic content of her visions is, in part, a strategically anti-Lollard gesture aimed at heading-off the potential dangers of a conspicuous religious literacy (female literacy being associated around this time with Lollardy). Joan M. Nuth also considers Julian in terms of anxieties about orthodoxy, though in a rather more generalized way than Watson does, see *Wisdom's Daughter*, pp. 16–22.

[58] The absence of any early manuscripts of LT is highly suggestive in this context. Perhaps those that did exist fell victim in some way to the heresy-hysteria of the fifteenth and especially the early-sixteenth century, or the Reformation and its long political aftermath, or both (see Swanson, *Church and Society*, pp. 350–63).

Julian's repeated assertions of her loyalty to the Church – though characteristically to the *teaching* of the Church – testify to her desire to be accepted as orthodox and there is no evidence that she intends her writing to be taken as an overt doctrinal or political challenge to the medieval Church. Nevertheless it is true that her claim of personal divine illumination inevitably threatens to alienate her from – or, one might say, *within* – an orthodox ecclesiological context, and this at a time of heightened sensitivity about the whole question of orthodoxy and the relation of the individual believer to the Christian mysteries as mediated through the structures of the Church. As a lay-person writing on religious themes in the vernacular; as a woman; as a self-proclaimed, self-authenticating visionary, Julian attains a necessary but problematical singularity. She finds herself in a paradoxical situation. As we have already noted, the showings set her apart from others by the fact of their extraordinariness, but her perception of a message for her 'even cristen' (8.13) within the showings means that this very separateness becomes a function of her relationship with them. This imposes on her a need to find a way of overcoming the problem of separateness which will effectively confirm her positive relation to the Church but will not deny the integrity, and so the extraordinariness, of her personal experience.

The problem of separateness, of the gap between the institutional and the charismatic, is one which Julian must address if what she believes to be a divine message is to reach and convince its intended audience. Yet both the religious/political problem of separateness and the problem of Julian's need to overcome it, to close the gap between herself and her fellow Christians, are also problems of rhetoric. Through the experience of vision Julian is, as it were, born out of the womb of a tribal, pre-reflective Christian anonymity, the condition of those 'that never had shewing ner sight, but of the comon techyng of holy church' (9.13). She achieves troubled self-consciousness as a distinct religious subject, differentiated from the tribe but of necessity still identifying herself in relation to it.[59] This coming to birth as a differentiated subject of religious experience is correlated also with a coming to birth of Julian as a self-conscious author. For the reader, Julian's assumption of a differentiated personal identity is indivisible from, and readable in, her assumption of the autobiographical 'I'. The pressing problem for Julian, both as author and as religious subject, is that of straddling the gap between herself and

[59] Leigh Gilmore writes: 'autobiographical identity is always constructed through the changing and contradictory exigencies of the specific, and . . . the autobiographer's reinscription of and resistance to a [politically-authorized] model of selfhood is a dialectic that shapes self-representation', *Autobiographics*, p. 84.

her fellow Christians.[60] Communication implies differentiation from, but also a yearning towards, the other. Julian's visionary experience makes her in one sense an exile from the mundane, from the domestic hearth of conventional religion; her yearning for re-admission informs her theological themes and procedures so that the very manner of the text's construction can be read as an index of that desire.

But Julian's achieved self-consciousness and the significance this allows her to attach to her own contingent experience cannot be denied. They are, for her, non-negotiable. If Julian is to return home to tell her story, she must do so as an adult. Our concern in the rest of this book is to show that there is inscribed within the rhetorical and theological procedures of the Long Text Julian's attempt to 'come home' to her presumed audience without, so to speak, selling her soul in the process. Her mature preoccupations, as discernible in the reconstruction of past experience combined with her theological reflections on it, can be interpreted as answering to an anxiety about the value attachable to personal experience within the context of late medieval Catholicism. This can be called an anxiety about autobiography.

It is a central claim of this book that Julian's Long Text achieves form both rhetorically and thematically precisely in response to this anxiety about autobiography. The next chapter will attempt to show that in reconstructing her experience, Julian narrates a personal movement from what is presented as a culturally-conditioned, affectively pietistic and would-be exclusive relationship with Christ to a developed theological understanding of the way in which the human race, initially left outside the door while she concentrates on God, is mystically enclosed in Christ.

Chapters 3 and 4 will then examine in depth Julian's concern for the relation between Christ's union with the Church and his personal union with each individual member of it. These chapters will look very closely at her incarnational theology and its implications. They will claim that, in effect, Julian proposes the union of Christ with the individual to be the necessary basis of a mystical (rather than a merely institutional) ecclesiology. The mystical coinherence through Christ of the personal and the ecclesiological implies a dissolution of the gap between Julian as differentiated subject of religious experience and the total community of her fellow Christians. This amounts to an affirmation of the value of personal

---

[60] We could say that Julian seeks to establish a totalizing paradigm within which the religio-political tensions of her predicament might be theoretically/imaginatively resolved, or at least contained. See generally, Jesse M. Gelrich, *The Idea of the Book in the Middle Ages: Language Theory, Mythology and Fiction* (Ithaca and London, 1985).

experience which does not place that experience over against the Church but invites interpretation in terms of an interiorized ecclesiology.

Chapter 5 seeks to illustrate Julian's assertion of the value of the person, and of life *as lived*, by considering two rhetorical aspects of her text. First, we look at her use of an idiom of interiority which supports her concept of the person as a *mystical* subject, made capacious both by nature and by grace for the fullness divine life. Secondly, we consider what can be called the pastoral thrust of Julian's text, its avowed purpose of giving real assistance to real people amid the contingencies and exigencies of life in a fallen world.

All in all, it should become clear as the book proceeds that the heart of the Long Text is to be found in a certain affirmation of the personal, though not of the self-sufficient individual in some kind of existential isolation. Julian writes as a fifteenth century woman immersed in the Catholic culture of her time and place. Her understanding of 'the person' is therefore not derived – to speak perhaps rather broadly – from a Renaissance humanism, or from an 'enlightened', atomizing scientism, or from a romantic or existential subjectivism. Rather, her affirmation of the personal takes the form of a developed incarnational theology; of a distinctly mystical ecclesiology, with an emphasis on sacrament rather than polity; and a pastoral concern for life as it is lived in the context of Christian community, both local and universal. Julian – and therefore we – cannot touch the question of the personal without touching all of these things directly or indirectly.

2

A Journey into Christ

IN Chapters 2 and 3 Julian sketches something of the background to her visionary experience; and, more crucially for us, something of the nature of her pre-visionary aspirations and priorities. The mature Julian, as we have already noted, is evoking with the benefit of hindsight a past self of many years ago. The precise manner of this evocation is revealing of her considered, critical attitude to that earlier self, and of her sense of its location on a retrospectively-discerned trajectory of achieved human and spiritual development.

Julian's story begins, as we have seen, with an account of her prayer for 'iii gifts of God' (2.2), which is in effect a prayer for five gifts since the third is in three parts. The gifts are: 'mende of his passion', 'bodily sekenesse' (2.2) and the wounds of 'very contrition', 'kinde compassion' and 'willfull longing to God' (2.3). At the start of the text Julian portrays herself rapt in an intense personal devotion to Christ, concerned primarily for her own salvation and desiring an intensification of her religious experience. She feels she has come sufficiently far to make some rather bold requests of her divine lover – certainly, and no doubt sincerely, with the express intention of enhancing her devotion to him in this life, but also very much with an eye to her heavenly reward:

> I desired to have all manier peynes bodily and ghostly that I should have if I should dye, and with all the dreds and tempests of the fends, except the outpassing of the soule. And this I ment for I would be purged be the mercy of God and after lyven more to the worshippe of God because of that sekenesse; and that for the more speede in my deth, for I desired to be soone with my God. (2.3)

The phrase 'speede in my deth' could express a desire for early death, but might also carry the sense of 'be to my advantage when I die'. The latter sense is supported by a line in Chapter 3 where Julian states her hope that the near-mortal illness might bring her to a greater love of God on earth so that, as a consequence, she will receive 'the more knoweing and lovyng of

God in blisse of hevyn' (3.4). If there is sound logic here, from a religious point of view, there is also a kind of self-interest.

In narrating her requests for the three gifts Julian gives us a snapshot of her own spiritual state as she perceives it to have been at about the time of the showings in 1373; and the main features of the ST account are retained,[1] suggesting that the mature Julian still regards them as integral to her communication of the 'revelation of love' (1.1). There is an important sense in which this snapshot is preserved as a stratum throughout the text, Julian sustaining her representation of that naïve but questioning consciousness of hers which experienced the showings in the first place. Nevertheless, it is largely in the first third of the text, and especially in Chapters 2 and 3, that she attempts to evoke the precise nature of this (relatively) youthful consciousness. What is particularly disclosed in these chapters is a private world consisting in a self-contained relationship between Julian and Christ. He alone, or her projected religious ideal of him, is the focus of her entire human interest, and in the presence even of a mere representation of him other realities recede into a sinister, shadowy margin:

> After this my sight began to failen and it was all derke about me in the chamber as it had be night, save in the image of the cross wherein I beheld a comon light, and I wiste not how. All that was beside the cross was uggely to me as if it had be mekil occupied with the fends. (3.4–5)

The younger Julian's devotion to the person of Christ is principally characterized by a desire to be emotionally stirred to love him through as vivid as possible an inner realization of his suffering. If any kind of knowledge is sought ('mende of his passion' 2.2; 'knowledge of the bodily peynes of our saviour' 2.3) it is with the precise purpose of serving this emotional response to Christ's sufferings. It also needs to be remembered,

---

[1] There are, however, significant changes of detail, as noted in B. A. Windeatt, 'Julian of Norwich and her Audience', *Review of English Studies*, New Series, XXVIII (1977), pp. 1–17, especially Section I. The omission from LT of any reference to the virgin-martyr St Cecilia (ST chapter i, CW 204–5.46–9) is particularly striking, as is that of the following passage: 'not withstandynge that I leevyd sadlye alle the peynes of Cryste as halye kyrke schewys and techys, and also the payntyngys of crucyfexes that er made be the grace of god aftere the techynge of haly kyrke to the lyknes of Crystes passyon, als farfurthe as man ys witte may reche' (CW 202.14–19). Nicholas Watson discusses the inclusion of the latter within ST as evidence of specific religio-political pressures which he thinks must have dissolved somewhat by the time LT was written. It is partly on this basis that he suggests Julian may still have been writing LT as late as 1415, see Watson, 'Composition', especially pp. 657–83. The story of St Cecilia (a version of which Chaucer uses for his *Second Nun's Tale*) perhaps suggests an impulse on Julian's part to adduce in ST her credentials as a subscriber to mainstream popular piety.

especially since later development of the theme can obscure this point, that when Julian asks for the 'wounde of kinde compassion' (2.3) she does not have in mind a fellow-feeling for humankind in general, but 'compassion as a kinde soule might have with our lord Iesus' (punctuation slightly altered). As for her desire for a sickness almost unto death, although Julian does not explicitly relate it to Christ's own suffering, the context suggests that it should be read as a further intensification of her prevailing religious mood, emotional empathy seeking a degree of bodily replication: 'therefore I desired to suffer with him' (3.5).[2]

The kind of christocentric piety Julian displays here must owe a debt to that stream of affective spirituality classically defined by Richard Southern, which he sees partly exemplified in the writings of Anselm of Canterbury (1033–1109) but very much gathering force and intensity in those of Bernard of Clairvaux (1090–1153) and the early Cistercians, including English Cistercians like Aelred of Rievaulx.[3] In relating Julian to a particular mode of affective religion it is important to maintain a sense of her dynamic and idiosyncratic interaction with tradition; and just as important not to underestimate the fluidity of tradition itself as it meanders through history's mainstreams and backwaters. It is as well to remember, for example, that Bernard and Aelred had both been dead nearly two centuries by the time Julian was born in 1342/3. But it is

---

[2] The influence of the Pauline notion of a personal conformation to the death of Christ is surely to be discerned here, as much as any contemporary *imitatio Christi* impulse – see Philippians 3.10: 'That I may know him and the power of his resurrection and the fellowship of his sufferings; being made conformable [Vulgate: *configuratus*] to his death'. In this context it is interesting that Colledge and Walsh note Julian's replication of the syntax of the Vulgate version of Philippians 2.5. See their note to ST chapter x. 25. Whilst many of the scriptural (and other) allusions 'identified' by Colledge and Walsh can seem arbitrary or tendentious, I agree with them here. My general view is that St Paul is a crucial influence on Julian, as this book should make clear.

[3] See R. W. Southern, *The Making of the Middle Ages*, paperback reprint (London, 1993), Chapter 5, 'From Epic to Romance', pp. 210–44. Other important works in this field are: Colin Morris, *The Discovery of the Individual 1050–1200* (London, 1972) and Caroline Walker Bynum, *Jesus as Mother: Studies in the Spirituality of the High Middle Ages*, paperback edition (Los Angeles and London, 1984), especially Chapter III, 'Did the Twelfth Century Discover the Individual?', pp. 82–109 – Bynum modifies the analyses of Southern and Morris, identifying an 'equilibrium between interior and exterior, self and community' (p. 109). Eamon Duffy's *The Stripping of the Altars: Traditional Religion in England 1400–1580* (Princeton, New Jersey, 1992) is indispensable for an understanding of the parish-based spirituality of the late medieval period. For specific discussion of Julian herself in relation to traditions of affective piety see: Baker, *Julian of Norwich's Showings*, pp. 15–62; Vincent Gillespie and Maggie Ross, 'The Apophatic Image: the Poetics of Effacement in Julian of Norwich', in *MMTE: V* (Cambridge, 1992), pp. 53–77; and, particularly lucid and accessible, Jantzen, *Julian of Norwich*, pp. 53–73.

nevertheless worth trying, briefly, to gain some purchase on the affective tradition since there can be no doubt that Julian's writing adduces themes and attitudes which had been prevalent in various forms for a considerable period. Furthermore, it should help us understand a little more clearly what Julian is telling us about her youthful, pre-visionary self.

In general terms, then, this mode of piety, springing from what Southern identifies as an apparently major shift in religious sensibility, has as its focus the human, and especially the suffering Christ,[4] and it seeks to involve the individual in an intense emotional relationship with the incarnate Word. Here is Bernard meditating on the passion in his sixty-first sermon on the Song of Songs:

> Ego vero fidenter quod ex mihi deest, usurpo mihi ex visceribus Domini, quoniam misericordia affluunt, nec desunt foramina, per quae effluant. Foderunt manus eius et pedes, latusque lancea foraverunt, et per has rimas licet mihi sugere mel de petra, oleumque de saxo durissimo, id est gustare et videre quoniam suavis est Dominus.[5]

> [But as for me, whatever is lacking from my own resources I appropriate for myself from the heart of the Lord, which overflows with mercy. And there is no lack of clefts by which they are poured out. They pierced his hands and his feet, they gored his side with a lance, and through these fissures I can suck honey from the rock and oil from the flinty stone – I can taste and see that the Lord is good.[6]]

---

[4] 'Until this time [the late-eleventh century], the most important representation of the Crucifixion in Western Europe had expressed the sense of that remote and majestic act of Divine power which had filled the minds of earlier generation. But a change had been slowly creeping in, which led in time to the realisation of the extreme limits of human suffering: the dying figure was stripped of its garments, the arms sagged with the weight of the body, the head hung on one side, the eyes were closed, the blood ran down the Cross', Southern, *Making of the Middle Ages*, p. 226. Compare Southern's observation here that 'the arms agged with the weight of the body' with Julian's statement that Christ's body 'saggid for weyte be long tyme hanging' (17.25). Julian's evocation of the passion would certainly qualify as a 'realisation of the extreme limits of human suffering'. Gillespie and Ross, whilst convincingly exculpating Julian herself, note that affective piety (in the form of an over-imaginative, over-emotional compassion for Christ) 'had become a debased commodity in the late-fourteenth century', 'Apophatic Image', p. 61. This degeneration is also noted by Rowan Williams, *Wound of Knowledge*, p. 140; and by Simon Tugwell, *Ways of Imperfection: An Exploration of Christian Spirituality* (Springfield, Illinois, 1985), pp. 152–69. Tugwell provides an excellent account of affective traditions in their literary forms, and especially of the lyric form. He concludes with a largely negative assessment of Richard Rolle and Margery Kempe, who are both seen as representatives of a tradition getting stuck in its own inherent emotionalism.

[5] Sermo LXI.ii.4, *Super Cantica*, vol. II, p. 150.

[6] *On the Song of Songs III*, trans. Kilian Walsh and Irene M. Edmonds, with an intro. by Emero Stiegman (Kalamazoo, Michigan, 1979), p. 143.

The affective bond with Christ is not an end in itself but is intended, as Bernard understands it, to act as a bridge between flesh and spirit, 'seducing' the suggestible, volatile, carnal self into a love of God which begins on the intrinsically disorderly sensual level but is gradually refined to become something spiritual and ordered (and into which the sensuality is absorbed). Commenting on the scriptural command, 'You shall love the Lord your God with your whole heart, your whole soul and your whole strength',[7] he writes in another of these sermons, the twentieth:

> Mihi videtur, si alius competentior sensus in hac trina distinctione non occurrit , amor quidem cordis ad zelum quemdam pertinere affectionis, animae vero amor ad industriam seu iudicium rationis, virtutis autem dilectio ad animi posse referri constantiam vel vigorem. Dilige ergo Dominum Deum tuum toto et pleno cordis affectu, dilige tota rationis vigilantia et circumspectione, dilige et tota virtute, ut nec mori pro eius amore pertimescas . . . Sit suavis et dulcis affectui tuo Dominus Iesus, contra male utique dulces vitae carnalis illecebras, et vincat dulcedinem, quemadmodum clavum clavis expellit.[8]

> [It seems to me, if no more suitable meaning for this triple distinction comes to mind, that the love of the heart relates to a certain warmth of affection, the love of the soul to energy or judgement of reason, and the love of strength can refer to constancy and vigour of spirit. So love the Lord your God with the full and deep affection of your heart, love him with your mind wholly awake and discreet, love him with all your strength, so much so that you would not even fear to die for love of him . . . Your affection for your Lord Jesus should be both tender and intimate, to oppose the sweet enticements of sensual life. Sweetness conquers sweetness as one nail drives out another.[9]]

Here Bernard outlines his paradigm of mature love of God, a love integrating affection, reason and spirit. The re-ordering of affectivity is fundamental to this paradigm, notably in relation to the dynamics of moral conversion. Such a conversion could not get off the ground in any credible sense without a genuine engagement of the vital power of *eros*.

Bernard, of course, is writing out of and for the disciplined and somewhat privileged world of the twelfth century Cistercians. Yet the idea of a tender personal love for Christ, with its obvious human appeal, soon found its way into the bloodstream of Catholic religious culture in general, owing in large measure to the influence of the early Franciscans.[10] But to the extent that this form of christocentric piety entered the popular

[7] Deuteronomy 6.5.
[8] Sermo XX.iii.4, *Super Cantica*, vol. I, pp. 116–17.
[9] *Song of Songs I*, p. 150.
[10] See Southern, *Making of the Middle Ages*, p. 229.

imagination, it largely broke away from the influence – moderating or repressive, according to your point of view – of monastic spiritual theology, and took on a varied, sometimes wild and wilful, life of its own.

A notable literary flowering of this tradition in the English vernacular can be identified in that body of peculiarly intense and emotionally-engaging religious lyrics dating from the thirteenth to the early sixteenth century.[11] Although the poems encompass a variety of religious themes, that of the suffering Christ is prominent, and principally a Christ whose death is presented as an act of personal love for every individual. The lyric form, by its very nature, elicits an imaginative/dramatic self-insertion into the events with which it is concerned and so intensifies the personalizing dynamic of affective piety. This is true whether the poem sketches the narrative details of the passion in the form of an address to Christ:

> My dereworthly derlyng, sa dolefully dyght,
> Sa straytly upryght streyned on the rode;
> For thi mykel mekenes, thi mercy, thi myght,
> Thow bete al my bales with bote of thi blode;[12]

or if it is composed as a divine *planctus* uttered from the cross, a personal appeal aimed precisely at the heart, as in the fifteenth century poem from which the following verse is taken:

> Thus nakid am I nailid, O man, for thi sake.
> I love the, thenne love me. Why slepist thou? awake!
> Remember my tender hert-rote for the brake,
> With paynes my vaines constrayned to crake.
> > Thus was I defasid,
> > Thus was my flesh rasid,
> > And I to deth chasid,
> > Like a lambe led unto sacrefise,
> > Slayne was I in most cruell wise.[13]

Another dramatizing angle on the passion is provided by those lyrics either addressed to, or put into the mouth of, the Virgin Mary as a witness and sharer of Christ's suffering. She pre-eminently represents humanity unconditionally responsive to God. Her perfect disposition in that respect figures, albeit in an idealized fashion, precisely the disposition of love that affective piety tries to foster. Mary's responsiveness to God is amplified as a poetic theme through its expression in terms of her relation to Christ as

---

[11] I have relied here on the introduction and texts of ed. Douglas Gray, *English Medieval Religious Lyrics*, revised edition (Exeter, 1992).

[12] Gray, *Religious Lyrics*, no. 19, pp. 16–17.

[13] Gray, no. 27, pp. 26–7.

his mother. The following lyric, found in a late-fourteenth century manuscript, neatly fuses a religious notion of self-immolation (a Pauline
conformation to the death of Christ) and the sheer agony of a mother
for whom the possibility of sharing her child's death would be a relief:

> Wy have ye no reuthe on my child?
> Have reuthe on me ful of mourning!
> Taket doun on rode my derworthi child,
> Or prek me on rode with my derling!
>
> More pine ne may me ben don
> Than laten me liven in sorwe, and schame –
> Als love me bindet to my sone,
> So lat us deyyen both isame.[14]

Perhaps even more relevant than this lyric tradition to a consideration
of Julian's affective piety, especially given her life as an anchoress,[15] is that
other tradition of self-dramatizing engagement with the events of Christ's
life which finds expression in, for example, the prose meditations of
Richard Rolle, but probably more influentially in Aelred of Rievaulx's *De
Institutione Inclusarum*. This is a treatise on the anchoritic life written in the
form of a letter to Aelred's sister. It was translated into Middle English,
and whether or not Julian was familiar with the work itself, in any of its
versions, she has unquestionably imbibed Aelred's devotional spirit from
one source or another. The anchoress is urged to imagine herself
physically present at the main events surrounding Christ's earthly life,
placing herself with the Virgin Mary as she awaits the archangel Gabriel;[16]
passing on through Christ's life to his suffering and death, the drama of
which is a climactic focus; and finishing with the post-resurrection
meeting of Christ with Mary Magdalen. One vernacular version of this
treatise, found in a manuscript contemporary with Julian, assigns an

---

[14] Gray, no. 22, p. 18.

[15] There is no certainty on the question of whether or not Julian was an anchoress
when she had the showings or indeed when she wrote either of her two texts.
On the latter point, the religious and literary stature of LT in particular argues
strongly (though not definitively) for an answer in the affirmative: it seems so
much a product of contemplative leisure. For further discussion, and an
alternative suggestion which I think unlikely, see Sr Benedicta, 'Julian the
Solitary', especially pp. 27–9. On the more general question of Julian's relation
to the anchoritic tradition, see Denise Nowakowski Baker, 'Julian of Norwich
and Anchoritic Literature', *Mystics Quarterly*, 19 (1993), pp. 148–60.

[16] In one vernacular tradition found in the fourteenth century Vernon manuscript,
the anchorite's cell and the Virgin Mary's private chamber, the room of the
annunciation, are conflated: 'And ferst goo in-to þy pryue chaumbre wit oure
lady Marie, wher schee abood þe angel message . . .'. *Aelred of Rievaulx's De
Institutione Inclusarum*, ed. John Ayto and Alexandra Barratt, EETS, o.s., 287
(Oxford, 1984), p. 39, lines 555–6.

urgent, imperative tone to the authorial voice as it reinforces the reader's own re-creation of the events in question. Here the meditation centres on Christ's agony in the garden of Gethsemane:

> Wher-aboute standest þu, suster? Ren to, for Godys sake, and suk of þe swete blessyde dropes, þat þey be not spild, and wyþ þy tounge likke awey þe dust of hijs feet.[17]

Another passage brings to mind Julian's desire to place herself in the company of 'Crists lovers' (2.3) at the foot of the cross:

> . . . wyþdraw þe fro þoo wummen þat stondeþ aver, as þe gospel sayþ, and wit Marie, moder and mayde, and seynt Jhon, also a clene mayde, so [sic] sadlyche to Cristes cros and *byhold avysily* [my emphasis: the phrase is reminiscent of Julian, see 11.17, 'I beheld with avisement'] how þilke face, þat angeles haueþ delyt to loke in, is bycome al dym and paal. Cast also þyn eȝe asyde to Maries cher, and loke how here fresche maydenly visage is al to-bollen and forsmoteryd wit terys. Lord, suster, whoþer þu schalle stonde by-syde wit drie eȝen, whanne þu sikst so manye salte teris lassche adoun so vnmesurably ouer here rodye chekes?[18]

The literary illusion here is of objectively real, present events in which both author and reader are implicated. This rhetoric of *anamnesis* might be said to dovetail with the quite distinct sacramentalism of the high Middle Ages which was fuelled to a significant extent by scholastic disputes over the nature of the eucharist.[19] What seems fundamentally at issue in these disputes is the need to find a credible way of affirming that Christ's saving acts, though historically particular, are susceptible of real re-enactment throughout time. For the one who meditates on the mysteries of Christ, as for the one who participates in the sacraments, mere time and space dissolve.

[17] *De Institutione Inclusarum*, p. 46, lines 842–4.
[18] *De Institutione Inclusarum*, pp. 48–9, lines 943–51.
[19] The fact that arguments about the precise nature of Christ's presence in the eucharist were central to the scholastic debates of the high Middle Ages testifies to the cultural and religious prestige attaching to the notion of sacrament. Helpful considerations of this and related questions can be found in: Miri Rubin, *Corpus Christi: The Eucharist in Late Medieval Culture* (Cambridge, 1991), especially ch. 1, pp. 12–63; Brian Stock, *The Implications of Literacy: Written Language and Modes of Interpretation in the Eleventh and Twelfth Centuries* (Princeton, New Jersey, 1983), especially ch. 3, pp. 241–325 – Stock shows how arguments about the eucharist also generated far-reaching debate about nature, language, epistemology and hermeneutics; more succinctly, see Evans, *Philosophy and Theology*, pp. 97–108; and for an important sense of the pastoral and community dimension of sacramental culture, see Duffy, *Stripping of the Altars*, Part I, and Glasscoe, *English Medieval Mystics*, pp. 18–24.

Brief mention should also be made here of the monastic concept of *lectio divina*[20] since it has a particular bearing on the way the interiorization of the scriptures, including the scriptural stories which form the basis of Aelred's meditations, is understood to bring the human subject into a personal, existential relation to the mysteries of faith, thus making these mysteries really present in their spiritual meaning and power. This laying open of the self to divine mystery is achieved by reading the Bible in an attitude of faith, by memorizing texts, and by a process of mental rumination in which emotional response (tasting, savouring[21]) is preferred to the more cerebral kinds of analysis. We can reasonably infer a significant, if not necessarily immediate, relation between this practice and both the affective fervour of the lyrics and the elaborate meditations commended by Aelred.

It is precisely the dramatizing character of both the lyric and the

---

[20] On *lectio divina*, see especially Jean Leclercq, *The Love of Learning and the Desire for God: A Study of Monastic Culture*, trans. Catharine Misrahi, revised second edition (London, 1978). Leclercq writes: 'For St Jerome as for St Benedict, the *lectio divina* is the text itself which is being read, a selected passage or a "lesson" taken from Scripture. During the Middle Ages, this expression was to be reserved more and more for the act of reading, "the reading of Holy Scripture"'', p. 89; '. . . the reader usually pronounced the words with his lips, at least in a low tone and consequently, he hears the sentence seen by his eyes . . . This results in more than a visual memory of the written words. What results is a muscular memory of the words pronounced and an aural memory of the words heard. The *meditatio* consists in applying oneself with attention to this exercise in total memorization; it is, therefore, inseparable from the *lectio*. It is what inscribes, so the speak, the sacred text in the body and the soul', pp. 89–90; 'This way of uniting reading, meditation and prayer, this "meditative prayer" as William of St Thierry calls it, had great influence on religious psychology. It occupies and engages the whole person in whom the Scripture takes root, later on to bear fruit', p. 91. (By way of illuminating 'secular' comparison' see George Steiner, *Real Presences* (London, 1990), p. 9: 'In reference to language and the musical score, enacted interpretation can also be inward. The private reader or listener can become an executant of felt meaning when he learns the poem or the musical passage by heart. To learn by heart is to afford the text or music an indwelling clarity and life-force. Ben Jonson's term, "ingestion", is precisely right. What we know by heart becomes an agency in our consciousness, a "pace-maker" in the growth and vital complication of our identity . . . Accurate recollection and resort in remembrance not only deepen our grasp of the work: they generate a shaping reciprocity between ourselves and that which the heart knows. As we change, so does the informing context of the internalized poem or sonata.' It is perhaps surprising that Steiner makes no mention of the *lectio divina* tradition in this context.)

[21] Leclercq writes: 'This repeated mastication of the divine words is sometimes described by the use of the theme of spiritual nutrition. In this case the vocabulary is borrowed from eating, from digestion, and from the particular form of digestion belonging to ruminants. For this reason, reading and meditation are sometimes described by the very expressive word *ruminatio*', *Love of Learning*, p. 90.

meditative tradition, with their translation of doctrinal truth into forms which offer the devout reader/audience imaginative admission into the story of Christ,[22] which can have a particular bearing for us on what Julian suggests about her own devotional sensibility as it was at the time of the showings. In her narration of that earlier stage, the mature Julian portrays her adult spiritual life as being initially characterized by a strong impulse towards self-dramatization:

> As in the first methought I had sume feleing in the passion of Criste, but yet I desired more be the grace of God. Methought I would have beene that time with Mary Magdalen and with other that were Crists lovers, and therefore I desired a bodily sight wherein I might have more knowledge of the bodily peynes of our saviour, and of the compassion [G: of] our lady and of all his trew lovers that seene that time his peynes, for I would be one of them and suffer with him. (2.3)

In offering us this glance back into her own past, Julian evokes the mental and emotional horizons of a stage which is understood to have been transcended and is now critically considered in relation to quite other horizons. There is significance in the selection she makes of details from her own experience,[23] as also in the manner of their representation.[24] Julian's literary re-creation of her former self is dominated by the memory of a set of religious aspirations that are evidently consonant with the tradition of affective spirituality we have touched upon. They emerge within a broad, common culture in which the personal and

---

[22] A dramatizing instinct is strong in numerous medieval English artistic-religious productions, notably the mystery plays, but also in such works as *Piers Plowman* and those of the *Pearl*-poet. The influence of the liturgy, the common and popular religious inheritance par excellence, should not be overlooked here. See especially Glasscoe, *Medieval English Mystics*, pp. 18–24 (cited above, n. 19); with specific regard to the influence of liturgy (in this case the canonical hours) on Julian herself, see Glasscoe, 'The Time of Passion: Latent Relationships between Liturgy and Meditation in Two Middle English Mystics [Julian, and Richard Rolle]', in ed. Helen Phillips, *Langland, the Mystics and the Medieval English Religious Tradition* (Cambridge, 1990), pp. 141–60.

[23] '. . . there is the infinitely complex process of deciding what from a lifetime's experience is to be included, what left out, what and whom and where and when to be emphasized, what subordinated', Robert C. Elliott, *The Literary Persona* (Chicago and London, 1982), p. 71.

[24] 'In his [Peter Abelard's] *Historia Calamitatum* the events of his own life are selected and presented as analogous to a text, the correct interpretation of which reveals the demonstration of God's grace at every step to correct and chastise his beloved, exceptional sinner . . . What *was* is subsumed in what was *meant*: the history of Abelard's misfortunes becomes readable only in retrospect as a series of symbolic events in which the hand of God can be discerned, guiding and directing an elemental drama of pride, fall, and redemption', Ruth Morse, *Truth and Convention in the Middle Ages: Rhetoric, Representation, and Reality* (Cambridge, 1991), p. 168. The emphases are my own.

emotional appropriation of doctrine is facilitated by imagination. Although, in the passage from Chapter 2 quoted immediately above, Julian is speaking of a *supernaturally*-induced remembrance of the passion, we can see it as a desire for an intensification of the imaginative form of recollection, something she herself seems to imply: 'methought I had sume feleing in the passion of Christe, but yet I desired more' (2.2). The extraordinariness of Julian's request for a 'bodily sight' (2.3) of the passion will be dealt with below. Here it is important to note that her impulse to play a part in the passion story as it is enacted on the stage of the imagination, to add herself to the select band of 'Crists lovers' who were the privileged historical witnesses of his actual death, has come to her as part of the mainstream religious inheritance of the pious faithful in the fourteenth century, whether in the cloister or outside it.

The placing of Julian in a broad context of christocentric affective spirituality is a preliminary gesture which provides the opportunity for the important question of what kind of personal interaction there is between Julian herself – more specifically, the past self Julian seeks to represent – and this religious mentality. Such a fluid, historically-protracted religious tradition cannot be regarded as merely subordinating individuals for the purpose of its own transparent manifestation through them. Whilst Julian is undoubtedly subject to religious/cultural conditioning, her appropriation of traditional aspirations for an imaginative realization of the passion story is idiosyncratic. It is readable in terms of a peculiarly strong self-dramatizing instinct which draws her to exploit, in a striking and extreme way, the inherently dramatic potentialities of contemporary piety.

The requests for a 'bodily sight' (2.3) of Christ's passion and a 'sekenesse . . . so herde as to deth' (2.3) are, in the Paris manuscript, acknowledged to be 'not the commune vse of prayer' (CW 288.35). Whilst it is not within the competence of this book to make judgements about the quality and sincerity of Julian's religious life, that phrase, 'not the commune vse of prayer', can point us to a particularly telling emphasis in the text's evocation of her pre-visionary state. Her desire for a bodily sight of the passion can be interpreted as a craving for some kind of self-separation, an untethering from the common run of those for whom the 'commune vse' of prayer is sufficient. Escaping from them, Julian wishes to enter a special region where she can relate to Christ as one of a very select band of his lovers, including the Virgin Mary and St Mary Magadalen. This is not in itself an original mood. Anchoritic literature, including *De Institutione Inclusarum*[25] and *Ancrene*

---

[25] See *De Institutione Inclusarum*, p. 33, lines 294–8: 'And Lord, wheþer it seme a grete woundour to þe, in þe whiche þu schuldest haue a veyn-glorie, þat þu hast forsake to wedde a monnes sone for þe loue þat þu hast to be Cristes spouse? Is

Wisse,[26] habitually commends Christ to the anchoress as a lover to whom she, having been separated from the contagion of the world, should be exclusively devoted, and as one by whose love she is ennobled. Another treatise, *Hali Meiðhad* ('Holy Virginity'), is notable for its praise of consecrated virginity as a spiritualized form of social advancement. For example, the virgin is depicted as inhabiting a tower ('Zion') – that is, her virginity – from the heights of which she looks down on widows and married women.[27] Julian's own writing, perhaps surprisingly, does not have any real emphasis on a personalized 'bridal mysticism'[28] (the mature Julian is too conscious of *ecclesiology* for that), nor on virginity as such. But in Chapter 2 she does represent her earlier self as being swept by powerful emotional currents, and with all the relatively unexamined enthusiasm of youth, into religious postures which themselves presuppose a belief in the possibility, and indeed legitimacy, of taking up an avowedly privileged position in relation to the person of Christ. The request for a supernatural vision is an extraordinary one; Julian knows this and says so, but the request is made nonetheless. It is eloquent testimony to the fundamental characteristic of her pre-visionary approach to Christ: the conviction that hers is a special case.

This instinct for singularity only reinforces itself through Julian's desire to come as close as possible to death without actually dying:

hit a gret woundour þat þu hast forsake styngyngge lust of body for þe swete sauour of maydenhood?'

[26] In *Ancrene Wisse*, meditation on the passion is momentarily transposed into an erotic key: 'þencheð ȝef ȝe ne ahen eaþe to luuien þe king of blisse þe tospreat swa his earmes toward ow & buheð, as to beoden cos, duneward his heaued', *Ancrene Wisse: Parts Six and Seven*, ed. G. Shepherd, revised edition (Exeter, 1985). The author seems here to be drawing on an apparently common contemporary pious notion, possibly Cistercian in origin, of Christ leaning down from the cross in order to embrace the meditating believer. See Shepherd, n. to p. 27, line 4, given on p. 64; also, Tugwell, *Ways of Imperfection*, p. 164, where Caesarius of Heisterbach (died 1240) is cited as the source of the tradition; but see also the fifteenth century engraving reproduced in Jean Leclercq, *Bernard of Clairvaux and the Cistercian Spirit* (Kalamazoo, Michigan, 1976), p. 168, which points to an association of Bernard with this tradition.

[27] 'And bitacneð þis tur þe hehnesse of meiðhad, þe bihald as of heh alle widewen under hire ant weddede baðe. For þeos, ase flesches þrealles, beoð i worldes þeowdom, ant wunieþ lahe on eorðe; and meiden stont þurh heh lif i þe tur of Ierusalem', *Hali Meiðhad* in *Medieval English Prose for Women: Selections from the Katherine Group and Ancrene Wisse*, ed. Bella Millett and Jocelyn Wogan-Browne (Oxford, 1990), pp. 2–5, including facing translation.

[28] Grace Jantzen identifies 'subdued erotic imagery', especially in relation to Julian's request for three wounds (2.3) – see *Julian of Norwich*, especially pp. 62–7. Julian does use bridal imagery sparingly in both an ecclesiological (51.82) and a mystical sense (52.81).

The iid came to my mynde with contrition, frely desireing that sekenesse so herde as to deth that I might, in that sekeness, vnderfongyn all my rites of holy church, myselfe weneing that I should dye, and that all creatures might suppose the same that seyen me; for I would have no manner comfort of eardtly life. (2.3)

The rest of humanity is apparently so insignificant to Julian at this stage that its only function in her proposed personal drama would be, as she imagines it, to provide nameless, faceless witnesses of it; with, presumably, just one minor speaking-part for the priest who would come to administer the last rites. When she does actually come to describe the 'death-bed' scene in the Long Text it is striking that she edits-out the Short Text references both to the child (acolyte?)[29] who accompanies the priest and to her own mother.[30] This tidying-up has the obvious stylistic advantage of producing a more focused narrative; but it can also be said to be entirely consonant with the general impression given here that the only figures of any real significance at this point are Julian and her personal fantasy-Christ.

Notwithstanding the ostensible genuineness of her conscious pious intentions,[31] or of her formal and explicit submission to God's will,[32] and perhaps above all the fact that she ingenuously seeks to number herself among 'Crists lovers' (2.3), the picture that emerges in Chapters 2 and 3 has Julian, not Christ, at the centre. The vehemence and extraordinariness of her desires suggest an energetic emotional drama in which Julian is the main actor. Chapter 2 especially can seem an exhausting litany of desire, almost every line containing some expression of Julian's needs, wants or hopes, of which these are only a few: 'I desired a bodily sight'; 'for I would be one of them'; 'frely desireing that sekenesse so harde as to deth'; 'I would have no manner comfort of eardtly life'; 'I desired to have all manier peynes bodily and ghostly'; 'I desired to be soone with my God' (all 2.3). Even in these few phrases we can detect a distinct note of extremity: 'no manner comfort'; 'all manier peynes'.

In sum, Julian characterizes her early piety in terms of an intense personal devotion to Christ; but the manner of her narration invites us to look beneath the surface of explicit religious aspiration and consider something of the psychological and moral dynamic informing it. This is a stage of great feeling, of self-consciousness and also self-dramatization, of

---

[29] CW 208.23–4.

[30] CW 234.29

[31] 'it was for I would haue leued to loueved god better and longer tyme', CW 289–90.9–10.

[32] 'These ii desires of the passion and the sekenesse I desired with a condition, sey[ing] thus: 'Lord, thou wotith what I would – if it be thy will that I have it; and if it be not thy will, good lord, be not displeased, for I will nought but as thou wilt', 2.3.

struggle and strain. Julian wants to see Christ; she wants to be wounded; she yearns to taste death (but only *taste*). Her human nature, her 'flesh' in the Pauline sense,[33] is doing its best to create an authentic religious experience but aching for something beyond its unaided capacities. Her narrative indicates that this 'something beyond', which we can understand as the showings themselves, is only attained when Julian has passed through a severe psychosomatic crisis: the very illness, she would have us believe, for which she had prayed.

Julian's concern in Chapters 2 and 3 with presenting a picture of emotionally-charged religious exertion inevitably produces a particular focus on herself, keeping Julian as agent at the centre of the picture. By contrast, the showings which follow are ascribed to the direction action of God himself. On Julian's part, exertion is still necessary in the form of sustained attention to what she sees and hears. But this exertion is represented as effectively short-circuiting her all-too-human impulse to feed egoism by means of religious self-dramatization. Beyond Chapter 3, Julian's self-representation becomes less that of a religious narcissist than of a *responding* self, evoked in tension with a pre-eminently untameable and independent reality: the reality of God as manifested through the showings. Julian's early piety is understood to have had its place in giving her a certain religious orientation, but of infinitely greater moment to her is the illumination received from God in the showings themselves, and subsequently in a lifetime of meditation on them.

The next section of this chapter will be concerned to show that in narrating her engagement with the *visionary* figure of Christ crucified, Julian discloses the story of her personal movement from a self-dramatizing, individualistic piety to a spirituality marked by a developed ecclesiological awareness. This story is also readable as an attempted theological and rhetorical negotiation of the gap between herself as a visionary and the community of her 'even cristen'.

His Body, the Church

Julian's writing is generously peppered with discreet and reverent nods in the direction of the Church's dogmatic authority, such as the following from Chapter 9:[34]

> But in althing I leve as holy church levith, preachith and teachith; for the feith of holy church the which I had aforn hand understonden and, as I

---

[33] See especially Romans chs 7–8.
[34] And many others, e.g: 9.13, 14; 10.16, 17; 26.37; 30.41; 32.45; 34.47; 46.65; 52.83; 53.85.

hope, by the grace of God wilfully kepte in use and custome, stode continualy in my sight, willing and meneing never to receive onything that might be contrary therunto. (9.14)

The importance Julian attaches to being perceived as orthodox should not be underestimated; but she does not let her text lean for legitimacy on a merely formulaic submissiveness to ecclesiastical authority. Her sense of the Church is much more inward to the text and is bound up with the exigencies of her position as one who is isolated by her extraordinary experience but feels an obligation to overcome that isolation without compromising her personal vision. We are concerned here with the way Julian attempts to bring her readers within the parameters of this theological vision by making the narration of her response to Christ simultaneously a narration of her deepening perception of the Church as his mystical body. In this way the Church, to which she and her contemporary audience are assumed to belong, is identified with the Christ of Julian's private revelation. To the extent that she can secure this identification through language she can claim a genuine theological basis for the minimization of distance between herself and her audience. The visionary Christ, who could have symbolized Julian's privileged isolation from the community of her fellow Christians, comes to symbolize, and to be represented as the instrument of, her discovery of a mystical union-in-Christ with that community.

A crucifix

If there is a fixed point in Julian's universe, a constant link between the *within* of her shifting subjective consciousness and the *without* of social structures and ecclesiastical jurisdiction, it is the crucifix which is set before her eyes by the priest who comes to minister at her supposed deathbed:

> He sett the cross before my face and seid: 'I have browte thee the image of thy maker and saviour. Louke thereupon and comfort thee therewith.' (3.4)

The solemn character of this injunction, and the context in which it is given, should not be overlooked.[35] Any medieval Catholic would recognize the formal and ecclesiological nature of the scene: the last visitation of the priest to a dying parishioner, a woman already anointed for the final journey ('on the fourth night I tooke all my rites of holy church', 3.4). The presentation of the crucifix would be enough to trigger an associative reaction in the mind of a contemporary reader. This is the moment of personal crisis for which the whole of life is a preparation and, as with

[35] See Duffy, *Stripping of the Altars*, pp. 313–16.

other rites of passage, it is a matter for the Church. Whatever else it might represent, Julian's fixing of her gaze on the cross is an act of obedience to ecclesiastical authority. In consenting to look 'in the face of the crucifix' (3.4) Julian willingly places herself in a conscious and positive relation to the Church, represented by the priest and people around her; and by the crucifix itself, the totem of the tribe.

But in Chapter 19 this willing obedience is tested. Fixity of concentration is taking its toll on the 'dying' patient and Julian is strongly tempted to look away from the crucifix. She says, 'In this I wold a lokyd up of the cross' (19.28); she wants to but dare not, believing that 'whyl I beheld in the cross I was seker and save'. She will not 'put [her] soule in perel' by reneging on her solemn assent to look at the crucifix in obedience to the Church.

Seeking its advantage at what is obviously a susceptible point – Julian's natural instinct to make herself more comfortable – temptation comes as a 'profir' (19.28) in her reason, suggesting that she 'Loke up to hevyn to his Fader'. Perhaps doing so would relieve her physical discomfort, but she sees in it something more sinister. This is a temptation to disobedience, urging her to set aside the priest's injunction, something which would cause a rupture in the relationship between Julian and the Church, and so place her outside that salvific context at this gravest of moments.[36] Disobedience to the priest would amount to an abandonment of faith in

---

[36] The concept of obedience to a spiritual father is a crucial one, whether we are speaking of professed religious or of lay-people; and whether the context is that of sacramental confession or extra-sacramental spiritual direction. On the evil of *disobedience* see, for example, Richard Rolle, *The Form of Living* in ed. S. J. Ogilvie-Thomson, *Richard Rolle: Prose and Verse*, EETS, o.s., 293 (Oxford, 1988), pp. 3–4, lines 29–34; and *The Book of Privy Counselling* in Hodgson, *Cloud of Unknowing*, p. 91, lines 25–40 and p. 92, lines 1–2. For 'confessor' Julian uses the revealing term 'domysman' (39.53) which conjures up an image of the sacrament of confession as a rehearsal (and in fact more than merely a rehearsal) for the last judgement, the 'doom', with the priest acting as judge *in persona Christi* – a context could hardly be more charged with consequence. The role of spiritual father seems to have been distinct from that of the confessor, being more about dispensing advice than giving absolution for sin (though it was surely possible, and perhaps usual, for one person to assume both roles in relation to a given individual). Nevertheless, it is likely that the prestige attaching to the priest in the sacramental setting would carry over into the sphere of spiritual counselling, so that the relationship of confessor to penitent can be understood as a defining one even in technically non-sacramental contexts. Leigh Gilmore suggests that Julian has interiorized the political and religious authority represented by the figure of the confessor and so she [Julian] 'interprets and represents *The Revelations* within the context of the confession she would later make', *Autobiographics*, p. 117; for the full argument see Gilmore, pp. 106–20. Gilmore makes some very astute points, but I think that LT, notably in its more magisterial and speculative sections, does transcend Gilmore's confessional box (so to speak).

Christ, her 'maker and saviour' (3.4), who alone gives access to 'his Fader' (19.28):

> And than saw I wele with the feyth that I felte that ther was nothyn betwix the crosse and hevyn that myght have desesyd me. Either me behovyd to loke up, or else to answeren. I answered inwardly with al the myghts of my soule and said: 'Nay, I may not, for thou art my hevyn.' This I seyd for I wold not; for I had lever a ben in that peyne til domysday than to come to hevyn otherwyse than by him; for I wiste wele that he that bonde me so sore, he sholde onbynde me whan that he wolde. (19.28)

The Church presents the crucifix to Julian precisely to activate and support her faith in Christ as saviour and redeemer. According to Eamon Duffy, the texts of services associated with the dead and dying in the late Middle Ages had as their 'consistent emphasis . . . the power and will of God to save, and . . . the all-sufficiency of the merits of the crucified Christ for the sinner';[37] but this is a Christ inescapably encountered within the Church. It is crucially important, at the (supposed) moment of death above all, that Julian does not trust her own merits or her own judgement. When she says that 'ther was nothyn betwix the crosse and hevyn that myght have desesyd me' we can sense her wavering, seeing no harm in looking upwards, rather in the way, perhaps, that Eve saw no harm in taking the fruit from the tree.[38] Julian, however, resists this temptation and keeps herself within the bounds of what has been ordained by lawful authority, trusting in the objectivity of the Church's sacramental nature rather than in her own isolated and unreliable subjectivity.[39] Salvation and security are guaranteed by Christ, in the Church, and the physicality of the artefact before her eyes mediates this guarantee to Julian's besieged sensuality, eliciting the assent of faith. The

---

[37] *Stripping of the Altars*, p. 314.
[38] Genesis 3:6.
[39] I disagree with Domenico Pezzini's assertion that 'Julian, like many other medieval mystics, does not derive her spirituality from the sacraments', 'The Theme of the Passion in Richard Rolle and Julian of Norwich', in ed. Piero Boitani and Anna Torti, *Religion in the Poetry and Drama of the Late Middle Ages in England* (Cambridge, 1989), p. 64. Any claims that Julian's spirituality is exclusively derived from the sacraments or is entirely dominated by them (or by sacramental *ritual* as such) would clearly be excessive. But I certainly hope this book as a whole will show how ecclesiology and sacramental theology are important conditions of Julian's experience and of the text's production. Strangely, Pezzini does note Julian's awareness of the biblical and patristic language and imagery traditionally associated with the sacraments, but sees this merely as an indication of her 'highly-refined theological education' (p. 64), rather than evidence of her immersion in, and personal need of, a sacramental culture.

importance attached to Julian's focus on the crucifix reads all the more clearly as a self-conscious signal of Catholic orthodoxy when taken in the context of contemporary Wycliffite hostility to the veneration of religious images.[40]

If the crucifix represents a point of contact between Julian's subjectivity and the 'objective' order of the medieval Church, it also functions in the narrative as an external correlative of her inner experience. It witnesses to Julian's continuous personal identity, providing a link between her pre-visionary and visionary state. Within the visionary state itself, it registers the alteration of her perceptions:

> In this sodenly I saw the rede blode trekelyn downe fro under the garlande, hot and freisly and ryth plenteously, as it were in the time of his passion that the garlande of thornys was pressid on his blissid hede . . . (4.5)

What Julian presents herself seeing here is not an independent vision of Christ's passion that makes the crucifix in front of her redundant, but that same crucifix mysteriously animated. Her use of the definite article to designate 'the rede blode' and 'the garlande' draws our attention to what is already there, to aspects of the depiction of Christ which, though not actually specified earlier, we would have assumed to be displayed on a (painted?) crucifix. The miraculous, therefore, is shown to enter the contemplative space created by Julian's attention to the crucifix and to appropriate this physical artefact as the locus of revelation.[41]

Within the hierarchy of perception that Julian adduces in relation to the showings – 'bodily sight . . . word formyd in my understondyng . . . gostly

[40] Nicholas Watson writes that 'Lollard opposition to images began to give cause for orthodox alarm in the early 1380s' but that 'it was not until about 1400 that an individual's attitude to images came to be treated as a kind of litmus test, one of the most accurate indices of his or her orthodoxy', 'Composition', p. 664. On this basis Watson argues for a post-1380 dating for ST, citing especially Julian's inclusion in ST of her respect for the iconography of the medieval Church (see CW 202.15–17, and n. 1, above). One Wycliffite text allows 'lewed men to haue a pore crusifix', ed. Hudson, *English Wycliffite Writings*, p. 83, line 13. But this same tract then goes on to attack the more extravagantly ornamented images, and the general tone of the piece leans towards a vehement iconoclasm that strikes at the heart of popular medieval Catholicism – the 'pore crusifix' is very much a concession. It is important to remember, also, that the presentation of the crucifix to Julian takes place in a sacramental, or at the very least a quasi-sacramental, context that is itself affirmative of orthodoxy.

[41] See Nicholas Watson, 'The Trinitarian Hermeneutic in Julian of Norwich's *Revelation of Love*', in *MMTE: V* (Cambridge, 1992), p. 84: 'Julian's experience was . . . a disparate series of glimpses of Christ's Passion, *strung like beads along her life-saving gaze at a crucifix*, and interspersed with other, more abstract sights, as well as with a few pregnant words passed from Christ to her and sometimes back again' (my emphasis).

sight' (9.14)[42] – her vision of the crucified Christ, of the crucifix in a state of animation, belongs to (though it is not wholly definitive of) the category of 'bodily sight'. Her representation of this primary level of vision begins with the passage from Chapter 4 quoted above and proceeds intermittently until, in Chapter 21, the experience is dramatically transposed when Christ suddenly appears transfigured in the glory of the resurrection. This change manifests itself indivisibly as a change in the crucifix-figure and in the nature of Julian's engagement with it/him. Significantly, Julian reminds us that she was at this point still 'beholdyng in the same crosse' (21.31). Even the risen Christ is Christ *crucified* and risen.

In the narration of this change in her visionary experience we can also read, at what might be termed the 'ghostly' level of the text, the story of a qualitative shift of consciousness which opens up for Julian new possibilities of spiritual understanding and initiates a process which has theological as well as rhetorical implications. The transformation of her relation to Christ can be seen as representing a transformation of her relation to her presumed audience of 'even cristen'. In order to understand the shift signified in Chapter 21 (which we take, following CW, to mark the beginning of the ninth showing[43]), it will be necessary first of all to examine the vision of Christ's passion which generates it. Attention will be paid to the precise manner in which Julian reconstructs her bodily sight of Christ's death throes so that we can read in it her implied, mature commentary on a religious sensibility which, whilst long out-grown, is now understood, and presented to the audience, in relation to a pattern of intellectual and spiritual development that has unfolded since.

---

[42] Watson notes that the categories of 'bodily sight' and 'gostly sight' have antecedents in Augustine, thus suggesting a 'continuity between [Julian's] revelation and visionary tradition'. But he goes on to say: 'as soon as we look in detail at the interpretive problems posed by Julian's revelation, it becomes clear how inadequate this ['Augustinian' hermeneutic], taken on its own, must prove to be. For in practice Julian finds herself describing almost as many kinds of "sight" and other divinely-inspired experiences, and invoking almost as many kinds of exegesis with which to interpret them, as her revelation can be separated into distinguishable visionary moments', 'Trinitarian Hermeneutic', p. 86. This article is very suggestive indeed. Regrettably, I came across it too late to take full account of its important implications.

[43] There is confusion between P and S1 over the precise beginning of the ninth showing. I incline intuitively to the view of Colledge and Walsh that Chapter 21 marks the beginning of the showing roughly speaking. The words 'he chongyd his blissfull chere' seem to signal the decisive shift, a new impetus of revelation, though S1 does not register it as such. I do appreciate Marion Glasscoe's concern about over-confident editorial interventions in CW, but am not ultimately convinced by the way S1 reads. It can be argued that with such late manuscripts a certain interpretative licence is justified, especially since scribes are themselves interpreters of a kind. For more on this see Glasscoe, *English Medieval Mystics*, p. 266, n. 39; and CW, p. 95, for an argument I find fairly persuasive.

Vision

Earlier in this chapter we identified a certain self-dramatizing quality in Julian's pre-visionary religious experience as she represents it, a straining beyond the boundaries of conventional piety, beyond the 'commune vse of prayer' (CW 288.35–6), in pursuit of extraordinary divine favour, namely 'a bodily sight' of 'the bodily peynes of our saviour' (2.3). It was also suggested that Julian's near-mortal illness can at least partly be read, in faithfulness to Julian's own mature self-awareness, as representing a quelling of this largely egocentric, self-generated religiosity; and as marking her discovery of the possibility of self-transcendence through responsiveness to God. Her self-involvement is disrupted by the experience of vision which brings into the reckoning a wholly other, untameable reality. Regardless of what we post-Enlightenment sophisticates might make of the showings themselves, they are presented by Julian precisely as supernatural revelation, and a supernatural *source* of revelation is thereby posited. By means of the peculiar vividness of her narration of Christ's death throes Julian seeks to register her experience of becoming a *responding* subject, of being mesmerized by something (taken to be) absolutely outside herself.

We have already attempted to place the pre-visionary Julian in relation to medieval traditions of affective meditation on the passion of Christ and it would indeed seem reasonable to approach her description of this central religious event with these traditions in mind.[44] However, whilst we certainly can locate in her account some vestiges of pious idiom, what is most striking about Julian's passion narrative is that it is not really narrative at all.[45] It does not, for example, correspond to the extended specimen meditations of an Aelred of Rievaulx or a Richard Rolle, in which the story is imaginatively realized scene by scene, with attention to times, localities and personages in attendance. Such meditational techniques necessarily involve individuals in their own mental world of images and feelings. Julian, on the other hand, seeks to reconstruct

---

[44] See Gillespie and Ross, 'Apophatic Image', for a subtle, and itself creative, discussion of Julian's own creative relation to affective traditions. They write that 'Julian creates in her text a dialogue with conventional images' but, as it were, deconstructs them so that they do not end up 'fettering her showings into an earthly order of signifying'. The images are 'apophatic', affirming similitude but denying it at the same time. For more on the problematics of signifying the ineffable, see Vincent Gillespie, 'Postcards from the Edge: Interpreting the Ineffable in the Middle English Mystics' in ed. Piero Boitani and Anna Torti, *Interpretation: Medieval and Modern* (Cambridge, 1993), pp. 137–65.

[45] Roland Maisonneuve writes 'Elle n'assiste pas à un événement historique qu'elle contemple, et qui ressurgit sous ses yeux' ['She does not assist at an historical event which she is watching, and which is playing itself out again before her eyes', my translation], Roland Maisonneuve, *L'univers visionnaire de Julian of Norwich* (Paris, 1987), p. 160.

what she understands to be a very different kind of experience. The primary difference of course is that her vision is triggered by, and plays upon, an object in the external environment; so that Julian's evocation of Christ's passion is what we can call *iconic* rather than narratorial, recreating the intense focus of Julian as viewing subject[46] rather than constructing a detailed story. The passion as a whole is implied by certain effects apprehended on the animated crucifix.

It is instructive to extrapolate the basic features of this primary visionary level of the text. In broad terms, Julian first of all sees the bleeding of Christ's head (4.5); then she sees the agony and humiliation of the passion represented in his face, which is, appropriately, shown covered with dry blood (10.14–15); her eyes are then drawn downwards to Christ's torso which is bleeding so profusely that there is scarcely anything to see except blood (12.19). The next visionary moment, at this level of bodily sight, signals a logical progression in that, having seen the body massively haemorrhaging, she now sees it dry and bloodless, at the point of death. Once again she focuses first on the head, especially the lips, and then on the rest of the body. The body is drying within because of lack of blood, and on the outside due to the sharp, cold wind (16.24–5). As a result of this process of drying, Julian observes the figure of Christ losing its human identity to such an extent that, finally, she can compare it/him to a cloth in the wind, and the texture of his skin to that of an old, worn-out table.

Julian's depiction of Christ's suffering is substantially comprehended in what we can imagine as two animated pictures: in the first picture his face and body are streaming with blood, in the second they are drying and shrivelling. The fact that the passion should be reduced to what are in effect just two graphically realized images detached from the distracting conditions of narrative procedure is immensely significant in terms of what Julian thereby implies about her former self and its mode of experience. Through the vividness of these pictures she recreates an intensity of focus, thus drawing attention to the distance which is necessarily implied between the Christ-figure as object and herself as subject.[47] The sense of Christ as object is intensified by the introduction of

[46] Maisonneuve rightly notes that Julian especially displays a need to *see* [une sorte d'obsession de voir], *L'univers visionnaire*, p. 126.

[47] Maisonneuve notes, for example, that in Chapter 12 Julian reduces the whole evocation of the passion to two images: flesh and blood – see *L' univers visionnaire*, p. 161. One question Maisonneuve (surprisingly) does not ask is: might there not be a eucharistic implication here? On a rather different plane, see also Ewa Kuryluk, *Veronica and her Cloth* (Oxford, 1991), p. 209: 'The vision of Christ's dried-up skin reflects the nature of mystical experience which, oscillating between the extremes of fullness and nothingness, ecstasy and mortification, empties out and annihilates the object of its desire.' For interesting comment about taboos attaching to blood, and about bodiliness in general as (for Julian) a sphere of, rather than an obstacle to, religious experience, see

domestic similes (described below). The very invocation of these images reinforces a sense of visualization that is crucial to this part of the text. Christ is lovingly, attentively contemplated, but remains absolutely out of reach, unengageable. It is also striking that these images are not present in the Short Text. Their introduction would seem, therefore, to form part of Julian's mature commentary on the nature of her original bodily sight of Christ's passion in May 1373.

The first three similes occur in Chapter 7, expanding ST's suggestive, though spare and rather unvisual, characterization of Christ's blood. The similes are as follows:[48]

(i) The grete dropis of blode fel downe from under the garland like pellots semand as it had cum out of the veynis . . . (7.10)

(ii) The plentioushede is like to the dropys of water that fallen of the evys after a greate showre of reyne that fall so thick that no man may numbre them with bodily witte. (7.10–11)

(iii) And for the roundhede, it were like to the scale of heryng in the spreadeing on the forehead. (7.11)

Just as Julian's evocation of the passion as a whole is detached from the exigencies of expansive narrative, so this too-close, surreal characterization of Christ's blood is momentarily detached from the integral image of the crucified saviour. Christ is atomized; the attributes of his blood are allegorized as discrete similes: pellets, drops of water, scale of herring.[49] Having introduced these similes, Julian immediately gives a recapitulation of them:

These iii come to my [G: mynde] in the tyme: pellots, for roundhede, in the comynge out of the blode; the scale of heryng, in the spreadeing in the forehede, for roundhede; the dropys of evese, for the plentioushede inumberable. (7.11)

Maria R. Lichtmann, ' "I desyrede a bodylye syght": Julian of Norwich and the Body', *Mystics Quarterly*, 17 (1991), pp. 12–19; also, Robertson, 'Medieval Medical View of Women', especially pp. 153–6.

[48] See CW 210.11–14; and 217.1–4.

[49] See Gillespie and Ross, 'Apophatic Image', p. 65: 'Like the disruption and deconstruction of a picture consequent on fixed attention to a small part, she dismantles the bleeding into a series of discrete images: pellets, rain, and herringbones (c. 7, p. 8). The images suggest an urge to "domesticate" the horror of the passion . . . the effect of her gesture to conventional analogy is paradoxically to imbue the domestic and mundane with the force of the original image and with the substance of its subsequent significations. By making immanence more openly manifest, Julian also reclaims these homely images as gateways into the apophatic.'

The atomizing function of the language in this section is reinforced by this self-conscious gesture, suggesting, as it does, observation, abstraction, classification, didactic summary. We are not so much to take note of the flow of blood in integral relation to Christ himself as of the images, the formulae, into which the attributes of his blood have been converted. The effect is to intensify Julian's rhetorical objectification of the suffering Christ, by means of which is implicitly posited an absolute divide between herself as viewing subject and the Christ-figure as viewed object.

There are, as already mentioned, a couple of other striking domestic similes employed by Julian in her narration of the passion and it is worth looking at them a bit more closely and contextualizing them. In Chapter 17 Julian conveys the gruesome physical disfigurement that marks the culmination of Christ's passion, chiefly through a description of how the crown of thorns has cut into his head, detaching pieces of skin and hair from the skull:

> And ferthermore I saw that the swete skyn and the tender flesh, with the heere and the blode, was al rasyd and losyd abov from the bone with the thornys where thowe it were daggyd on many pecys, as a clith that were saggand, as it wold hastely have fallen of for hevy and lose while it had kynde moysture . . . (17.25)

Later in this chapter, more clearly in P than in SS, the image of the ragged, sagging cloth with which this passage ends is developed so as to signify not just one effect of the passion but the whole event. Julian says that Christ 'was hangyng vppe in the eyer as men hang a cloth for to drye' (CW 363.39–40); he is reduced to the level of an anonymous, discardable household item. This identification follows close on the heels of another simile in the preceding paragraph (taking P's reading again) where the texture of Christ's dry and 'rympylde' skin is likened to that of a 'drye bord when it is agyd' (CW 363.36–7).

To recapitulate, Julian's imagistic re-working of this part of the text – these three similes, as already indicated, are not found in the Short Text – secures by implication the sense of Julian as a distinct, separate viewing subject. The Christ-figure is presented precisely as an object of visual attention, and Julian's experience of visual attentiveness is conveyed through her use of immediate, visualizable domestic imagery. The images of the cloth in the wind, and of the old worn-out table are especially effective, not only in their heightening of a sense of the visual but also in the subtle way in which they dovetail with the theological theme of Christ's self-emptying, his *kenosis*. The crucifixion is thus evoked as a depersonalizing process in which the supremely living person, whose blood Julian initially saw flowing 'hote and freisly and ryth plenteously'

(4.5), descends to the status of a dead object, a *thing* to be characterized in terms of other *things*.

Julian's depiction of the passion also represents an attempted recreation of the mode of religious consciousness within and through which her initial experience was mediated. Her Christ at this stage is substantially the figure on the crucifix, the parts of his body usually being designated by the definite article: 'the face' (10.14), 'the body' (12.19), 'the pretious blode' and 'the swete flesh' (16.24). The importance of the crucifix as a physical artefact has already been noted; as has the subject/object dichotomy implied by the reconstruction of an intense visual focus, aided by the deployment of domestic imagery. In sum, Julian characterizes her initial visionary perception of Christ as being of someone utterly separate from herself, a distinct bodily entity, the compelling object of her attention but not otherwise engageable in a personal way.

Dialogue

In Chapter 21[50] there is a qualitative change in Julian's vision of the crucified Christ. Expecting to witness the actual moment of his death, as the logical conclusion of what has gone before, she is instead surprised by a complete transformation of the image in front of her:

> And ryth in the same tyme that methowte, be semyng, the life myght ne lenger lesten and the shewyng of the end behovyd nedis to be, sodenly, I beholdyng in the same cross, he chongyd his blissfull chere. The chongyng of his blisful chere chongyd myn, and I was as glad and mery as it was possible. Than browte our lord merily to my mynde: 'Wher is now ony poynte of the peyne or of thin agreefe?' And I was full merry. (21.30–1)

The alteration in the crucifix before her – 'the same crosse' – registers a shift in Julian's mode of religious experience so that the cross is effectively presented as a mirror of consciousness, something also suggested here by the phrase, 'The chongyng of his blisful chere chongyd myn.' The most notable characteristic of the change initiated here is not simply that the crucifix now exhibits the joy of the resurrection rather than the anguish of the passion. This alone would not represent a qualitative change in the *mode* of Julian's experience because what we might call the absolute cinematic divide would remain between the animated crucifix as object and Julian as viewing subject. What is signalled in Chapter 21 is a degree of reciprocity between Julian and the image, something which clearly signifies a breach of that divide. The breach is widened in Chapter 22 as

---

[50] See above, n. 43.

Christ engages Julian in conversation, taking up her own verbal response and weaving it into the revelation itself:[51]

> Than [G: seide] our good lord Iesus Christe, askyng: 'Art thou wele payd that I suffrid for thee?' I said: 'Ya good lord, gramercy. Ya good lord, blissid mot thou be!'. Than seyd Iesus, our kinde lord: 'If thou art payde, I am payde. It is a ioy, a blis, an endles lekyng to me that ever I suffrid passion for the; and if I myht suffre more, I wolde suffre more.'
>
> (22.31–2)

By this stage in the text Julian has already received two divine locutions: 'herewith is the fend overcome' (13.20) in the fifth showing; and 'I thanke thee of thy travel and namely of thy youthe' (14.21) in the sixth showing. She does not represent herself making a direct verbal response to either of these statements. They are themselves iconic, apodictic, requiring nothing from her but reverent acceptance, and so it would seem appropriate to assign them to the level of 'word formyd in my understondyng' (9.14) in Julian's hierarchy of perception, rather than to that of bodily sight which mainly pertains to her apprehension of the animated crucifix. But in Chapter 22 these two levels of perception are more or less fused so that the words of Christ are presented by Julian as more overtly bound up with her contemplation of the image on the crucifix. The divine words are not, in this instance, disembodied and needless of reply. On the contrary, they seek to initiate a dialogue.

The reciprocal, conversational nature of the experience in Chapter 22 builds on the momentum of the previous chapter and registers Julian's attainment of a new, dynamic level of personal relationship with the Christ-figure. Taken in context of her total experience, both as a visionary and as a writer, this moment (the 'moment' of Chapters 21 and 22) would appear to be seminal. As we shall see in an examination of Chapter 24, and with broad reference to other parts of the text, it also initiates a narrative in which the deepening of Julian's personal relationship with Christ is represented indivisibly as a process in which she makes a fuller discovery of Christ's relation to humanity-that-is-to-be-saved, to 'the general man' (79.127) as she will put it later. Through this process she discovers a unity in Christ between herself and her presumed audience of fellow Christians, a unity upon which the rhetorical character of the text as a whole is predicated and through which it claims an intrinsic theological authorization. To put all this another way, just as the crucifix registers an alteration of her relation to Christ, so it registers a change in

---

[51] The breaching of the divide between Christ's world and Julian's is consonant with that blurring of distinction, within the text, between revelation and commentary. See Watson, 'Trinitarian Hermenuetic', p. 95.

her relation to the *Church* with which, as we have noted, that same cross is her formal link in this death-bed setting.

The transformation of the Christ-figure in Chapter 21 marks the beginning of the ninth showing, which also subsequently includes the short conversational sequence between Julian and Christ as quoted above. This showing last from Chapter 21 to Chapter 23 inclusive. The tenth showing (Chapter 24 only) develops out of the ninth as Julian's dialogue with Christ becomes a journey into his wounded side.[52] The altered mode of perception this involves can be compared to virtual reality techniques which create an illusion for the viewer of moving within a three-dimensional space:

> Than with a glad chere our lord loked into his syde and beheld, enioyand; and with his swete lokyng he led forth the understondyng of his creture be the same wound into his syde withinne. And than he shewid a faire delectabil place, and large enow for al mankynd that shal be save to resten in pece and in love. And therwith he browte to mende his dereworthy blode and pretious water which he lete poure al oute for love. And with the swete beholdyng he shewid his blisful herte even cloven on two. (24.35)

Julian is led progressively deeper into Christ, 'into his syde withinne', the depth of her penetration being correlated with an enlargement of perception. Therefore, although the literary illusion here is substantially of the discovery of a space within the Christ-figure, it is, more significantly, the means by which Julian conveys her discovery of a space within herself, the realization of a cognitive potential. According to the logic of the image, understanding grows to the extent that it is led further into Christ.

The precise character of Julian's vision in Chapter 24 transmits unmistakable signals to the reader as to the particular nature of Julian's enlarged understanding, as to what exactly it is that she has freshly discovered. Her reference to Christ's 'dereworthy blode and pretious water' clearly indicates the price of redemption: Christ's death. But there is a further significance. According to a conventional understanding going back at least to Origen (185–254)[53] and developed influentially

---

[52] The notion of entering Christ's wounded side is not uniquely Julian's. Compare the tenth showing with the Middle English *De Institutione Inclusarum* in MS Bodley 423: 'Crepe in-to that blessed syde where that blood and water cam for the, and hyde the ther as a culuer in the stoon, wel likynge the dropes of his blood, til that thy lippes be maad like to a reed scarlet hood', p. 22, lines 863–6. Aelred and Julian share an affective quality, but Julian is finally much more ecclesiological and soteriological in emphasis. See also n. 57, below.

[53] Olivier Clément quotes Origen: 'Christ has flooded the universe with divine and sanctifying waves. For the thirsty he sends a spring of living water from the

by Augustine,[54] an understanding dependent on a particular exegetical approach to certain key Johannine passages, as Eve was created from the side of Adam whilst he slept, so the Church, the new Eve, was created from the side of Christ, the new Adam, as he 'slept' on the cross. This birth of the Church was signified by the blood and water that flowed from the pierced side of Christ; these symbolized baptism and the eucharist, the core sacraments.[55] Medieval iconography illustrates this by representing the Church as a queen, the new Eve, standing at the foot of the cross, holding a chalice into which the blood and water stream.[56] The ecclesiological ramifications of Julian's journey into Christ's side should not be overlooked. Her movement into Christ is depicted in such a way as to signify also a movement into the heart of the Church and the discovery of a union with her fellow Christians, effected through the mystical Christ in whom all are to be enclosed. It is precisely in the body of Christ – literally so, in terms of her vision – that Julian discovers the Church, that 'faire delectabil place . . . large enow for al mankynd to resten in pece and in love' (24.35).[57] She shows herself being drawn away from a narrow isolationist piety in which a rather iconic, static Christ is appropriated as an object of her exclusive attention, into a state of religious consciousness in which her engagement with Christ as a living person is shown to be instrumental in bringing her to a new and dynamic relation with the Church as an essentially spiritual reality, Christ's mystical body.

The contrasting use of one particular image in two separate instances reinforces the ecclesiological significance that comes to be attached to the Christ-figure, and it also acts as a bridge between what we can term respectively the *iconic* and the *reciprocal* mode of Julian's visionary experience. The image is one we have already encountered as it occurs in Chapter 17. There, Christ is described as 'hangyng vppe in the eyer as

wound which the spear opened in his side' (*Commentary on Psalm 77*); and 'From the wound in Christ's side has come forth the Church, and he has made her his bride' (*Commentary on Proverbs*), Clément, *The Roots of Christian Mysticism: Text and commentary*, trans. Theodore Berkeley and revised by Jeremy Hummerstone (London, 1993), p. 96.

[54] 'Dormit Adam ut fiat Eva, moritur Christus ut fiat Ecclesia. Dormienti Adae fit Eva de latere; mortuo Christo lancea percutitur latus, ut profluant sacramenta quibus formetur Ecclesia', *Tractatus in Evangelium Johannis*, ix. 10.

[55] For a modern (and utterly committed) recapitulation of this ecclesiological/exegetical tradition, see Hans Urs von Balthasar, *Mysterium Paschale*, trans. Aidan Nichols (Edinburgh, 1990), pp. 126–36.

[56] See Emile Mâle, *The Gothic Image: Religious Art in France of the Thirteenth Century*, trans. Dora Hussey, paperback reprint (New York, 1972), pp. 187–90.

[57] *The Orcherd of Syon* similarly conflates the notions of entering Christ's wounded side and of discovering one's neighbour (morally and spiritually): 'In þat opyn wounde of my sones herte ȝe schulen fynde þe feruent boilynge charite of me and of ȝoure neiȝbore . . .', p. 281, lines 4–6.

men hang a cloth for to drye' (CW 363.39–40), and the implications of this visual characterization of the humiliated saviour have been discussed. In Chapter 28 – again, only in the Long Text – the image of the cloth develops a new significance which nevertheless depends on its earlier association with Christ. Julian writes:

> Gods servants, holy church, shal be shakyn in sorows and anguis in this world *as men shakyth a cloth in the wynde*. (28.39, my emphasis)

The Church is, like Christ, a cloth in the wind, persecuted by 'men' (the 'world', no doubt, in the Johannine sense); more than this, mystically the Church *is* Christ.[58] It is a united body – 'holy church' – and suffers communally; but it is made up of individuals – 'Gods servants' – who must expect personally to participate in that suffering, to be 'lakid and dispisyd in thys world, scornyd, rapyd and outcasten'. There is adumbrated here a notion of the individual believer as being fully representative of the Church, an ecclesiological microcosm. It is a notion which, we hope to show, gathers density of significance in relation to Julian's concern to recreate her own personal religious experience, and to communicate the fruits of her own mature reflection on that experience.

Compassion

Julian presents her first clear realization of the union between Christ and Church (and by implication, between Christ and individual-as-Church) as part of the ninth showing, placing it at just that moment when she narrates the sudden change in the crucifix before her, that change which signals the initiation of a new kind of engagement with the Christ-figure:

> The chongyng of his blisful chere chongyd myn, and I was as glad and mery as it was possible. Than browte our lord merily to my mynde: 'Wher is now ony poynte of the peyne or of thin agreefe?' And I was full merry. I understode that we be now, in our lords menyng, in his crosse with hym in our peynys and our passion, deyng; and we wilfully abydyng in the same cross with his helpe and his grace into the last poynte, sodenly he shall chonge his chere to us, and we shal be with him in hevyn. (21.31)

The second part of this quotation (from 'I understode . . .') is not in the Short Text, nor is the material making up the rest of Chapter 21 as it

---

[58] This transposition of the cloth-image is remarked upon by Roland Maison-neuve, *L'univers visionnaire*, p. 102; and by Marion Glasscoe, *English Medieval Mystics*, p. 241.

develops the theme of the identification between Christ and his people. The greater importance and more rigorous development of this theme in the later version points to its having a particular significance for Julian's intellectual and religious development, and specifically for her mature rhetorical project.

Julian presents her own response to Christ undergoing a change consonant with her understanding of his identification with the Church. Her intense compassion for the suffering Christ – 'there was no payne that might be suffrid leke to that sorrow that I had to se him in peyne' (17.27) – is transposed so that it becomes a movement of compassion for the members of his body, the earthly Church, suffering the pain of sin:

> Thus I saw how Criste hath compassion on us for the cause of synne. And ryte as I was aforn in the passion of Criste fulfillid with peyne and compassion, like in this I was fulfilld a party with compassion of al my even cristen . . . (28.39)

Christ, the head, loves his body, the Church; and Julian, united with the head, loves the body through a participation in that same love. In P the distinction between the compassionate Christ and the compassionate Julian is momentarily, and tellingly, elided at this point:

> . . . in this *I* was in party fulfyllyd with compassion of alle my evyn cristen, for fulle wele *he* lovyth pepylle that shalle be savyd . . .
> (CW 408.4–5, my emphases)

Later in this same chapter, taking up a line from the Short Text which inevitably assumes fuller resonance here, Julian develops this theme by affirming that genuine human compassion is the outward expression of an inward union with Christ:

> And than I sawe that ech kynde compassion that man hath on his even cristen with charite, it is Criste in him (28.40)

In all this we may understand Julian to be, as it were, narrating the story of how her request for 'the wound of kinde compassion' (2.3) has been answered: in the first instance by the gift of 'compassion as a kinde soule might have with our lord Iesus' (4.5, punctuation slightly altered), and then by that compassion being redirected towards her 'even cristen' as she identifies with Christ in his compassion for them. She is thereby assumed into the *meaning* of the passion.

The characteristically Pauline phrase 'in Christ' denotes a theological idea which is crucial to the development of Julian's thought and to her activity as author. Christ is the principle of unity between Christians and so is understood by Julian to be the principle of unity between herself as author and her presumed audience of 'even cristen'. Her mature conception of the Church, as we have to some extent seen and will see more clearly later, is fundamentally theological and mystical rather than hierarchical or juridical. Her concern is for the realities of the Christian faith as they apply to all, regardless of status or degree. It is instructive to contrast Julian's approach to the Church with that of some of her continental visionary contemporaries, notably Bridget of Sweden and Catherine of Siena who both address problems of clerical ungodliness, often quite fiercely.[59] Julian's sense of the Church is, on the other hand, much more thoroughly and consistently *ecclesiological* than ecclesiastical. And it is precisely through a deepened perception of the equable and unifying love of Christ in the Church that Julian finds herself – a woman, a non-cleric – free to address her readers with the authority of charity,[60] according to her conscientious understanding of God's will. By working into her text a conception of the union of all Christians, specifically *her* union with her *audience*, in the mystical body of Christ, she creates an acoustic within which her authorial voice can achieve a distinctive resonance. This sense of union, or more appropriately *communion*, emboldens Julian to adopt quite freely a rhetorical stance by which her insights are presented not merely as significant for her personally but universally significant. This is most clearly seen in her deployment of plural pronouns in the first person – 'our', 'we', 'us' – throughout the text:[61]

> This sheweing was made to lerne our soule wisely to clevyn to the goodnes of God. And in that time the custome of our prayeing was browte to mende: how we use, for lak of understondyng and knowing of love, to make many menys. (6.8)

Sometimes there is a shift between singular and plural forms, as in the following lines from Chapter 10:

[59] For example, Bridget of Sweden reports St John the Baptist as criticizing a rich bishop in the following terms: 'he is like to an ape: firste, for his clethinge couers not þe parti þat suld be preue; þe secound, for with his fingers he touches filthe and þan laies þaime to his mouthe; þe þirde, for he hase a mannes visage, bot it was colour of vnresonabill bestis; þe fourt, for all if he haue handes and fete, зete he fowles with clai both fingers and handes . . . his besines is all aboute worldli þinges and fleshli, þat suld noзt be sene in a bishop for euell ensampill of oþir', *The Liber Celestis of St Bridget of Sweden* I, ed. Roger Ellis, EETS, o.s., 291 (Oxford, 1987), p. 211, lines 20–5, 28–30. See also *Orcherd of Syon*, pp. 273–316, for Catherine of Siena's protracted attack on clerical corruption (sodomy representing the absolute moral nadir, pp. 279–82).

[60] In ST chapter vi Julian claims charity as her motivation: 'sotheleye charyte styrres me to telle зowe it', CW 222.43–4.

[61] B. A. Windeatt draws attention to a shift from a preponderance of third person grammatical forms in ST to the use of the more inclusive 'we' in LT. See Part I of Windeatt, 'Julian of Norwich and Her Audience'.

And thus I saw him and sowte him, and I had him and I wantid hym. And this is, and should be, our comon werkeyng in this [P: life], as to my sight. (10.15)

This tendency to universalize is not absent from the Short Text, a fact which suggests that Julian has a sense from quite early on of the wider significance of her private experience. The extreme pitch of anxiety we identified in chapter vi of the Short Text is partly generated by the inward pressure to communicate the revelation; and her task as author is to negotiate herself into a position from which that act of communication can be made as credibly and inclusively as possible. It is in the Long Text that the fruits of this negotiation are made clear as Julian's rhetoric takes on an even greater universalizing, and indeed speculative, boldness:

Our hey fader, God almyty, which is beyng, he knew us and lovid us fro aforn any tyme; of which knoweing, in his mervelous depe charite be the forseing endless councel of all the blissid Trinite, he wold that the second person shuld becom our moder, our brother and our savior. Wherof it folowith that as verily as God is our fader, as verily God is our moder. Our fader [G: wyllyth], our moder werkyth, our good lord the Holy Gost confirmith. (59.96)

This is only one passage in which the 'simple creature that cowde no letter' (2.2) demonstrates a magisterial command of her theological material together with an equally magisterial linguistic facility which together exude a remarkable degree of rhetorical confidence, especially if we glance back to the anxiety so evident in Short Text chapter vi. It seems reasonable to propose that Julian's confident, self-assured relation to her presumed audience is largely predicated upon, and made instrumental through, her mature conception of the essential unity-in-Christ of all Christians.

'one new man'

This chapter has been concerned to show that in reconstructing her relation to the figure of Christ crucified Julian narrates her own movement from pious individualism to an inclusive compassion rooted in her developed understanding of Christ's identification with the Church. As we have said, to the extent that she can secure this identification in credible rhetorical terms she can represent a bridging of the gap between her own visionary isolation and the body of Christian believers. Julian's consciousness of her relation to the Church has been noted at the beginning of this Chapter, in her obedience to the priest's injunction that she should keep her eyes fixed on the crucifix at the end of her bed. The visionary experience as a whole is thus given location with the parameters of legitimate ecclesiastical jurisdiction. It is also striking that, in Chapter 66, Julian's faith in the veracity of the showings is revived and confirmed only because the cleric who comes to see her takes them seriously, whilst Julian initially dismisses them as the ravings of a sick woman (66.108).[62] In these two examples of her dependence on and submission to the clergy, Julian reconstructs for her audience the sense of her relation to the Church which pertains to the particular stage of her religious development within which the showings were originally experienced. Authority and hierarchy are foregrounded as major determinants of Julian's relation to a reality that seems largely external to her rather than intrinsic, a relation between separate entities (Julian; the Church) which must, on Julian's part, be experienced either positively through obedience to legitimate authority or negatively through disobedience to it. The absolute dichotomy she evokes between herself as viewing subject and the crucifix as viewed object – the crucifix which has been placed before her *by the Church* – is suggestive of the mature Julian's perception of her past self's somewhat externalized and undeveloped ecclesiological awareness. The shift in the ninth showing from the iconic to the reciprocal, from vision alone to vision and dialogue, is equally suggestive of a fresh dynamism entering Julian's relation both to Christ and the Church.

But it is the tenth showing, in which Julian imaginatively enters the side of Christ and discovers there 'a fair delectabil place . . . large enow for al mankynd that shal be save to resten in pece and love' (24.35), that especially conveys this fresh dynamism. She no longer just gazes at the Christ-figure, or converses with it, but instead plunges into it and so discovers the spiritual inwardness and unity of the Church, its reality in Christ which the outward structures of authority and hierarchy only serve and upon which they depend. No suggestion is made here that Julian abjures the juridical in favour of the mystical. Rather, we might say that it is by passing through the narrow door of the juridical that Julian discovers the wider pastures of a mystical ecclesiology. Her literary representation of this movement invites the reader to pass through the narrow door of Julian's contingent personal experience into the limitless world of the showings, to discover there the mystical Christ in whom all evil separateness is dissolved. The antecedents of Julian's distinctive christological/ecclesiological mysticism are substantially Pauline:

> For [Christ] is our peace, who has made us both one, and has broken down the dividing wall of hostility . . . that he might create in himself one new man in place of two, so making peace, and might reconcile us both to God in one body through the cross, thereby bringing the hostility to an end.[63]

[62] See Riddy, ' "Women talking about the things of God" ', especially pp. 114–15.
[63] Ephesians 2:14–17, RSV.

In narrating Julian's personal movement from individualism to compassion, from piety to ecclesiology, the text rhetorically enacts a dissolution of that particular separateness which is an inevitable condition of her vocation as both visionary and author.

The quotation from the letter to the Ephesians given above cites Christ crucified as the 'one new man' in whom all are united, and the vision of the crucified Christ as a specific, and a specifically ecclesiological, symbol of unity is at the heart of Julian's textual universe. This does not mean, however, that Julian eschews the personal and particular in favour of a generalized ecclesiology. In Chapter 28 it is striking that she maintains a sense of Christ's identification with the Church as a whole, together with a sense of his identification with the individual: 'Gods *servants*, holy church, shal be shakyn in sorows and anguis and tribulations as men shakyth a cloth in the wynde' (28.39, my emphasis). One body, many members. Christ crucified indivisibly represents both the body as a whole and each individual member of it, 'ech person that he lovyth to his bliss for to bringen' (28.39). The persecution of Christ's Church is manifested in the suffering of real individuals on the ground, those who are 'lakid . . . dispisyd . . . scornyd, rapyd and outcasten'. The union of Christ and the Church is not an abstraction; rather, it is actualized through his personal union with each member of that Church. The individual and the Church as a whole are coinherent, not separate entities in competition with each other. And this coinherence, this mystical unity, is effected through 'the charity of God' made available in Christ:

> the charite of God makyth in us such a unite that whan it is trewly seen no man can parten himse[l]fe fro other. (65.105)

Looking to the larger textual picture, Chapter 28 adumbrates a theological vision that will find the source of a fully mystical ecclesiology in the believer's unbreakable personal union with Christ. The fact of this union means that there is attached to the individual as such an absolute and non-negotiable value in the context of the Church. Julian's development of this theme of personal union with Christ – her development, to put it another way, of a distinctive and rigorous incarnational theology – is the subject of our next two chapters, which form a diptych and should be taken together. Julian's precise theological thinking in this area has clear implications in view of her task of presenting her own experience, and her own reflections on that experience, as being of real religious benefit to other Christians. In an important sense, as we have already noted, it represents her development of an implicit theological justification of autobiography.

3

Incarnation (I):
A Lord and a Servant

THE PRESENT chapter and the one immediately following it examine Julian's theological explication of the bond between Christ and humanity. Both chapters are given the main title 'Incarnation' and should be treated as a diptych. This doubleness reflects the procedure by which Julian herself evokes that reciprocity which is essential to the classic notion of incarnation: Christ assumes a human nature; human beings are enabled thereby to participate in Christ's divine nature. The present chapter considers Christ's willing solidarity with human beings in obedience to his Father. It offers a substantial account of the example of the lord and the servant (Chapter 51), and follows Julian as she draws out of that example an intricate understanding of this solidarity. The next chapter examines that section of the text which grows specifically out of the example (substantially Chapters 52–65), and considers Julian's account of what Christ's solidarity implies for human beings themselves, namely a real sharing of the divine life. It pursues Julian's subsequent development of the theme of humanity's relation to God, examining her concept of the theological structure of the human person as such, and relating this to her theme of divine motherhood. It is hoped to show above all in this diptych that the real union between Christ and humanity – whether considered in terms of the Church as a whole, or of the individual as a kind of ecclesiological microcosm – is Julian's dominant preoccupation.

The reader is asked to bear in mind our precise intention in giving a (relatively) detailed account of Julian's theology. If her theology can be accounted 'autobiographical' in the sense that it is rooted in her personal experience, and also in that it bears witness to her religious and intellectual development over time, that same theology also serves an autobiographical and personal function in providing Julian both with a means of self-projection and a philosophical defence of her very act of self-projection. It seems reasonable, therefore, to propose that the actual *character* of Julian's theology is of the essence in all this. As she clearly understands it, the inestimable value attachable to the human person as such is derived from the incarnation of Christ. The individual human being is literally unthinkable, unconceptualizable, apart from him. Within the parameters of such an understanding, the experience of even the most discardable nobody can be said to achieve a unique significance demanding of respect. In Julian's case, since her authority to address an audience on spiritual matters cannot be derived from ecclesiastical office, from the Church *juridically* understood, it must be derived from her own experience as a bona fide member of that Church *mystically* understood along the lines her text both implicitly and explicitly proposes. The paradigm Julian offers – integrating ecclesiology and personal mysticism with incarnational theology – would represent the optimum conditions for the acceptance of her own human credentials as both visionary and author, if an audience might be persuaded to take it.

We will need in this and the following chapter to try and be something like as systematic in examining Julian's theology as she is herself in its construction. Whilst Julian is capable of writing with anecdotal vividness and humour, and has a poetic gift for realizing subjects in a visual way, when it comes to the more explicitly and ambitiously theological section of the text her method is quite formal and logical, and perhaps more subtly self-consistent than she is sometimes given credit for. This method seems to demand a willingness on the part of the reader to proceed in an orderly fashion and not to imagine that Julian's remarkably coherent theological vision can be apprehended or put together in any old order. Her verbal precision and consistency, her cumulative layering of meaning upon meaning, and the intricate self-allusiveness of her text are a constant challenge to any reader; and a specific rebuke to those of us inclined to allow Julian's often delightfully rhythmical and supple syntax to carry us further *thematically* than we have earned the right to go. Since it will be impossible, in discussing Julian's theology of the incarnation and all that flows from that, to avoid altogether an impression of 'working through' the text, it is hoped that the reader will keep in mind the larger rationale for this as outlined above, and find that the end fully justifies the means.

As already indicated, this first chapter of our diptych focuses on Julian's example of the lord and the servant, and finds in it the source of Julian's incarnational theology and her ecclesiological mysticism. But since the example is presented in the text as having been given to Julian in response to her anxious concern about God's attitude to human sinfulness, that is a question we will need to consider first.

Sin and Blame

Christ's union with humanity is qualified by Julian (and by Christian tradition in general) as a *saving* union, answering precisely to humanity's need for salvation, notably from sin in the form of deliberate human wickedness; but also from sin in the wider sense, as that from which proceed all the world's imperfections, and everything that is negative and painful in human life. The question of sin increasingly vexes Julian from the third revelation onwards, intruding on her experience of vision; but the intrusions act also as catalysts of further revelation.

In the first showing Julian experiences the joy of the Trinity, a foretaste of heaven:

> And in the same sheweing sodenly the Trinite fullfilled the herte most of ioy. And so I understood it shall be in hevyn withoute end to all that shall come there. (4.5–6)

This positive experience of the divine modulates in Chapter 5 into the vision of the 'littil thing, the quantitye of an hesil nutt in the palme of my hand' (5.7),[1] an image of the whole created order, of which Julian is told three things: 'the first is that God made it, the second is that God loveth it, the iiid is that God kepith it'. She realizes in this that creation has its being through the love of God and that 'his goodness comprehendith all his creatures and all his blissid works, and overpassith without ende' (5.8).[2]

---

[1] Roland Maisonneuve's comments on this image of the little thing in the palm of Julian's hand are subtle and suggestive: 'La symbolisation est . . . très originale par l'espèce d'identification qui se fait entre la main de Julian et la main de Dieu . . . Il y a, par là, association de l'homme à l'action continuelle de Dieu en sa création. La création est comme confiée à l'homme. De plus, en cette identification Dieu-Julian, par l'intermédiaire d'une main, est manifestée la divinisation de l'homme que Dieu poursuit à travers l'histoire et en chaque âme, et par ce symbole de Tout-Puissance l'assurance que cette déification sera conduite à son terme', L'univers visionnaire, p. 107. ['The symbolism is particularly original on account of its identification of God's hand with Julian's . . . By that identification, humanity is shown to be involved in God's continual activity within creation. Creation is as though entrusted to humanity. Furthermore, in this identification of God and Julian, as mediated through the image of the single hand, there is indicated the divinization of humanity, which God seeks throughout all ages and within each soul; and through this image of divine omnipotence, the assurance that this process of divinization will be brought to its proper completion', my translation.]

[2] The goodness of God is a crucial theme of Julian's, notably in the chapters (4–9) in which the first showing is described and meditated upon. Significantly, Chapter 9 opens with the words, 'For the shewing I am *not* good' (9.13, my emphasis), thus giving negative emphasis to the proper and positive goodness of God. In her illuminating essay, 'The Goodness of God: A Julian Study', in ed. Helen Phillips, *Langland, the Mystics and the Medieval English Religious Tradition* (Cambridge, 1990), pp. 85–95, Ritamary Bradley makes the large but convincing claim that 'the meaning of [Julian's] visions grows out of contemplating goodness, which is the unifying subject' (p. 85); and she links Julian's concern with goodness to influential *auctoritatis* such as Augustine, Pseudo-Dionysius, Thomas Aquinas and Bonaventure.

The third showing recapitulates this cosmic vision and (taking CW's reading here) points not only to God's presence in all things but his active power:

> And after this I saw god in a poynte, that is to say in my vnderstandyng, by which syght I saw that he is in althyng. I beheld with avysement, seeyng and knowyng in that syght that he doth all that is done.
>
> (CW 336.3–6)

Again we have a positive experience of the divine, and this is very much to be kept in mind as we move on to the question of sin. There is a dialectical character to Julian's engagement with the showings, a dynamic tension between seeking and beholding from which the momentum of experience is shown to derive. Her overwhelming perception of God's goodness in creation, as presented in the first and third showings, does not fit unproblematically into Julian's mental world. Her response to the third showing makes this clear enough. Whether the 'poynte' in which God is seen is understood spatially or temporally – perhaps the terms should be read as a metaphoric enigma, an apophatic refusal of category[3] – the nature of that experience seems primarily to be one of inner realization: God is present in all things[4] and God does all things.[5] This would appear to be the most obvious example in the text of what Julian means by 'gostly sight' (9.14), an experience of 'seeyng and knowyng' which, transcending *ratio*, corresponds to *intellectus*[6] in the

---

[3] On apophasis, and the problematics of expressing/engaging the ineffable, see generally, Gillespie and Ross, 'Apophatic Image', especially pp. 53–8; also, Gillespie, 'Postcards from the Edge'.

[4] Brian Davies quotes from Thomas Aquinas, *Summa Theologiae*, Ia. 8. I: 'God exists in everything . . . Since it is God's nature to exist, he it must be who properly causes existence in creatures, just as it is fire itself that sets other things on fire . . . Now existence is more intimately and profoundly interior to things than anything else, for everything as we said is potential when compared to existence. So God must exist and exist intimately in everything', *The Thought of Thomas Aquinas* (Oxford, 1992), p. 99.

[5] Thomas Bradwardine could be an influence here; if so, probably an oblique one. G. R. Evans writes: 'God, says Bradwardine [in his *De Causa Dei*], knows everything specifically, and his knowledge is complete. It is also eternal and immutable, and he knows past, present and future alike. Everything which God knows is actively moved by him. His knowledge is therefore an active force. Nothing can happen unless God wills it. Even what he "permits" is his act', *Philosophy and Theology*, p. 84.

[6] For an excellent, concise presentation (drawing on Boethius and Thomas Aquinas) of the distinction between *intellectus* (higher reason) and *ratio* (lower reason), see C. S. Lewis, *The Discarded Image: An Introduction to Medieval and Renaissance Literature*, paperback reprint (Cambridge, 1985), p. 157. The notion of *intellectus* has a Platonist/neo-Platonist pedigree and relates to a stress on *nous* or 'mind' as that in human beings which opens out onto transcendent reality. This leads in Plotinus, and sometimes in those influenced by him (including the

sense of a non-discursive, spiritual intuition. But Julian does not merely bask here in a delicious state of mystical illumination. Beholding stimulates seeking, and her response to the third showing is a questioning one, intellectual in the modern sense, as she thinks to herself, 'What is synne?' (11.17).

Even at this moment of mystical intuition, when we might have expected a sense of unitive plenitude and of a dissolution of boundaries, Julian presents herself standing apart as self-conscious observer and interrogator. God's all-comprehending presence and activity seem to admit of a mysterious fissure, an independent space in which Julian's question, 'What is synne?', emerges as a telling sign of her habitation of that ontological gap; and as a sign, therefore, of a certain separation from God. The incompleteness of union this implies between God and Julian is a manifestation of her fallen condition. It should be noted that no rational explanation of sin itself is given at this point, or indeed at all.[7] Julian is simply encouraged to trust that God, who 'doth althing be it never so litil', is leading everything to its appointed fulfilment. She places a reply in

Greek Fathers, and Augustine), to a certain emphasis on purification of intellect as constitutive of spiritual advancement as such. For discussion of this, see Andrew Louth, *The Origins of the Christian Mystical Tradition: From Plato to Denys* (Oxford, 1981), especially pp. 8–10 and 44–7; see also Williams, *Wound of Knowledge*, pp. 64–70. It is, however, important to note that in the context of later (i.e. western medieval) spiritual traditions, the idea of an intellectual ascent to God is modified by a degree of affectivity, leading to an emphasis on *will* rather than intellect. This affective dimension (not always wholly absent, of course) seems to have emerged partly in reaction to a growing scholastic culture which appeared, especially to someone like Bernard of Clairvaux, to assert by implication that reality was only construable – and God only engageable – according to paradigms that suited the academic élite; on this, see, for example, Sister Edmée, 'Bernard and Abelard', in ed. Benedicta Ward, *The Influence of Saint Bernard* (Fairacres, Oxford, 1976), pp. 89–134. This reaction, if it is entirely correct to call it that, is evident in the religious 'personalism' of the reinvigorated monastic movement of the twelfth century. It is in fact William of St Thierry, the Benedictine-become-Cistercian, who, in his phrase, 'amor ipse intellectus est' ('love itself is understanding'), expresses most succinctly the anti-scholasticism (not anti-intellectualism) of many in the monastic world – see William of St Thierry, *The Golden Epistle*, trans. Theodore Berkeley with an introduction by J. M. Déchanet (Kalamazoo, Michigan, 1980), p. 68, para. 173, and n. 6. In the fourteenth century it is clear that this suspicion of the scholastic mood has influenced the *Cloud*-author, who writes (with his characteristic emphasis on will/desire), 'For whi [God] may wel be loued, bot not þouȝt', *Cloud of Unknowing*, p. 14, line 22. It is possible to argue that Julian's writing represents an attempted integration of the rational and the affective – as Marion Glasscoe notes: '[Julian's] is a language which expresses the emotions of faith but has a tough rational sub-structure to convey the illumination of understanding by that faith', *Revelation*, intro. p. xvi.

[7] See Chapter 1, n. 35, above. Julian's ST apostrophe to sin (CW 271.26–36) is not retained in LT.

God's mouth, rounded off with a rhetorical question that balances her own enquiry but does not exactly answer it on its own terms:

> 'Se I am God. Se I am in althing. Se I doe althyng. Se I lefte never myne hands of myn werks, ne never shall, withoute ende. Se I lede althyng to the end that I ordeynd it to fro withoute beginnyng be the same might, wisdam and love that I made it. How should anything be amysse?'
>
> (11.18–19)

The problem of sin re-emerges in the thirteenth showing and with greater personal import as Julian recognizes in it the one obstacle to complete union with God. The question of 'why by the gret forseyng wysdam of God the begynnyng of synne was not lettid' (27.38) is something that has been troubling her, and in Chapter 27 the inner tension is apparent: 'mornyng and sorow I made therfor without reason and discretion'. The term 'discretion' has a particular resonance within medieval spiritual tradition, denoting the art of appropriate conduct, a sensitivity to whatever might be done in a practical way to make a person more supple in responding to God; including, negatively, a concern for what ought to be repudiated or avoided. Discretion recognizes human limitations and is therefore associated with humility. The art of discretion operates through a precise sifting of the possible in terms of the morally and spiritually desirable – a kind of reality-testing – and as such is a function of reason. Julian herself speaks here of 'reason and discretion' and the coupling is not arbitrary.[8] For the twelfth century Richard of St Victor, discretion (Joseph) is the first offspring of reason (Rachel). But within the context of a person's spiritual life, the inherent limits of rationality must be understood. Reason operates within a demarcated sphere and is orientated towards practicality, appropriate conduct; and the acceptance of this intrinsic limitation is itself an act of discretion enabled by reason. Transcendent divine truth is beyond reason's direct apprehension, and certainly beyond its mastery, and it is important that the rational intellect should know its place. Julian's 'mornyng and sorow' (27.38) betray her frustration at not being able to ascend *by reason* to a plane of spiritual reality where sin might be understood fully in its relation to God. The energy squandered in this frustration leaves her unable to use reason (in the form of discretion) at its appropriate level in the practical service of faith. Her perturbation over the question of sin is symptomatic of her wrong-headedness, her irrationality; which is to say

---

[8] At this point I am emphasizing Julian's implicit concern with human sinfulness as taking the form of irrationality; and of irrationality itself as taking the form of indiscretion and inappropriate conduct. But see also Chapter 1, n. 34, above.

that she is, as Augustine understood himself to be, hampered by sin itself in her search for the truth about sin.[9]

The response Julian receives in the thirteenth showing in relation to the conundrum of why sin was not prevented in the beginning is, as in the third showing, another baffling non-explanation. God is clearly not willing to argue. Rather, there is an assertion, as before, of his leading of creation to its appointed end. But there is in addition a qualitative increment of revelation assigning a positive role to sin within that providential dispensation:

> But Iesus, that in this vision enformid me of all that me neydyth, answerid by this worde and seyd: 'Synne is behovabil, but al shal be wel, and al shal be wel, and al manner of thyng shal be wele.' (27.38)

God's apparent refusal to collude with Julian's search for rationally digestible explanations is further represented in this chapter by his expansion of the signifying power of the word 'sin' beyond its restricted, conventional sense of deliberate moral transgression so that it appropriates a complex of meanings embracing the sufferings of Christ and of humanity:

> In this nakid word 'synne' our good lord browte to my mynd generally al that is not good, and the shamefull dispite and the utter nowtyng that he bare for us in this life, and his dyeng, and al the peynys and passions of al his creatures, gostly and bodyly . . . (27.38)

Julian's search for an explanation of sin really takes her no further than the crucifix at the end of her bed as she discerns there an enigmatic, non-conceptual interpretation of her sinful, suffering condition, and that of humanity generally. Sin is not merely a problem for Julian to solve, analyzable in terms of the relative culpability pertaining to discrete moral transgressions. Rather, to paraphrase Kierkegaard, sin is the very thing she is in: the unstable, possible, incomplete condition of a self not 'transparently grounded in the power which established it'.[10] It is a

---

[9] I allude to Augustine's Confessions, VII.v (7): 'Et quaerebam, unde malum, et male quaerebam et in ipsa inquisitiones mea non videbam malum', Skutella, p. 129, lines 22–3; 'I searched for the origin of evil, but I searched in a flawed way and did not see the flaw in my very search', Chadwick, p. 115. The English translation here does not convey the lexical looping by which Augustine signifies his *a priori* entanglement in evil: 'unde *malum* . . . *male* quaerebam . . . no videbam *malum*'.

[10] Søren Kierkegaard, *The Sickness Unto Death*, trans. Alastair Hannay (Harmondsworth, 1989), p. 127: 'No human being is able to say, of his own and by himself, what sin is, for sin is the very thing he is in'; and p. 165: 'in relating to itself and in wanting to be itself, the self is grounded transparently in the power which

condition of ontological vulnerability of which the figure of the crucified Christ is here understood to be the definitive image, a mirror of human suffering and of the desecration of innocence.

But sin is also 'behovabil' (27.38). In the new dispensation of grace it is transfigured through Christ into the meeting place between God and humanity, and therefore has become the very premise of salvation for the predestined. Relation to God is effected according to the dynamics of the economy of salvation in which the horror of sin is innocently assumed by the second person of the Trinity in obedience to the Father. The Word, who from the beginning was in the form of God,[11] speaks to humanity in the form of sin:

> For our sake [God] made him to be sin who knew no sin so that in him we might become the righteousness of God.[12]

As Son Christ is the image of the Father, as incarnate Word he takes on 'the likeness if sinful flesh'.[13] His death on the cross marks him out as a 'curse',[14] executed 'outside the camp'.[15] He thus allows himself to he consigned to the solitude of that ontological desert which is humanity's alienation from God, the place Augustine (after Plato and Plotinus) calls *regio dissimilitudinis*, the Land of Unlikeness.[16] Sin, therefore, as Julian must learn, is now to be comprehended in the contemplation of Christ crucified.

In the cross are focused the paradoxes of the Christian universe. It represents God's judgement against sin but is also the definitive sign of his love for sinners, a sign of redemption. It also focuses a paradox that comes to have particular significance for Julian: the fact that humanity is at once guilty of sin but regarded by God as blameless, 'childer, inocentes and vnlothfull' (28.40). For Julian, to live towards God under the

---

established it. Which formula in turn, as has frequently been remarked, is the definition of faith.'

[11] John 1:2; Philippians 2:6.

[12] II Corinthians 5:21. Also note Julian's Chapter 27: 'In this nakid word "synne" our lord browte to my mynd generally al that is not good, *and the shamfull dispite and the utter nowtyng that he bare for us in this life, and his dyeng*' (27.38, my emphasis).

[13] Romans 8:13.

[14] Galations 3:13.

[15] Hebrews 13:13.

[16] See Confessions, VII.x (16): 'et inveni longe me esse a te in regione dissimilitudinis', Skutella, p. 141, lines 7–8; 'And I found myself far from you "in the region of dissimilarity" ', Chadwick, p. 123. The phrase is from Plato's *Statesman* (see Chadwick, p. 123, n. 22) and has reached Augustine via Plotinus (see Louth, Origins, p. 42). From Augustine, the phrase was taken up by Bernard of Clairvaux – see Etienne Gilson, *The Mystical Theology of Saint Bernard*, paperback reprint (Kalamazoo, Michigan, 1990), p. 45 and also n. 43 (pp. 224–5).

conditions of time is to be taken up into a dialectic of sin and mercy, a dialectic represented in the double significance of the cross as both judgement and redemption. Christ crucified represents the individual – and the Church – suffering the pains of sin in a fallen world, but this suffering is interpreted in the light of the resurrection:

> I understode that we be now, in our lords menyng, in his crosse with hym in our peynys and our passion, deyng; and we wilfully abydyng in the same cross with his helpe and his grace into the last poynte, sodenly he shall chonge his chere to us, and we shal be with hym in hevyn.
>
> (21.31)

Julian is concerned with the kind of world human beings find themselves in, a world that is diseased in its very structure and at all levels, but most crucially within the human person as such, in the separation of substance from sensuality. Sin is not a problem to be solved but a condition to be lived in and through. It is of the nature of life lived under the conditions of time that sin, consequent upon human weakness and spiritual blindness, will be part of the equation: 'I shal do nothyng but synne' (36.49). In Chapter 32 Julian mentions a 'grete dede' (32.44) which will be performed by the Trinity on the last day, making all things well. In addition to this, however, there is a second 'dede that shall be done' (36.49) by God, and which 'shal lastyn . . . in werkyng onto the last day', a miracle of redemption worked out through time, bringing the negativity of sin to work positively within a lifelong process of spiritual recuperation, restoring the unity between substance and sensuality. But again, this work takes place within time and is therefore characterized as temporal, incremental, not once-for-all. Human development towards interior harmony, never completed in this world, derives from a dialectic of sin and mercy/grace. The wound of sin is a wound of possibility.[17] This is not to say – and Julian herself affirms this – that sins should be deliberately committed in order to expedite the process of salvation. Rather, the point is that individuals have to be reconciled to the kind of world they are in, a world in which sin is linked ineluctably to a structural fault and so is, to some extent at least, inevitable. As Denise Baker has pointed out, Julian's approach to evil, and therefore sin, is teleological rather than aetiological.[18] Julian, that is, comes to be concerned less with the origin and nature of sin as such than with its accommodation within those processes which are leading believers to the fulfilment God intends for them.

Prayer, as Julian understands it, expresses a longing for union with

---

[17] The image of the 'wound of possibility' is Kierkegaard's and is cited in Steiner, *Real Presences*, p. 173.

[18] D. N. Baker especially notes Julian's difference from Augustine in this respect – see Chapter 1, n. 35, above.

God, a longing precisely predicated on the fact of separation from him. Her discussion of prayer (Chapters 41–43), which logically follows her discussion of sin, can be regarded as the pastoral heart of the text, touching on the practical implications of the revelation for those who wish to take it seriously. This section of the text will be considered in Chapter 5 of this book, and in relation to what seems to be the primary guiding principle of the text: that personal experience matters supremely.

Chapters 44–49 continue the broad theme of sin, looking particularly at how God himself regards sinners. Julian is unable to see any wrath in God, and this perception, together with her previous realization of the insubstantiality of sin, leads her to the conclusion that even the notion of God's forgiveness of sin – so utterly central to Christian teaching – is ultimately a kind of benign illusion, an anthropomorphism. God, in fact, does not forgive people because he does not blame them for sin in the first place. Human beings project onto God the wrath that is in themselves:

> For this was an hey mervel to the soule, which was continuly shewid in al, and with gret diligens beholden: that our lord God, anempts hymself, may not forgevyn, for he may not be wroth – it were impossible. For this was shewid: that lif is all groundid and rotid in love, and without love we may not levyn; and therfore to the soule that of his special grace seyth so ferforth of the hey mervelous godenes of God, and that we arn endlesly onyd to hym in love, it is the most impossible that may ben that God shuld be wreth, for wreth and frendship be ii contraries; for he that westeth and destroyith our wreth and makyth us meke and mylde, it behovyth neds to ben that he be ever on in love, meke and mylde, which is contrarious to wreth . . . (49.69)

But whatever understanding Julian presents herself attaining through the showings, she does not neglect to remind us that her own personal sinfulness leaves her continually a prey throughout her visionary experience to an obtuseness both intellectual and spiritual. In Chapter 50 we find Julian still subject to the contrariousness of her sinful condition, unable to rest with the assurance she has been given that 'al shal be wel' (27.38) and once again sliding into a regressive rationalism that would reduce divine mystery to a manageable formula. Having perceived no wrath in God, and seeing him apportion no blame to human beings on account of sin, Julian's problem in Chapter 50 is that she cannot reconcile all this either with her own experience of guilt or, perhaps more crucially, with what she takes to be orthodox Catholic doctrine:

> For I knew be the common techyng of holy church and be myne owne felyng that the blame of our synne continuly hangith upon us, from the first man into the tyme that we come up into hevyn; than was this my mervel, that I saw our lord God shewand to us no more blame than if we

were as clene as holy angelys be in hevyn. And atwix these ii contraries
my reason was gretly traveylid by my blyndhede . . . (50.71)

Julian is again looking for the kind of answer that has already been denied
her. She has fallen, as it were, from unity into multiplicity, from a
spiritually intuitive contemplation of the truth in God into a feverish
and exhausting mental struggle with irreconcilable 'contraries'. Her
greatest anxiety is that, unless the problem is resolved in some way, she
will 'be left in onknowyng how he beholdyth us in our synne' (50.71).

This question of what exactly is God's own perspective on humanity's
fallen state is central to the example of the lord and the servant, which
follows in Chapter 51 and is presented as a direct divine response to
Julian's anxiety about this matter. As on previous occasion, the response
she receives is not a rationally appropriable formula. Instead she is
presented with an enigma, a narrative vision shown 'full mystyly'
(51.72), as through that obscuring glass which, for St Paul, denotes the
incompleteness of human knowing – 'we see now through a glass in a
dark manner'.[19] This is a vision so pregnant with meaning that Julian tells
us she has been schooled inwardly about it for 'xx yeres after the tyme of
the sheweing, save iii monethis' (51.74) and can refer to it even after all
that time as providing her not so much with an ABC as 'the *begynnyng* of
an ABC' (51.79, my emphasis).[20] But despite her claim for the theological
inexhaustibility of the example, she does make an attempt to explicate it
for her audience and, in doing so, sets out to produce an integrated, large-
scale interpretation of sinful humanity's relation to God, and to one
another, through Christ.

The Lord and the Servant – Julian's Primary Experience

Although Chapter 51 is by far the most substantial chapter of the Long
Text, the basic narrative details of the showing with which the chapter
opens take up less than a fifth of the whole, after which Julian says, 'And
at this poynte the shewing of the example vanishid' (51.73).[21] The showing

---

[19] I Corinthians 13:12 [Vulgate: 'videmus nunc per speculum in aenigmate'].

[20] Nicholas Watson presents the phrase 'the begynning of an ABC' as referring to
the total revelation, and not just to the example of the lord and the servant as the
context makes quite clear: 'Also *in this mervelous example* I have techyng with
me, as it were the begynnyng of an ABC' (51.76, my emphasis). See Watson,
'Trinitarian Hermeneutic', p. 84.

[21] The example of the lord and the servant has attracted significant critical
attention (though less than might have been expected given its obvious
weight within the text). For example, see: Baker, *Julian of Norwich's Showings*,
pp. 83–106; Jantzen, *Julian of Norwich*, pp. 190–200; Glasscoe, *English Medieval
Mystics*, pp. 246–55; Nuth, *Wisdom's Daughter*, pp. 27–34. Also useful, and more

is presented here in bare, simple terms (especially by comparison with later elaborations) and with only a few interpretative comments which appear to her represent her initial reactions to the experience and so, in a certain sense, to belong to it. We need to focus here on Julian's narrative of her primary experience of the showings since on it depend the rest of this pivotal Chapter 51 and subsequent chapters. Despite the appearance of lapsing from interpretation into mere narration it will be helpful to follow Julian particularly closely here since this is a part of the text in which the reader is well advised to make a heavy investment.

Julian says she perceived this showing in two modes: 'gostly in bodily lyknes' (51.72) and 'more gostly without bodyly lyknes'. The former term would seem to refer to her perception of the actual images presented to her mind, the word 'gostly' indicating the supernatural origin of those images and the fact that they do not have an external, physical location – by contrast with her vision of the crucifix in a state of animation. The latter term suggests her intuition of inner meaning and here designates only the first stage of a continuing process. For the present we are specifically concerned with the first, the narrative itself, if narrative is quite the word for this minimalist cameo which could be realized as three static pictures, like a sequence in the stained glass window of a medieval cathedral. This image is fitting in that it conveys, first, a definite form analogous to the fixity of the example's basic elements; and, second, a variation of illumination by fitful sunlight which would correspond to the enigmatic disclosure of meaning through these basic elements.[22]

The first picture is devoid of action and is dominated by the benignity and Buddha-like restfulness of the seated lord:

> The lord sittith solemnly in rest and peace, the servant standyth by, aforn his lord reverently, redy to don his lords will. The lord lokyth upon his servant ful lovely and swetely . . . (51.72)

The readiness of the servant, however, does suggest a tension towards that decisive moment of action when the lord gives his command and the

scholarly than the title would suggest, is Ritamary Bradley, *Julian's Way: A Practical Commentary on Julian of Norwich* (London, 1992), especially pp. 98–123. Despite its title, J. P. H. Clark, 'Time and Eternity in Julian of Norwich', *Downside Review*, 109 (1991), pp. 259–76, is substantially concerned with the example of the lord and the servant, relating it to the theology of Augustine and Duns Scotus – sadly, the hefty portions of untranslated Latin text will prove an obstacle to most readers of this article.

[22] In slight contrast, but similarly, Marion Glasscoe notes: 'It [the example of the lord and the servant] combines the static representational qualities of an icon, and the fluidity of allegorical narrative, to focus an intuitive understanding of the redemptive work of love, at the heart of the Incarnation, through which Christ and man are one in the game of faith', *English Medieval Mystics*, p. 246.

servant obeys with alacrity, a moment which is frozen in the next picture of the sequence:

> mekely he [the lord] sendyth hym to a certain place to don his will. The servant, not only he goeth, but suddenly he stirtith and rynnith in grete haste for love to don his lords will. (51.72)

This lends itself to a stylized, iconic realization, the lord's right hand raised in a gesture of command, the servant caught in an attitude of enthusiastic obedience, on his toes, knees bent, lurching away from his master.

The sequence ends with a bathetic picture of the servant's crash-landing in a 'slade':

> And anon he fallith in a slade and takith ful grete sore. And than he gronith and monith and waylith and writhith, but he ne may rysen ne helpyn himself be no manner wey. And of all this the most myscheif that I saw him in was faylyng of comforte; for he cowde not turne his face to loke upon his loving lorde, which was to hym ful nere, in whom is ful comfort; but as a man that was febil and onwise for the tyme, he entended to his felyng, and induryd in wo . . . (51.72)

While this passage is not merely iconic, stressing as it does the emotional trauma of the servant's fall, it does nevertheless represent the amplification of a simple, uncomplicated narrative-picture: 'he fallith in a slade'.

Julian's basic outline of the primary experience of the showing does not end as simply and suggestively as it begins. Instead, focusing on the suffering servant, she launches into a categorizing mode of description which suggests self-conscious analytical distance more than a baffled exposure to the enigmatic. In addition to the very significant fact of the servant's inability to 'turne his face to loke upon his loving lorde', Julian perceives that the servant suffered 'vii grete peynes' which can be summarized as follows:

  (i) bruising (51.72);
  (ii) bodily heaviness;
  (iii) weakness;
  (iv) blindness of reason, and mental stupor, 'so ferforth that almost he had forgotten his owne luf' (51.73);
  (v) inability to rise;
  (vi) isolation;
  (vii) the pain of lying in a 'lang, hard and grevous' place.

Although this list reads as part of an interpretative amplification, the interpretation is presented as belonging to the initial experience. Julian is suggesting that her primary analysis of the servant's pains is to be considered as an intrinsic part of the example itself, part of the primary 'text' which the reader is asked to digest so that later exegesis will be understood.

Also narrated as part of this initial experience of the showing is Julian's inability to perceive any fault in the servant, and her understanding that the lord assigns no blame to him. She has a double perception of both figures. The servant appears in a state of degradation but is also seen to be 'as onlothful and as good inwardly as whan he stode afor his lord redy to don his wille' (51.73). Below the surface his love for the lord, his 'good will', is intact, though he is unconscious of it. The lord, too, is 'shewid double' (51.72). Outwardly his countenance is one of 'grete ruth and pety' (51.73) on account of the outward pains of the servant. But inwardly the lord has a countenance of joy 'for the worshipful resting and nobleth that he will and shall bryng his servant to'.

Julian's narration of her primary experience is brought to a decisive end with the words, 'And at this poynte the shewing of the example vanishid' (51.73); and God then 'led forth myn vnderstondyng in syte and in shewing of the revelation to the end'. The primary level of this experience, outlined thus far in Chapter 51, is perhaps best described as an embryo, which over 'xx yeres . . . save iii monethis' (51.74) has been filled out with meanings according to the dynamics of Julian's inner experience over that period of time. The image is apposite in that it can suggest the kind of open-endedness implied in the phrase 'the begynnyng of an ABC' (51.79) which she assigns even to her mature understanding of this showing. She will later say that there is no higher stature than childhood, spiritually speaking.[23] The process of discovery never ends but is always beginning.[24]

Adam

In the process of interpreting the example of the lord and the servant, one of Julian's earliest intuitions is that the servant represents Adam. But this realization, far from satisfying her, increases the sense of enigma:

> methowth [the example] was goven me for an answere to my desir, and yet cowth I not taken therin ful vnderstondyng to myn ese at that tyme; for in the servant that was shewid for Adam, as I shall seyn, I saw many dyvers properties that myten be no manner wey ben aret to single Adam. (51.74)

[23] 'And I vnderstode non heyer stature in this life than childhode, in febilness and fayleing of myte and witte', 63.103.

[24] 'And than shall the bliss of our moder in Criste be new to begynnen in the ioyes of our God; which new begynning shal lesten without end, new begynnand', 63.104.

Any preconception Julian may have had of what a representation of Adam ought to be and ought to show has not been fulfilled. In the first place, this Adam is completely detached from the biblical narrative. There is no serpent-tempter and no Eve. Although the servant does sustain a fall, with the obvious suggestion of *the* fall, his descent into the slade is not presented as a moral transgression. Sin, as such, is mysteriously absent. In contrast to Adam's (and Eve's) act of disobedience in eating the fruit of the tree of knowledge, as described in Genesis 3, the servant acts only in obedience to the lord's command and it is the sheer energy and unreflectingness of his willing response to the lord's command which lands him in trouble.[25] The lord, for his part, is perceived by Julian to 'commenden and approven' (51.75) the servant's good will. The example, therefore, as Julian comes to realize, cannot simply be read as a stylized reworking of the Genesis story. Julian is enlightened to some extent by interpreting Adam in general terms as representative of the whole human race. This, of course, frees her from an otherwise inhibiting dependence on Genesis, and from the impossible task of accommodating the servant solely to 'single Adam' (51.74):[26]

> The lord that sate solemnly in rest and in peace I understond that he is God. The servant that stode aforn the lord, I understode that it was shewid for Adam, that is to seyen, on man was shewid that tyme, and his fallyng, to maken that therby understonden how God beholdeth [P: alle manne] and his fallyng; for in the syte of God al man is on man and on man is all man. (51.75)

Julian, however, does not find in this identification of the servant with the human race any solution to the main problem: how is it that humanity's fall from grace is evoked without reference to sin and culpability, and

[25] For a comparison between Julian and Anselm on the question of Adam's culpability, see Baker, *Julian of Norwich's Showings*, pp. 91–3. Baker notes that in his *Cur Deus homo*, which includes something remarkably similar to Julian's example of the lord and the servant, Anselm assigns culpability to the servant where Julian does not (though in Anselm's scenario the servant/Adam is specifically ordered not to throw himself into a pit which the lords points out to him).

[26] It was a theological commonplace that the whole human race was seminally present in Adam. As Augustine has it: 'Made an exile from thence [i.e. paradise] after his sin, he bound also his offspring, whom by sinning he had marred in himself as root, in the penalty of death and damnation; with the result that all the children born of him and of the wife condemned with him (her through whom he had sinned), being born of the carnal conscupiscence which was imposed as a penalty akin to their disobedience, were infected with original sin . . .', *Saint Augustine's Enchiridion*, trans. Ernest Evans (London, 1953), p. 24. See also St Thomas Aquinas, *Summa Theologiae: A Concise Translation*, ed. Timothy McDermott, paperback edition (London, 1991), pp. 263–7. For critical comment, see Baker, *Showings of Julian* of Norwich, p. 92; and Evans, *Augustine on Evil*, p. 5.

indeed 'represented' in the opposite terms of obedience and blame-lessness respectively? The showing, we recall, is given to Julian in response to her fear of being 'left in onknowyng how he beholdyth us in our synne' (50.71). It appears, in confirmation of what she has already understood about there being no wrath in God and about forgiveness itself as a kind of benign illusion, that God perceives no sin in humanity at all. There is in the showing a sense of *distance* between Adam and God, but not of moral transgression as such. This would seem to contradict the teaching of the Church, as well as Julian's own feeling 'that the blame of our synne continuly hangith upon us'. She has to take another inter-pretative leap, helped by tradition, identifying the servant also as Christ, the second (or last) Adam.[27]

Christ

The first association of Christ with the servant comes in the following passage, just after Julian has amplified her initial description of the lord's countenance which she has perceived doubly as outwardly compassion-ate and inwardly joyful:

> And the lovely lokeing that he loked upon his servant continuly, and namly in his fallyng, methowte it myte molten our herts for love and bresten hem on to for ioye. The fair lokyng shewid of a semely medlur, which was mervelous to beholden: that one was ruth and pety, that other was ioye and bliss. The ioy and bliss passith as fer reuth and pite as hevyn is aboven erth. The pite was erthly and the blis was hevenly. The ruth in the pite of [the] Fadir was of the falling of Adam, which is his most lovyd creatur: the ioy and bliss was of his dereworthy Son, which is evyn with the Fadir. (51.75–6)

The doubleness of the lord's atttitude to the servant's fall corresponds to the simultaneous, double signification of the servant as Adam and Christ. The lord's compassion is aroused by the outward reality, which is the pain of fallen humanity; but his joy is on account of the inward reality, which is the unbroken love of Christ expressed through his obedience. The fact that both falls are signified through the one figure of the servant suggests that inward and outward are constituent parts of an integrated whole: one man, one humanity, complete in Christ.

Julian understands that Christ's identification with redeemed human-ity, which is in effect Christ's identification with the Church, is fully enacted within each individual: 'al man is on man and on man is all man'

---

[27] 'For by a man came death; and by a man the resurrection of the dead. And, as in Adam all die, so also in Christ all shall be made alive', I Corinthians 15:21–2; 'The first man Adam was made into a living soul; the last Adam into a quickening spirit', I Corinthians 15:45.

(51.75). In later chapters, as we shall see, she develops what can be called her 'the-anthopology', central to which is a theologically-grounded conception of the human person as being composed of a higher, or inward, part – substance – and a lower, or outward, part – sensuality. In Chapter 19 Julian has already stressed the superiority of the inward over the outward:

> The outeward party is our dedely fleshede which is now in peyne and wo, and shal be in this life . . . The inward party is an highe, blissfull life which is al in pece and in love . . . And in this I saw sothly that the inward party is master and soverayn to the outeward . . . That the outeward part shuld draw the inward to assent was not shewid to me; but that the inward drawith the outeward by grace, and bothe shal be onyd in blisse without end by the vertue of Criste: this was shewid. (19.29)

Examined retrospectively in the light of Chapter 51, these lines have a particular resonance. The 'outeward party' of each person corresponds to Adam's 'dedely fleshede which is now in peyne and wo'. But because of 'the vertue of Criste', made available through his work redemption, the 'inward party' is now a source of grace and 'high, blissfull life' to the 'outeward party'. In the example of the lord and the servant, the servant-as-Christ is understood as appropriating Adam's outwardness, something Julian conveys through her description of the servant's outward appearance. By taking human form, Christ communicates to Adam his own divine inwardness, the perfect love which is his own participation in the Trinity:

> Outward, he was clad simply as a labourer which wer disposid to travel . . . His clothyng was a white kirtle, sengil, old and al defacid, died with swete of his body, streyte fittyng to hym and short, as it were an handful benethe the knee, bar, semand as it shuld sone be weryd up, redy to be raggid and rent . . . And inward, in him was shewid a ground of love, which love he had to the lord was even like to the love that the lord had to hym. (51.76–7)

In this conjunction of human outwardness and divine inwardness Adam is recreated as Christ, a literary as well as a theological transformation. This is even more clearly disclosed in the way Julian develops the image of the servant's clothing. In the above quotation it represents human flesh which has laboured throughout history under the constraints of fall-enness, something made clear by the epithets applied to the clothing – 'old', 'defacid', 'died with swete', 'streyte fittyng', 'short'. Julian will later interpret these epithets thus:

the steythede is povertye; the eld is of Adams waring; the defaceing of swete, of Adams travel; the shorthede shewith the servant labour.

(51.79)

Hard labour is the exigent biblical penalty of sin, a result of humanity's post-lapsarian destitution, its 'povertye'. If Adam had not squandered his rich inheritance through disobedience he would not have to 'labour and toil . . . all the days of [his] life'[28] and his appearance would not be filthy and dishonourable.

The servant's clothing – Adam in his outwardness – is assumed by Christ. This represents the incarnation, Christ's entry into a fallen world. It also represents the passion, not understood merely as a discrete event separable from the incarnation but a working-through of the incarnation itself. Even before the servant hurries to do the lord's will, the crucifixion is implied and anticipated. Julian flashes back to her own account of the passion:

> Be that his kirtle was in poynte to be raggid and rent is vnderstonden the sweppys and the scorgis, the thornys and the naylys, the drawyng and the draggyng, his tender flesh rendyng; as I saw in sum partie, the flesh was rent from the hedepanne, falland in [G: pecys] into the tyme the bledyng failyd; and than it began to dryand agen, clyngand to the bone.
>
> (51.80)

The fact that the 'kirtle' is 'in poynte to be raggid and rent' suggests sinful humanity on the verge of redemption. The murderous violence done to Christ's own flesh becomes, in God's plan of salvation, a tearing-up of the old humanity to make way for the new. It is important to see the continuity here between the experience of Adam-as-sinner and Christ-as-redeemer. Paradoxically, the murder of the innocent Christ represents both the definitive expression of humanity's sinfulness and the very possibility of a recuperated, glorified humanity.[29] This new humanity is

---

[28] Genesis 3:17.
[29] It would be difficult to exaggerate the significance of this particular paradox in the context of Julian's theological universe. What we have here is the concept of sin as 'behovabil' (27.38) being applied to christology and soteriology. In relation to the individual, what the paradox suggests is that although the one who commits sin is in a sense murdering Christ, in the divine plan this murder is made salvific, so that sin itself becomes the premise of salvation. Reflecting on the relationship between Julian's image of the scourged Christ and scourging as an image of sin ('Synne is the sharpest scorge that any chousyn soule may be smyten with', 39.53), Debra Scott Panichelli writes: 'In this imagery of scourging and blood, we find our common ground with the mediator, Christ. In the scourge of sin, our blood mingles with his. The wound is our common dwelling-place, since the scourging of Jesus is the scourging of all souls. The further implication is that when our sins scourge his body, it is so that his blood can wash away our sins. This is an important reciprocity: Jesus is the vessel for

97

signified, as we shall see below, by the servant's being clothed in a luxurious new robe.[30] The filthy, threadbare robe of the pre-redemption stage focuses this continuity: it is the fragile condition to which sinfulness has brought this garment which precisely facilitates its redemptive and recreative disintegration in the passion.

Christ-as-Adam works within the constraints of Adam's fallen condition, but is shown to be effective in turning that condition to good account. This theme is amplified in Julian's characterization of Christ's redeeming work in terms which rely on a correspondence between the servant-figure and the Adam of the Genesis narratives.[31] It is the servant's

the blood which is everflowing. The vessel has to be broken for the blood to flow. And the vessel can only be broken by the scourge of sin. Here again we hear the text echoing in an explanation of the statement, "sin is necessary [sic]"', 'Finding God in the Memory: Julian and the Loss of the Visions', *Downside Review*, 104 (1986), p. 314. More obliquely, see Sebastian Moore, *The Crucified Jesus is No Stranger* (New York, 1977). Moore's soteriology is distinctively psychological (with much talk of symbol and archetype, Jung seems more obviously in the background here than Freud); but there is an overlap with Julian that suggests he owes her a large debt. He writes, for example: 'In the ultimate order the ultimate sin, of crucifying the Just One, reverses itself, the victim giving life to the crucifiers. Sin, our deep, necessary, negative power, has no being. The only kind of "being" it can have is the sight of itself in its ultimate effect, the crucified . . . we have to experience God coming into us, taking our shape of sin, making explicit our sin, making sin work our salvation. The ultimate truth, which is God's unique embrace, is that the essential *effect* of sin – the crucified – is, identically, the healing', pp. 8–9. (For what it is worth, I am also curious about how a study of some of René Girard's ideas might affect our perception of Julian's thinking in this area. But this is something for the future, and maybe someone else.)

30 See Matthew 22:2–14, the Parable of the Marriage Feast, where the lack of a wedding garment leads to one guest's ejection. In *The Orcherd of Syon*, the exchange of a 'foule raggid coote' for a 'wedding coote' symbolizes the casting away of 'deedly synne' through the sacrament of confession – see *Orcherd*, p. 381, lines 19–22. A wedding garment, then, is the entry ticket to 'the Kingdom' (ecclesiological or/and eschatological).

31 Marion Glasscoe notes: 'The figure of the gardener links with economy a trio of medieval iconographical motifs: the activities of fallen Adam/everyman as a labourer, Christ the true gardener cultivating the virtue of the Church, and God as the gardener planting Christ, the tree of love, in the heart of man', *English Medieval Mystics*, p. 250, and see also p. 267, n. 49 and n. 50. In *The Orcherd of Syon* the eponymous orchard is, first, the Church, in which the priests are 'tilieris' (see p. 276, especially lines 22–5); second, it is the human soul, of which 'fre chois' is the 'gardener' (see p. 336). Reminiscent of this latter is Langland's Tree of Charity which is rooted in the garden of the human heart, a garden tended by 'Liberum Arbitrium' (i.e. free will/choice) – see *The Vision of Piers Plowman*, ed. A. V. C. Schmidt, corrected and revised reprint (London, 1984), Passus XVI, lines 1–94, pp. 198–201. Wolfgang Riehle identifies scriptural antecedents from the Book of Proverbs and the Song of Songs for the image

task to restore fruitfulness to Eden, to release within man's being the 'rivers of living water'[32] and so, in the language of the prophets, to make the desert bloom:[33]

> And than I understode that he shuld don the gretest labor and herdest travel that is – he shuld ben a gardiner; delvyn and dykyn, swinkin and swetyn, and turne the earth upsodowne, and sekyn the depnes, and wattir the plants in tyme. And in this he shuld continu his travel and make swete flods to rennen, and noble plenteous fruits to springen, whych he shuld bryng aforn the lord and servyn him therwith to his lykyng. (51.77)

In Genesis, the garden of Eden, well watered and fruitful, represents humanity's innocent friendship with God in the original creation, but because of the fall this garden has become a dried-up wilderness ('cursed is the earth'[34]), the parched land of humanity's separation from God.[35] The lord, representing God the Father, sits 'on the erth barren and desert, alone in wildernes' (51.75), an image Julian uses to show that this state of separation is not complete but that humanity continues to be sustained by God's presence and power: 'I saw that he is in al things' (11.17).[36] She stresses this further by indicating that the 'tresor that was in the erth' (51.77–8), the 'mete . . . louesom and plesyng' (CW 530.187) which represents humanity, and which the servant is commanded to bring to the lord, is nevertheless 'groun[dyd] in the lord in mervelous depenes of endles love' (51.77–8). This expresses the fact that humanity, in Julian's view, is simultaneously united with God in substance but separate from him because of a sensuality that has lost its moorings in the inward part of human nature. The language of simultaneous presence and absence is

of the soul as a garden – see Riehle, *The Middle English Mystics*, trans. Bernard Standring (London, 1981), p. 161, and p. 215, n. 187.

[32] John 7.38.

[33] Most obviously Isaiah 35:1–2.

[34] Genesis 3:17.

[35] Langland's Will finds himself in a wilderness when he first dreams: 'Thanne gan I meten a merveillous swevene-/That I was in a wilderness wiste I nevere where', *Piers Plowman*, Prologue, lines 11–12, p. 1. Unlike the sunny and fertile Malvern hills, suggestive of a world at ease with itself (unreflecting, smug?), the dream-wilderness suggests the morally barren condition of sinful humanity. Will falls asleep to the pleasant scenes around him but, in terms of the moral and spiritual order, wakes up to *reality*. For an interesting cultural overview of medieval notions of wilderness, see the chapter entitled 'The Wilderness in the Medieval West', in Jacques Le Goff, *The Medieval Imagination*, trans. Arthur Goldhammer, paperback edition (Chicago and London, 1992), pp. 47–59.

[36] Marion Glasscoe writes: 'the lord is dressed in blue robes and sits in a brown wilderness, thus representing the steadfast presence of God in the heart of man', *English Medieval Mystics*, p. 248; and see Davies, *Thomas Aquinas*, pp. 98–101.

reminiscent of Augustine: 'ecce intus eras et ego foris . . . mecum eras, et tecum non eram'[37] ['behold, you were inside and I was outside . . . you were with me and I was not with you'[38]]. Through the paradox of humanity being at once separated from God and inalienably grounded within him, Julian dislodges the ostensible linearity of her exegesis of the example. We have seen the servant lurching away from the lord and landing in a ditch, but the image in question here would have us imagine him plunging *into the lord* in search of lost humanity. This is perhaps an apophatic gesture on Julian's part, a reminder that the rational intellect's tendency to look for tidy, logical explanations must ultimately be refused since reason is not up to the job of perceiving spiritual truth.[39] Explanations – narratives – are provisional guides. Julian herself has to learn this lesson more than once. The non-sequential, discrete images, of the servant's robe, of Christ-Adam as the gardener restoring fruitfulness to Eden, and of Christ plunging into the divinely-sustained fallen world to retrieve the lord's desired 'mete'; all in their own way signify redemption, the assimilation of the first Adam, fallen humanity, to the new Adam, Christ. In this way, and at other points, Chapter 51 puts up some resistance to linear analysis or allegorical decoding.

Nevertheless Julian does resort to a more formally didactic procedure as she attempts to summarize what she understands about the double identity of the servant as both Adam and Christ; and, one suspects, to prevent the exegesis of the example from running away in too many directions, something in which she is perhaps not entirely successful. The section in question is central to the whole text – this sense is reinforced by Julian's self-consciously magisterial tone – and merits significant attention:

> In the servant is comprehendid the second person in the Trinite; and in the servant is comprehendid Adam, that is to say, al man. And therfore whan I say 'the Son', it menyth the Godhede which is even with the Fadir, and whan I sey 'the servant', it menyth Christs manhood which is rythful Adam. Be the nerehede of the servant is understode the Son, and be the stondyng on the lefte syde is vnderstod Adam. The lord is the Fadir, God. The servant is the Son, Christ Iesus. The Holy Gost is even love which is in them both. (51.78)[40]

---

37 *Confessions*, X.xxvii (38), Skutella, p. 237, lines 16–19.
38 Chadwick, p. 201.
39 For an eloquent discussion of the way Julian uses imagery to resist a hegemony of linear logic, see Gillespie and Ross, 'Apophatic Image'.
40 Arguments that Julian adduces Christ and not herself as the principal didactic authority (see Chapter 1 n. 32, above) need to be weighed against the didacticism of passages such as this in which Julian appears to speak as teacher *in propria persona*.

Having affirmed unequivocally the simultaneous relation of the servant to both the Trinity and Adam, Julian startlingly ties Adam's fall into sin to Christ's descent into the womb of the Virgin Mary, almost conflating them:

> Whan Adam fell, God Son fell; for the rythfull onyng which was made in hevyn, God Son myte not [CW: be separath] fro Adam, for by Adam I understonde all man. Adam fell fro lif to death into the slade of this wretchid world and after that into hell. Gods Son fell with Adam into the slade of the mayden wombe, which was the fairest dauter of Adam, and therfor to excuse Adam from blame in hevyn and in erth; and mytyly he fetchid him out of hell . . . for in all this our good lord shewid his owne Son and Adam but one man. (51.78)

The slade into which the servant falls (as initially recounted at the beginning of Chapter 51) now has several layers of meaning. It signifies the post-lapsarian world as a whole, from which we should infer all the attendant exigencies of life lived under the conditions of time. Time and space constitute the sphere of incarnation and passion. The 'slade' is also the womb of the Virgin, and in this particular respect has a double significance. On the one hand it is the place where the Word takes human flesh and so begins his submission to the ravages of time in a fallen world. To this extent it identifies him with Adam's vulnerable condition and signifies the sorrowful aspect of the incarnation, Christ's real sharing of the human lot. But the slade/womb also stands for the positive, soteriological aspect of these mysteries. The Virgin's womb, as the one fertile field in the wilderness of space-time, is furrowed and seeded by the Holy Spirit to be the womb of the new creation through which all might be reborn in Christ.[41] So the image of the slade telegraphically signifies the three crucial aspects of redemption: the human experience of sin; the love of God expressed and made operative through the incarnation and passion of Christ; and the possibility of humanity's rebirth. This density of signification is reinforced in the way Julian collapses temporality at this point in order to indicate that the incarnation and passion of Christ, whilst having specific historical location, are spiritually effective for the

---

[41] Through the images of flower and fruit, a number of medieval vernacular lyrics associate the Virgin Mary with natural fecundity. See Gray (ed.), *Religious Lyrics*, especially nos. 55–65, pp. 57–73. This was no doubt partly inspired by the exclamation of Elizabeth, 'blessed is the fruit of thy womb' (Luke 1:4) – in the Vulgate this is 'et benedictus fructus ventris tui' and forms part of that ubiquitous prayer, the 'Ave Maria'. For an image of Mary as a *field* sown with Christ as unviolently as the dew falls (echoes of Isaiah 45:8), see Gray, no. 6, pp. 4–5: 'He cam also stylle ther his moder was/As dew in Aprylle that fallyt on the gras.' On this particular lyric, and more generally on popular late-medieval devotion to the Virgin, see Duffy, *Stripping of the Altars*, pp. 256–65.

recuperation of all the pre-destined throughout time: 'Whan Adam fell, God Son fell'.

As so often with Julian's theological discourse, it is important here not to be seduced into an inappropriate literalism by trying to square with the human experience of time what Julian can mean by the simultaneous descent of both Adam and Christ into the 'slade'.[42] She is attempting to show the mysterious, if incomplete, coinherence of the world of time with the world of eternity, and she uses the language of coincidence in a poetical way in order to represent a necessary link between the respective destinies of Christ and Adam, whether Adam is considered in general as the whole human race, or in particular as the individual person. Her primary intention is to assert the reality of that 'rythfull onyng' between Adam and Christ:

> for in al this our good lord shewid his owne Son and Adam but one man. The vertue and the goodnes that we have is of Iesus Criste, the febilnes and the blindnes that we have is of Adam; which ii wer shewid in the servant. (51.78)

Julian's assertion that 'our good lord shewid his owne Son and Adam but one man' (51.78) represents the answer she has discovered to her previous anxiety about how God 'beholdyth us in our synne' (50.71). It discloses in a nutshell the dynamic heart of her theological vision; which is also to say that it discloses the theological basis of her appeal to the presumed audience.

At one level of Julian's elusive example of the lord and the servant we have the parable of the Prodigal Son christologically recast. Christ himself travels into the 'far country' of humanity's sinfulness in order to unite himself with fallen Adam and so, in his own divine strength, to take Adam home to the Father.[43] The homecoming is indivisibly Christ's and humanity's, and, as in the parable, the question of blame is beside the point:

> And thus our good lo[r]d Iesus taken upon him al our blame; and therfore our Fadir may, ne will, no more blame assigne to us than to his owen Son, derworthy Criste. (51.78)

The father in the biblical parable seeks to restore his son's proper dignity by having him dressed in the best robe. This is echoed – deliberately, one suspects – in the case of Julian's servant-figure who exchanges the 'old kirtle, steyte, bare and short' (51.80), the emblem of Adam's slavery to sin, for a luxurious new robe, 'fair . . . white and bryte', a mark both of his own

---

[42] For parallels in Augustine, see Clark, 'Time and Eternity', p. 267.
[43] Luke 15:11–32.

restoration to the full dignity of divine sonship, and of Adam's rehabilitation as son in the Son:

> Now stondith not the Son aforn the Fadir as a servant dredfully, unornely clad, in party nakid, but he stondith ever rythe, rechely clad in blissfull largess . . . (51.81)

Julian's concern to emphasize that Christ's identification with Adam represents his enclosure of all humanity within himself – not merely of the 'historical' Adam of Genesis – points again to the notion of a mystical union with Christ as constituting the true bond between human beings in the new creation of grace. Towards the end of her exegesis of the example, and with a clear Pauline allusion, Julian adduces the concept of the Church's spiritual reality as the mystical body of Christ:

> for all mankynd that shal be savid be the swete incarnation and blisful passion of Criste, al is the manhood of Criste; for he is the hede and we be his members . . . (51.79)[44]

The Church in eschatological terms is the sum of redeemed humanity united in Christ. Looking forward to this final consummation, Chapter 51 ends with what we might call the apotheosis-in-Christ of this collective Adam.[45] The servant, in his glorified state, is described as being 'rechely clad in blissfull largess, with a corone upon his hede of pretious richess' (51.81). This crown signifies redeemed humanity, 'the Fadirs ioye, the Sonys worshippe, the Holy Gost lekyng'. But it is also the crown of the bridegroom, a correspondence suggesting itself between this image and that of the crowned bridegroom of Isaiah 61.10.[46] It

[44] See I Corinthians 12:12, and Ephesians 4:15–16; and also, CW 537, n. to line 256.

[45] The notion of the 'deification' of human beings (in Christ) is especially emphasized in Eastern Orthodox mystical tradition which tends to stress the positive relation between the divine and and human realities, rather than the radical bifurcation so mourned-over in the Augustine-influenced West – see Vladimir Lossky, *The Mystical Theology of the Eastern Church*, paperback reprint (Cambridge, 1991), especially pp. 196–216. For generous citation from the Greek Fathers on this notion, see Clément, *Roots of Christian Mysticism*, pp. 263–9. The temper of Julian's text, with its emphasis on substantial union, leans somewhat towards an 'Eastern' optimism, though it clearly evinces 'Western' preoccupations with sin, passion and redemption. I do not say that Julian has been directly influenced by Greek-patristic sources, though many texts had long filtered through into the Latin West, notably into the monastic world – see Ferruccio Gastaldelli, 'Proposed Inventory for the Greek Fathers in the Library of Clairvaux', in ed. M. Basil Pennington, *One Yet Two: Monastic Traditions East and West* (Kalamazoo, Michigan, 1976), pp. 401–4. Of course we ought not to overstate the differences between Eastern and Western Christianity – it is perhaps above all a question of tone, of characteristic expression.

[46] Isaiah 61:10: 'as a bridegroom decked with a crown'.

should be remembered that St Paul, whom Julian has already obliquely quoted in this chapter and on the same theme,[47] describes the relationship between husband and wife as analogous to that between Christ and the Church respectively. The marital symbolism is made explicit, and unambiguously ecclesiological, in the climactic final passage which doubly recalls the book of the Apocalypse. It suggests both the marriage feast of the Lamb[48] and the eschatological transfiguration of the earthly Church into the place where God dwells with humanity, the New Jerusalem which comes down from heaven like a bride dressed for her husband – the bride prepared by God for his own son.[49] Separation becomes marital union; the desert becomes a city.

> Now is the spouse, Gods Son, in peace with his lowid wife, which is the fair mayden of endles ioye. Now sittith the Son, very god and very man, in his cety in rest and peace, which his Fadir hath adyte to him of endles purpose; and the Fadir in the Son, and the Holy Gost in the Fadir and in the Son. (51.81)

This vision of eschatological unity, in which all evil separateness between God and humanity and between person and person is healed, in which wilderness is converted into the city of God, also supplies Julian with a powerful symbol of the essential unity-in-Christ which is implicitly proposed as that which might underwrite her text's, and therefore her life's, claim for serious Christian attention. But that is by no means the end of Julian's theological vision; and therefore by no means the final extent of her implicit theological apologia for the prophetic task she understands herself to have been given.

---

[47] See n. 44, above.
[48] Apocalypse 19:7–9.
[49] Apocalypse 21.

4

Incarnation (II):
The City of God

JULIAN's explication of the example of the lord and the servant draws on a number of iconographical and exegetical traditions. Christ is presented by turns as servant, gardener, bridegroom; at times he is presented clearly under the aspect of divinity, at times under that of suffering humanity. The cumulative effect of Julian's writing in Chapter 51 is to suggest the interchangeability of Christ and Adam in the context of salvation: 'for Iesus is al that shal be savid and al that shal be savid is Iesus' (51.79). As the figure of Adam conventionally stands for all humanity, so the figure of Christ-as-Adam stands for the assimilation of all humanity to Christ: 'for all mankynd that shal be savid be the swete incarnation and passion of Criste, al is the manhood of Criste'. This Christ is the 'perfit man' (57.92) in whom is mystically knit 'ilk man that shall be savid'.

As we have noted, the ecclesiological ramifications of Julian's exegesis are clear, and borne out in her allusions to biblical passages of ecclesiological import; and these together reinforce the emphasis of Chapter 51, which is on securing a sense of the union between Christ and *humanity-as-a-whole*. The figures in the example are stylized and archetypal, the shifting 'narrative' a tissue of scriptural mythology, the language conventionally allusive and symbolical. It is a broad canvas painted in bold strokes, certainly rich in detail but subsuming particulars into a general picture. But within Chapter 51 we can detect signs of the way in which the theme of Christ's union with Adam will be developed in subsequent chapters. There are two crucial indicators.

The first is Julian's explanation of the lord/Father's sitting 'on the erth barreyn and desert' (51.76) which she says signifies that 'he made mans soule to ben his owen cyte and his dwellyng place'. God's union through Christ with redeemed humanity is also – primarily – a personal union operating at the level of 'mans soule'. The new Jerusalem of Apocalypse 21, which we have noted as an ecclesiological image, here becomes anagogically the city of the soul, denoting personal, mystical union with God. The image is taken up again at the end of the Chapter 51, as

105

we have seen, with Christ seated 'in his cety in rest and peace, which his Fadir hath adyte to him of endles purpose' (51.81). This implied conflation of Church and individual soul is certainly not unique to Julian, but it has a particular significance given her concern for the relation between personal experience as a source of shareable religious truth and the Church as the authoritative mediator of both truth and grace.

The second indicator of the way Julian will pursue the theme of Christ's union with Adam is found at the end of the chapter, in the bridal imagery already identified. It will suffice to say that anyone familiar with medieval spiritual traditions will recognize that the ecclesiological image of Christ as the spouse of 'his lowid wife . . . the fair mayden of endles ioye' (51.81) asks also to be interpreted as an image of Christ's mystical union with each believer, a bifocal exegetical convention reaching back at least to Origen[1] and taken up with poetical enthusiasm by Bernard of Clairvaux.[2] In Chapter 52, a conflation of the personal and the ecclesiological is neatly suggested by the plural pronoun, 'our': 'God enioyeth that he is our very spouse, and our soule is his lovid wife' (52.81).

In view of the clear mystical connotations of the images of city and wife there is adumbrated in Chapter 51 a concern for Christ's union with the individual believer, a theme explored with remarkable consistency and vigour in subsequent chapters. This represents a reversal, though not a rebuttal, of the notion of humanity assimilated to a total Christ: the stress is now to be on how Christ is assimilated to the individual.[3] This implies what can be called a move from macro- to micro-ecclesiology. Christ's union with the Church is understood to be constituted by his mystical union with real, particular individuals. The mystical nature of the Church is earthed in the contingent history of each person. Julian makes both ecclesiology and personal mysticism, and her attempt to unite them, answerable to a distinctly incarnational theology that attaches an inalienable value to personal experience in its coinherence with that of Christ.[4] The individual is *minor ecclesia* in Peter Damian's phrase (he is actually talking about hermits), a microcosm of the Church.[5] In examining Julian's

[1] See Louth, *Origins*, pp. 52–74.
[2] That is, of course, in his sermons on the Song of Songs.
[3] Marion Glasscoe also notes that the shift from Chapter 51 to Chapter 52 marks, in broad terms, a shift towards anagogy and a concern for the 'soul of man' as the subject of a transformative process. See *Medieval English Mystics*, p. 252.
[4] For a suggestive discussion of the way (by contrast with Walter Hilton) Julian's epistemology and her imagining of Christ combine to produce, in effect, a distinctive affirmation of the incarnation, see Tarjei Park, 'Reflecting Christ: The Role of the Flesh in Walter Hilton and Julian of Norwich', in *MMTE: V* (Cambridge, 1992), pp. 17–37 (pp. 32–7 for Julian specifically).
[5] I have lifted this phrase of Peter Damian's from André Louf, 'Solitudo Pluralis', in ed. A. M. Allchin, *Solitude and Communion: Papers on the Hermit Life* (Fairacres, Oxford, 1977), p. 18.

development of theological themes in this area we are ultimately concerned with how these themes bear on Julian's representation of her own experience, and the intellectual fruits of that experience, as something of religious benefit for others.

The Personal as the Universal

Chapter 51, as suggested above, provides a fairly generalized sense of the union between Christ and humanity. Chapter 52, whilst ostensibly distinct (at least editorially speaking) from Julian's exegesis of the example of the lord and the servant, represents a continuation of that exegesis, but in another gear. The ecclesiological focus that we have at the end of Chapter 51 gives way here to a focus on personal experience, and on the 'soule' as the essential subject of that experience. Almost as though to press home the significance of the contingently *human*, Julian begins the chapter by invoking the traditional images of familial relationship by which the nature of the divine-human axis has conventionally been conveyed:

And thus I saw God enioyeth that he is our fader, God enioyeth that he is our moder, and God enioyeth that he is our very spouse, and our soule is his lovid wife. And Criste enioyeth that he is our broder, and Iesus enioyeth that he is our savior. (52.81)

In themselves these images (perhaps not that of the mother) might seem merely conventional, except that Julian introduces them all together and with no apparent logical connection between them. This, however, is not so much illogical as a-logical, and deliberately so. Relations between God and humanity might be dimly knowable by analogy, but analogy ultimately fails. One way to insure your readers against analogy's (and interpretation's) tendency towards closure is to keep shifting the analogical base-line by altering the image. The fact that Julian's images belong (punningly) to the same family – father, mother, spouse, wife, brother – actually means that the anti-analogical shift from one to another is all the more effective precisely because it subverts familial propriety. The relationship between the terms is not the one that obtains in the empirical world where, for example, if A is your mother, A cannot also be your father, or your spouse (barring Sophoclean turns of events). The power of signification is not permitted to accumulate in one privileged image, or one logical pattern of relationship. On the other hand, whilst Julian deploys these images in such a way as not to trap God in a box, the particular character of the images does have an important bearing on her main concern here, which is not so much to offer a description of God as to evoke the nature of the relationship between God and the human subject. Each of the images implies a notion of personal, familial relationship, and the generic consonance of the images supports this implication.

So Chapter 52 opens by bringing to our attention a certain sense of the primacy of the *personal*, and this sense is confirmed as the chapter proceeds. The previous chapter's large-scale scenario of fall and redemption, with its general (though not exclusive) stress on the entirety of humanity-being-saved as assimiliated to the total Christ, gives way here to a vision in which the realities of the Christian universe are focused in the experience of the individual. Of course Julian is writing here of a *typical* individual, and therefore of a universal figure. But there can be no doubt of her understanding that it is precisely *particularity-as-such* which is universal; and that it is the shifting economy of lived, personal experience that lends the currency of universalizing, abstract propositions its value. There is a pastoral note in this chapter, a concern for how life feels for the individual Christian believer, how the truths of faith are lived through and grasped – how the incarnation of Christ gives form, as it were, to the life and experience of each believer. In the first place, the example of the lord and the servant, assimilating the myth of fall (Adam) and redemption (Adam/Christ), is reinterpreted here as paradigmatic of personal experience:

> Al that shal be savid, for the tyme of this life, we have in us a mervelous medlur bothen of wele and wo. We have in us our lord Iesus uprysen; we have in us the wretchidnes of the mischefe of Adams fallyng, deyand. Be Criste we are steadfastly kepte, and be his grace touchyng we are reysid into sekir troste of salvation. And by Adams fallyng we are so brokyn in our felyng on divers manner, be synnes and be sondry peynes, in which we arn made derke and so blinde that onethys we can taken ony comfort. But in our menyng we abiden God and faithfully trosten to have mercy and grace; and this is [CW: his] owen werkyng in us. (52.81–2)

The echoes here of the example of the lord and the servant are obvious and deliberate: the falling of the servant into the slade ('the mischefe of Adams fallyng') and the resurrection of Christ ('our lord Iesus uprysen') through which Adam's tattered humanity is transfigured in glory. The 'mervelous medlur . . . of wele and wo' brings to mind the new clothing of the glorified Christ, which is described in Chapter 51 as being 'of a fair semely medlur . . . so mervelous that I can it not discrien' (51.80). There is a reference to the blindness suffered by the servant as he lies in the slade, unconscious of his own good will towards the lord. Also, there is a reminder that even in the slade the servant is sustained by the presence and power of the lord, and that it is the presence and power of the lord within the servant which keeps alive the sure hope of salvation:

> But in our menyng we abiden God and faithfully trosten to have mercy
> and grace; and this is [CW: his] owne werkyng in us. (52.82)

The word 'menyng' here could be translated as 'intention', and intention
understood as a function of the will. What Julian seems to be saying is that
the fallen servant/fallen humanity is sustained in relation to the lord by
the persistence of a good will towards him. She is implicitly referring to
the 'godly wil' mentioned in Chapter 37 (37.51), and which is referred to
again in Chapter 53 (53.85). It is central to Julian's theology and soteriology that there exists an unbroken union between the individual and
God at the level of substance, and that the individual therefore desires
complete union with God even when sin in the lower part of his or her
human nature obscures this fact.[6] Blinded by sin, the individual is
unconscious of the 'godly wil', just like the servant lying in the slade
who 'had forgotten his owne lufe' (51.73) because he was 'blinded in his
reason' (51.72).

As we have stated, Julian's concern in Chapter 52 is to show that the
example of the lord and the servant, interpreted christologically, is fully
applicable to the being and condition of each believer.[7] The example
derives its essential tension and interest, and indeed theological resonance, from a number of paradoxes – the servant being at once Adam and
Christ; the servant both separated from the lord and united to him; the
lord regarding his servant with ruth and pity, but also with joy. These
paradoxes point to a certain structuring of reality as observed by Julian

---

[6] Marion Glasscoe writes: 'The whole example [of the lord and the servant] thus
enacts a process of transfiguration which is at the heart of Julian's showings',
English Medieval Mystics, p. 252.

[7] The notion of a godly will that never gives its consent to sin has caused problems
for commentators eager to present Julian as dogmatically sound (from a
Catholic-Christian point of view). In the introduction to his translation of LT,
Clifton Wolters writes of the godly will: 'This is wishful thinking, and not the
teaching of the Church'; see *Revelations of Divine Love* (Harmondsworth, 1966),
introduction p. 37. A more sympathetic and scholarly approach, though still
rather defensive, is taken by Deryck Hanshell in 'A Crux in the Interpretation of
Dame Julian', *Downside Review*, 92 (1974), pp. 77–91. Hanshell notes Julian's own
crucial statement that 'we have all this blissid will hole and safe *in our lo[r]d Iesus
Christe*' (53.85, my emphasis). Judith Lang gives an excellent analysis of the
question in her article, ' "The Godly Wylle" in Julian of Norwich', *Downside
Review*, 102 (1984), pp. 163–73. Lang summarizes her own interpretation thus:
'The "godly wylle" in the predestined soul is to be found in the indwelling of the
Holy Trinity in that soul. The Second Person, carrying out the perfect will of God
in every soul, by this indwelling and by the Incarnation unites body and spirit in
its creation, and the soul to its Creator. The inpouring of grace by the Holy Spirit
actuates the obediential potency of that soul, so that it may freely unite its will to
the will of God. This action of the will manifests itself in the soul in sorrow for
sin, and in a longing for God expressed in prayer', p. 127.

within her peculiar religious perspective; though in speaking of 'structuring' it is crucial to avoid a suggestion of the static since Julian's religious universe is a dynamic one in which the polarities – evil/goodness, darkness/light, sin/mercy, dishonour/honour – are understood dialectically. It is a world in which sin is 'behovabil' (27.38) and where both 'wele and wo' (52.81) are made inextricably parts of the weave in the new garment of Christ's/Adam's glorified humanity (see 51.80).

These polarities of the Christian universe are focused, and made dialectically operative, within the being and experience of individuals. Julian is concerned with the way union with God co-exists with continuing human sinfulness, and this concern has a practical and pastoral character which explicitly adduces lived personal experience as the actual and true sphere of theology:

> And yet nevertheless whan this sweteness is hidde, we falyn ageyn into blindhede, and so into wo and tribulation on divers manner. But than is this our comfort, that we knowen in our feith that be the vertue of Criste, which is our keper, we assenten never therto, but we grutchin theragen, and duryin in peyne and wo, prayand into that tyme that he shewith him agen to us. (52.82)
>
> But we may wel be grace kepe us from the synnes which will ledyn us to endles pay[n]es, as holy church techith us, and eschewen venal, resonable upon our myte; and if we be our blyndhede and our wretchedness ony tyme fallen, that we redily risen, knowand the swete touching of grace, and wilfully amenden us upon the techyng of holy chuirch after that the synne is grevous, and gon forwith to God in love; and neither on the on syd fallen over low, encylnand to despeyr, no on that other syd ben over rekles as if we gove no fors, but nakidly knowing our feblehede, witeand that we may not stond a twincklyng of an eye but be keping of grace, and reverently cleven to God, on him only trostyng; for otherwise is the beholdyng of God, and otherwise is the beholdyng of man; for it longyth to man mekely to accusen hymselfe, and it longith to the propir goodnes of our lord God curtesly to excusen man. (52.83)

The general use in these passages of first person plural pronouns is symptomatic of Julian's instinct for universality, of her conviction that the 'revelation of love' (1.1) is for all. But this does not mean that her conception of humanity is merely generalized. As we have already noted, what is common to human beings in her view, what is *universal*, is precisely the irreducible particularity of contingent life. In Julian's universe the necessary dialectics of spiritual growth are derived from the individual's specific experience of falling and rising, of seeking and beholding; that is, from the whole dynamic interplay, in all its various forms, of human sinfulness and divine mercy. Each individual human existence is a sphere of creative tension, figured for Julian in the conflation of Christ and Adam:

> We have in us our lord Iesus uprysen; we have in us the wretchidnes of the mischefe of Adams fallyng, deyand. (52.81–2)

It is not the case that individuals must somehow insert themselves into the mystery of Christ-Adam by an effort of will. Rather, they can come to the knowledge that this mystery is being enacted within them. It is in this sense that Julian's text takes on a peculiarly revelatory function, if we understand this to refer not to a revelation of new truths or ideas but a disclosure of what was already there (though not evident to minds darkened by sin). Julian holds up a christological mirror to human experience. She offers her readers the possibility of making a 'true' interpretation of their own experience in the light of faith; just as the literary reconstruction of her own personal experience is presented as relying on what we have called a grace of interpretation.

In subsequent chapters Julian attempts to uncover and conceptualize the theological and ontological rationale informing the human experience of tension between what is constant in the individual's life – union with God; and what is variable – all that pertains to the person as a vulnerable, suggestible creature living and changing in space-time. Julian covers the former by the term *substance*, the latter by the term *sensuality*. In bringing her attention to focus on the structure of the person as such, Julian constructs a distinctly *interiorized* soteriology in which the drama of sin and redemption is enacted in the relation between the higher and the lower parts of the person – that is, between substance and sensuality respectively – such that not only is sin located in the personal sphere, as we would expect, but also the possibility of redemption:

> for the life and the vertue that we have in the lower parte is of the heyer, and it cummith downe to us of the kinde love of the selfe be grace. Atwixen that on and that other is ryte nowte, for it is all one love; which on blissid love hath now in us double werking; for in the lower part arn peynes and passions, ruthes and pites, mercies and forgevenes and swich other that arn profitable; but in the higer parte are none of these, but al on hey love and mervelous ioye, in which mervelous ioy all peynis are heyly restorid. (52.84)

As a spiritual descendant of Augustine, Julian sees the realization of personal union with God as indivisibly the healing of a fragmented self.[8]

It is important to note that our larger interest here is not so much in the

---

[8] G. R. Evans sums up Augustine's vision of a complete and integrated human being: 'in the future the perfect man will . . . be whole, full of *sanitas*, healthy and shining', *Augustine on Evil*, p. 165.

plausibility or otherwise of Julian's theological and philosophical positions as in her presentation of the human person as the scene of a complete enactment of the mysteries of salvation; such that any given individual might be understood to be *minor ecclesia*, a real and integral sacrament of the mystical body of Christ. The individual believer is more than merely a sign of the Church. His or her union with God in Christ is constitutive of the Church as such. It creates a unity between persons which is not merely a unity of common purpose or interest but a unity of charity in the richest sense, a mystical coinherence of the ecclesiological Christ and each particular human 'member', so that whole is fully present in every part. As Julian will say later:

> It is God will that I se myselfe as mekil bounden to him in love as if he had don for me al that he hath don. And thus should every soule thinkyn innward of his lover: that is to seyn, the charite of God makyth in us such a unite that whan it is trewly seen no man can parten himse[l]fe fro other. (65.106)

Crucially, this unity of charity exists both *within* and *between* all members of the Church.

The Individual's Substantial Union with God

In order to make credible her sense of the individual as *minor ecclesia*, Julian must establish that the union with God and each person is real, absolute and unbreakable. Of course in one sense the whole text has this as its aim, but in Chapters 53 and 54 the individual's substantial union with God is considered directly as the foundation of Julian's conception of the human person. Her starting-point is the now no longer troubling realization that God does not blame humanity for sin; the reason for this non-blaming being the persistence in sinful Adam of a good will towards God:

> I saw and understode ful sekirly that in every soule that shal be save is a godly wille that never assent to synne, ne never shalle; which wille is so good that it may never willen ylle, but eve[r]more continuly it will good and werkyth good in the syte of God. (53.83–5)

This 'godly wille' is, for Julian, the absolute soteriological fulcrum.[9] Without it there would be no hope and the servant lying in the slade would be a figure of damnation. But there is a danger of reifying the godly will and conceiving it as a piece of machinery, a kind of moral back-up

[9] See n. 7, above.

generator in the soul, still miraculously working when everything else has broken down.[10] Julian's overt aspirations to scholastic terminological rigour in this part of the text do not necessarily help in this respect. What is most important to realize is that the godly will is, for Julian, a person: Christ himself. United to each individual at the level of substance (another candidate for reification, if we are not careful), Christ is completely orientated in love towards the Father, and thus orientates the individual: 'we have all this blissid will hole and safe in out lo[r]d Iesus Christe' (53.84).

The godly will, therefore, signifies that orientation to God which is maintained within the individual as a function of his or her union with Christ. The theological rationale of this union is identified by Julian in the relation between creation and incarnation, a relation which relies on a certain Johannine-Pauline perception of Christ as the creative divine Logos:

> In the beginning was the Word, and the Word was with God, and the Word was God. The same was in the beginning with God. All things were made by him: and without him was made nothing that was made . . . And the word was made flesh. . . . [11]

> For in him were all things created in heaven and on earth, visible and invisible, whether thrones, or dominations, or principalities, or powers. All things were created by him and in him. And he is before all; and by him all things consist.[12]

Christ is, so to speak, the incarnate interface of eternity with space-time, through whom all things are both variously created and sustained in unity. The utter dependancy of creation on Christ-as-Logos is the basis of Julian's 'the-anthropology'. Each part of creation lives through Christ, but in the manner proper to it. Humanity, bearing the image and likeness of God, differs in kind from the rest of creation, being created to live in love with him. To be human is precisely to be implicated in relationship with the divine. What is more, this distinct and pre-eminent species of created

---

[10] Julian's concept of the godly will can be compared with (though not assimilated to) the Eckhartian 'spark', the *scintilla animae*, or *Fünkelîn*. For helpful comment on this aspect of Meister Eckhart's thought, see Williams, *Wound of Knowledge*, pp. 132–9; and Oliver Davies, *God Within: The Mystical Tradition of Northern Europe* (London, 1988), especially pp. 47–59. Davies includes a few pages (pp. 185–9) on Julian, but they are not his best.

[11] John 1:1–4. The Vulgate version of the phrase 'All things were made by him' is 'omnia *per* ipsum facta sunt'; and since 'per' can mean 'through' as well as 'by', the Latin is rather more suggestive than the English of the divine Word's intimate involvement in creation.

[12] Colossians 1:16–17. Vulgate: 'omnia *per* ipsum et in ipso creata sunt'. See n. 11, above.

113

nature is generically christological. Human nature was/is created in a primary sense for Christ himself so as to be shared with all human beings, the adopted children of the Father and Christ's own brothers and sisters. The incarnation, therefore, as an event in space-time, is not primarily understood as God's descent into human flesh on a soteriological mercy-mission, but as a manifestation of what is true from eternity: Christ is one with humanity.[13] His local and particular manifestation within the contingencies of space-time is a logical necessity of this identification:

> And be the endles assent of the full accord of al the Trinities, the mid person would be ground and hede of this faire kinde, out of whom we be al cum, in whom we be all inclosid, into whom we shall all wyndyn ... and thus is man soule made of God and in the same poynts knitt to God.
>
> (53.85)

The relationship between the humanity of Christ and that of all other human beings is not in the first place soteriological but generic, familial.[14] That it becomes soteriological under certain exigent conditions (as we shall see) is something else. Essentially, the generic relationship between Christ and humanity is part of God's eternal plan:

> God, the blisful Trinite which is everlastand beyng, ryte as he is endless from without begynnyng, ryte so it was in his purpose endles to maken mankynd; *which fair kynd first was adyte to his owen Son*, the second person. And whan he wold, be full accord of all the Trinite, he made us all at onys; and in our makyng he knitt us and onyd us to hymse[l]fe; be which onyng we arn kept as clene and as noble as we were made.
>
> (58.93, my emphasis)

Considered *sub specie aeternitatis*, the creative act whereby the primary humanity of Christ is produced is indivisibly (because God is one, eternal, indivisible) the creative act by which all human beings are produced, though in space-time individuals are discrete and disparate.

[13] For a persuasive argument that soteriology is a secondary factor in Julian's understanding of the incarnation, see J. P. H. Clark, 'Predestination in Christ According to Julian of Norwich', *Downside Review*, 100 (1982), pp. 79–91. Clark suggests the oblique influence of Duns Scotus (quoted, alas, in untranslated Latin) who takes the view that, as Clark puts it, 'the Incarnation cannot be considered merely as 'occasioned' by the Fall, but was for its own sake part of God's purpose from all eternity' (p. 88). I should like to emphasize, in slight contrast to Clark, that soteriology is clearly very important in Julian; though it need not be therefore understood as *explaining* the incarnation. My interpretation of Julian's position here would go something like this: God is always already united with human beings, but his presence becomes soteriological as a reaction to human sinfulness.

[14] Roland Maisonneuve is eloquent on this theme, speaking of Julian's Christ as the 'texture' of humanity-as-such, see *L'univers visionnaire*, pp. 215–34.

Whatever the plausibility, or indeed explicability, of the theology, it is quite clear that Julian is proposing that human beings are substantially united to God by simple virtue of their humanity itself. Everyone carries something like a christological DNA code. This does not make them divine, since human nature as derived from Christ remains a created nature, but it binds them to God precisely on account of the indissolubility of the bond between Christ's humanity and his divinity. Participation in this indissoluble bond is intrinsic to the christological code that human beings share:

> Wherfore he will we wettyn that the noblest thing that eve[r] he made is ma[n]kynd, and the fullest substance and the heyest vertue is the blissid soule of Criste. And furthermore he will we wettyn that his derworthy soule was preciousley knitt to him in the making; which knott is so sotil and so myty that is onyd into God; in which onyng it is made endlesly holy. Furthermore, he will we wettyn that al the soules that shall be savid in hevyn without end ar knitt and onyd in this onyng, and made holy in this holyhede. (53.86)

Julian goes on in Chapter 54 to insist on an identification between God and individual human beings that only just (but also absolutely) stops short of assigning actual divinity to human nature itself:

> Our soule is made to be Gods wonyng place, and the wonyng place of the soule is God, which is onmade. And hey vnderstondyng it is inwardly to sen and to knowen that God which is our maker wonyth in our soule; and an heyer vnderstondyng it is inwardly to sen and knowen our soule that is made, wonyth in Gods substance; of which substance, God, we arn that we arn. And I saw no difference atwix God and our substance, but as it were al God, and yet myn vnderstondyng toke that our substance is in God: that is to sey, that God is God, and our substance is a creture in God . . . (54.86–7)

God is divine by nature. Humanity is divine by participation, a participation facilitated by means of the primary humanity of Christ in which all share.

Faith and the Inner Drama of Salvation

Towards the end of Chapter 54 Julian's tone changes as she turns away from her direct concern with humanity's unbreakable, substantial union with God in Christ to consider how this looks from the point of view of life lived in space-time. To use Julian's own shorthand (and it *is* a kind of shorthand), the focus moves from substance to sensuality. She does not, however, simply make a clean thematic leap, as though substance and

115

sensuality were discrete entities. On the contrary, the modulation is deft, with the concept of faith as a linking-motif, since faith mediates between substance and sensuality:

> And our feith is a vertue that comith of our kynd substance into our sensual soule be the Holy Gost, in which al our vertuys comith to us – for without that no man may receive vertue – for it is not ell but a rythe vnderstondyng with trew beleve and sekir troste of our beyng that we arn in God, and God in us, which we se not. And this vertue with al other that God hat ordeynid to us command therin, werkith in us grete things; for Crists mercifull werking is in us, and we graciosly accordand to him throw the gefts and the vertues of the Holy Gost; this werkyng makith that we arn Crists children and cristen in liveing. (54.87)

Faith is a principle or power ('vertue') of mediation. It is, as the above quotation suggests, Christ dwelling and working within the human person, receiving the Father's love and gifts in the grace of the Holy Spirit. Faith, therefore, is to do with the dynamic of trinitarian divine life as it is mediated to individual human beings; and Julian comes in this part of the text to place more and more stress on the fact that relationship with Christ implies relationship with the whole Trinity. In Christ humanity bears the imprint of God, *imago dei*, and that imprint is necessarily trinitarian. Julian introduces the Augustinian language of the psychological trinity – memory, intellect, will – in order to affirm this:[15]

> Our feith cummith of the kynd love of our soule and of the cler lyte of our reson and of the stedfast mend which we have of God in our first makyng. (55.88)

Memory, intellect, will; respectively, 'the stedfast mend [remembrance; *memoria dei*] which we have of God in our first makyng', 'the cler lyte of our reson', 'the kynde love of oure soule'. These, of course, correspond respectively to the persons of the Trinity: Father, Son, Holy Spirit.

Whether we use the term *imago dei* or 'substance', the question here is precisely of the relation between humanity's divine origin (substance) and the experience of human beings in the exigent conditions of space-time (sensuality). We can go further than saying that Julian sees faith as the link between substance and sensuality, and say that she sees faith as substance-construed-soteriologically. To the extent that human nature is

---

[15] For an excellent and critical exposition of Julian's relation to Augustinian theory in this area, see Baker, *Julian of Norwich's Showings*, pp. 107–34. Louth, *Origins*, offers a helpful guide to Augustine's 'psychological' theory, especially in respect of its orientation towards the mystical – see pp. 146–58. The 'base-text' of all this is, of course, Augustine's *De Trinitate*, an English Version of which is to be found in *Augustine: Later Writings*, trans. John Burnaby (London, 1955).

fractured, the relation of substance to sensuality has a soteriological character. This is to say that if humanity falls into the slade of sinfulness (sinfulness in the widest sense – sensual life in a fallen world), the unbroken substantial union with Christ in those particular circumstances becomes, of necessity, dynamically operative as a principle of restoration and salvation. We can think of a chemical reaction that only occurs at a certain temperature. Faith is a term that denotes the divine presence become divine mission of salvation. Faith also denotes the extent of the individual's willing personal surrender to this salvific divine mission. Therefore, true to the nature of faith as *mediation* (a two-way street, as it were), it can be named as a mode of God's presence and active power within human subjects; or as a mode of the individual's response to God. It is both of these indivisibly.

Julian's concern with faith has drawn us into a distinctly soteriological landscape, and this landscape is clearly understood to be located *within the person*:

> And what tyme that our soule is inspirid into our body, in which we arn made sensual, also swithe mercy and grace begynyth to werkyng, haveing of us cure and kepyng with pite and love; in which werkyng the Holy Gost formyth in our feith hope that we shal cum agen up aboven to our substance, into the vertue of Criste, incresid and fulfillid throw the Holy Gost. (55.88)

It is worth looking closely at this passage. Here we have the example of the lord and the servant translated into Julian's quasi-technical theological vocabulary, a paradigm of creation-fall-redemption *personally* and *interiorly* understood. The descent of the servant into the slade is interpreted as the inspiration of the soul into the body, involving Julian's characteristic, and theologically tricky, virtual conflation of creation and fall. For the time that the servant is in the slade (the body, sensual life, space-time) he is separated from God. But this separation is not absolute since the servant is also Christ, Christ the redeemer/gardener, undertaking the work of salvation, the benefits of which operate in individuals through grace, which is the Holy Spirit – 'mercy and grace begynyth to werkyng'. Christ is 'mercy', the Holy Spirit is 'grace'. As Christ, the servant in the slade remains in union of will with the lord/Father, though unconsciously: 'But his will was *kept* hole in God sygte' (51.75, my emphasis). This is a reference (from the example itself) to the 'godly will', the inner presence of Christ by which the individual's orientation towards God is sustained, and indeed made dynamically, soteriologically operative within the sphere of sensuality and sinfulness: 'mercy and grace begynyth to werkyng haveing of us cure and *kepyng* with pite and love' (my emphasis). The hope that we shal cum agen up aboven to our substance, into the vertue of Criste, incresid and fulfillid throw the Holy Gost (55.88)

recalls the glorification of Adam in Christ as depicted in Chapter 51, the servant restored to the Father's side, no longer a servant but fully the Son, and with even greater dignity than before ('*incresid* and fulfillid throw the Holy Gost', my emphasis):

Now stondith not the Son aforn the Fadir as a servant dredfully, unornely clad, in party nakid, but he stondith aforn the Fadir ever rythe rechely clad in blissful largess, with a corone upon his hede of pretious richess . . . Now sittith the Son, very God and man, in his cety in rest and peace, which his Fadir hath adyte to him of endles purpose; and the Fadir in the Son, and tho Holy Gost in the Fadir and in the Son.

(51.81)

Julian's heaven is essentially *human beings becoming themselves* according to the christological genetic code by which divinity makes scope for itself within a created nature. Heaven may be 'up there' as an eschatological reality, but it is 'in here' already; and the nature of life 'up there' will be the full realization of the christological 'in here'. Julian conflates the two: we shal cum agen up aboven to our substance' (55.88).[16]

The Womb of this Life

The soteriological drama of the lord and the servant, implicitly containing within itself the christological drama of incarnation-death-resurrection-glorification, provides a paradigm through which personal experience can be theologically interpreted. In adducing the *person* as the scene of a full, integral enactment of the drama of salvation, it has been important for Julian to establish two things. First, that there is union of substance between Christ and human beings; second, that there is a mediation between substance and sensuality, a mediation that can be called 'faith' or given the name 'Christ'. But another crucial thing becomes clear between Chapters 41 and 65. However much Julian is confident of the transcendent

[16] The upward-inward movement is a distinctively Plotinian/neo-Platonist one, and subsequently Augustinian. As Andrew Louth writes: 'For Plotinus, the higher is not the more remote; the higher is the more inward: one climbs up by climbing in, as it were. Augustine's *tu autem eras interior intimo meo et superior summo meo* (thou wert more inward than the most inward place of my heart and loftier than the highest), with its suggested identification of the inward and the higher, strikes an authentically Plotinian note', *Origins*, p. 40. For a brilliant discussion of similar themes, see J. W. Pacey, *The Mystical Economy* (London, 1995), especially Chapter 3, 'Up and In, Down and Out', pp. 75–102.

mysteries of her religion (the nature of God; humanity's creation from eternity and substantial union of God in Christ; the eschatological future), her real interest for the purposes of the text is in how these mysteries bear upon humanity's mundane existence, and that at the personal level. Her theology has a practical orientation and range of reference. It accommodates a peculiarly dynamic, even dialectical view of human experience in which humanity is not merely understood as being immobilized in a state of sin and suffering from which it has to be rescued by the application of the correct remedy ('grace'). Rather, space-time itself represents a process in which vulnerable, suggestible human beings are caught up, a process of growth in which both suffering and sin are positioned dialectically in relation to the goodness of God:

> And all this bliss we have be mercy and grace; which manner of bliss we myte never had ne knowen but if that propertes of goodnes which is God had ben contraried, wherby we have this bliss; for wickidnes hath ben suffrid to rysen contrarye to the goodnes, and the goodnes of mercy and grace contraried ageyn the wickidnes, and turnyd al to goodness and to worship to al these that shal be savid; for it is the propurte of God which doith good agen evil. (59.95)

Life itself is the sphere of this battle between good and evil; and the individual person is the battleground, though it is God himself who fights by means of mercy and grace, mediated through 'Iesus Christ that doith good agen evil' (59.95).

But militaristic metaphors do not find a place in Julian's own store of tropes and she prefers the language of transformation to that of annihilation. As the passage previously quoted suggests, evil is not merely vanquished but 'turnyd al to goodnes and to worship' (59.95). The world is charged with the dynamic of growth, and needs both positives and negatives. The affirmation of the indispensability of the negative dialectical pole – sin/suffering – within Julian's ontological and existential scheme has the crucial effects of opening up the text to a positive sense of the contingencies of life lived in the sphere of space-time. This is because it precludes the presentation of a two-dimensional, 'static' soteriology in which Evil (or the Devil) is simply bashed on the head by *Christus Victor* and that's that. Such a scenario would not easily accommodate a sense of dynamism and tension, of God's engaging the individual precisely in the chaos and unresolvedness of terrestrial life. In the static scenario, time, space and bodiliness are accidentals; contingent human creatureliness, with all its passions, necessities and importunities, is for most practical purposes an obstacle to holiness;[17] and the issues

---

[17] See n. 4, above,

come down to an eschatological-juridical 'guilty' or 'not guilty': am I saved or not?[18]

By contrast, Julian's soteriology is characterized by a certain fluidity, a sense of organic development. The pertinent question in respect of human life is not so much about whether or not individuals are in a 'state of grace' in any juridical sense, but whether or not they are as fully caught up as they might be in that process of growth which is the operation within them of the soteriological Christ-in-the-Spirit. Or, to put it another way, whether they are managing not to impede the operation of mercy and grace:

> And all the gefts that God may geve to cretures he hath geven to his Son Iesus for us; which gefts he, wonand in us, hath beclosid in him into the time that we be waxen and growne, our soule with our body and our body with our soule [CW: . Eyther] of hem takeing help of other tylle we be browte up into stature as kynd werkyth; and than, in the ground of kind with werkyng of mercy, the Holy Gost graciously inspirith into us gifts ledand to endless life. (55.88)

To grow up as a human being is to grow into the full flowering of the christological genetic code, and all the particularities of life, including the negative particularities of sin and suffering, actually *count* as part of the process of growth. Salvation is not simply about restoring what has been lost, but about a process in which loss is turned to gain:

> ... that our sensualite be the vertue of Crists passion be browte up to the substan[c]e, with al the profitts of our tribulation that our lord shall make us to gettyn be mercy and grace. (56.90)

If at one end of the spectrum sin is 'al that is not good' (27.38), but appears as 'worshippe and profite' (28.40) at the other end of the spectrum, then somewhere in the middle it must be in a certain sense indifferent. Christ himself is the 'mene' between 'not good' and 'profite'. He absorbs and neutralizes sin[19] – 'behovabil' (27.38) is an equivocal

---

[18] In *Piers Plowman*, the motivating factor of Will's search is summed up in the request he makes to Holy Church (personified as an imposing woman): '"Teche me to no tresor, but tel me this ilke – /How I may save my soule ..."', Passus I, lines 83–4, p. 12. The image of possible damnation was kept graphically before the eyes of the faithful in the form of the doom-paintings of medieval churches. These normally spanned the area above the chancel arch, and thus faced the congregation directly. It is probable that for most people sheer familiarity blunted the edifying/terrifying effect of these paintings, but what is most important to note is the kind of pastoral priority such iconography represents. On doom-paintings, see Duffy, *Stripping of the Altars*, pp. 157, 187 and plate 55.

[19] 'Him [i.e. Christ] who knew no sin, he [i.e. God] hath made sin for us; that we

term – thereby converting it into tradeable capital within the economy of salvation.

The question of turning to profit is inseparable in this part of the text from the notion of 'werkyng', a term that denotes the inner divine activity through which substance (*imago dei*, Christ coinherent with Father and Spirit) relates soteriologically to dissociated sensuality:[20]

> And thus in our substance we arn full, and in our sensualite we faylyn; which faylyng God will restore and fulfill be werkyng [CW: of] mercy and grace plentiously flowand into us of his owne kynd godhede. And thus his kinde godehede makith that mercy and grace werkyn in us; and that kind godehede that we have of him abilith us to receive the werking of mercy and grace. (57.91–2)

The notion of *working* is suggestive of process and struggle, of the involvement of Christ-in-the-Spirit in the raw material of human experience. It also recalls the image from Chapter 51 of the servant-gardener:

> And than I understode that he shuld don the grettest labor and herdest travail that is – he shuld ben a gardiner; delvyn and dykyn, swinkin and swetyn, and turne the earth upsodowne, and sekyn the depnes, and wattir the plants in tyme. (51.77)

Here we have the historical Christ involved in the travail of incarnation/ passion, but also the mystical Christ operative *personally and interiorly* within each individual believer. The notion of Christ's interior travail comes into its own between Chapters 52 and 64, where the term 'werkyng' takes on a quasi-technical sense perhaps derived, whether directly or indirectly, from the dynamic sacramental theology of Thomas Aquinas. As Brian Davies says of Aquinas:

> In his view, a sacrament is not just something standing as a sign of what cannot be seen by the physical eye (though he certainly thinks it *is* a sign of what cannot be seen by the physical eye). It is also a process by which something is actually effected . . . 'The term "sacrament",' he explains, 'signifies the reality which sanctifies [and this means] that it should signify the effect produced.' His view is that in the sacraments God shows us what he does and does what he shows us.[21]

---

might be made the justice of God in him', 2 Corinthians 5:21; 'Who, his own self . . . bore our sins in his body upon the tree', 1 Peter 2:24.

[20] The concept of 'werkyng' is, in this context, inseparable from that of 'faith'.

[21] Davies, *Thomas Aquinas*, p. 351. Davies quotes here from *Summa Theologiae*, 3a. 60. 3 ad. 2. For further insight into Aquinas' sacramental theology, see *Summa Theologiae* (ed. McDermott), pp. 541–600.

Efficacy and process are key concepts here, as they are for Julian. She unites these concepts in the images of Christ-gardener and Christ-growing-to-maturity. To grow spiritually mature is to 'become' the mature Christ, but it is Christ himself (by virtue of his passion, which releases the grace of the Holy Spirit) who causes and promotes this growth. Significantly, too, Julian presents her mystical understanding of growth in the context of a recognizable ecclesiology with its conventional affirmation of sacrament and moral order. This has the useful double-edged effect of securing a sense of Catholic orthodoxy whilst at the same time emphasizing the rootedness of sacramental theology and moral order in the contingencies of particular lives:

> The next good that we receive is our feith in which our profittyng begynnyth; and it commith of the hey riches of our kinde substance into our sensual soule; and it is groundid in us and we in that throw the kynde goodness of God be the werkyng of mercy and grace. And therof commen al othir goods be which we arn led and savid; for the commandements of God commen therein in which we owe to have ii manner of vnderstondyng which are: his bidding to love them and to kepyn; that other is that we owe to knowen his forbyddings, to haten and to refusen; for in these ii is all our werkyn comprehendid. Also in our feith commen the seven sacraments ech folowing other in order as God hath ordeyned hem to us, and al manner of vertues; for the same vertues that we have received of our substance, gevyn to us in kinde, be the goodnes of God the same vertues, be the werkyng of mercy, arn geven to us in grace, throw the Holy Gost renued; which vertues and gyfts are tresurd to us in Iesus Christ . . . (57.92)

There is no reason to believe that Julian's affirmation of Catholic orthodoxy is less than ingenuous, or that her stated belief in the necessity of obedience to God's commandments is merely a placatory gesture towards Church authority and tradition. But her emphasis is not so much on how the ecclesiastical institution mediates the grace of God to the faithful, but on the way personal faith engenders an engagement with God that is made visible and incarnate through sacramental signs, and in moral form.

Sacrament and commandment pertain to the sphere of space-time, the nine-till-five of this world's day when the economy of salvation is in full swing, converting loss into profit through the working of mercy and grace. This is the period/space between humanity's creation-from-eternity and fulfilment-in-eternity:

> For al our life is in thre. In the first we have our beyng and in the second we have our encresyng and in the thrid we hav our fulfilling. The first is kinde; the second is mercy; the thred is grace. (58.94)

122

Julian's predominant concern is with the 'tyme of this life' (52.81), the tyme of 'encresyng' (58.94, see quotation above) which is also the time of Christ's continuing passion in the members of his mystical body:[22]

> Thus was our blissid lord Iesus nawted for us, and we stond al in this manner nowtid with hym; and shal done til we come to his blisse . . .
>
> (18.28)

Embodiment in space-time is the womb within which human beings grow towards their birth into eternity according to the pattern of the christological genetic code; and this code fulfils itself by means of a recuperative and transformative spiritual power ('vertue') derived from the incarnation and passion of Christ; that is, through the operation of mercy and grace (Christ-in-the-Spirit).

With a light but definite architectural touch, Julian records a suggestive transposition of her initial desire for a 'sekenes so herde as to deth' (2.3) into a desire 'to be deliverid of this world and of this life' (61.104). The word 'deliverid' used in the later chapter suggests that her initial desire for virtual death has been re-formulated as a desire for actual death, but death understood as *birth*. The former desire, as considered in Chapter 2 of this book, has a note of youthful idealism about it, perhaps indicative of an ego-driven desire for absolute experience. It implies a scenario in which the contingencies of bodily life chafe the idealistic young soul, generating in her an anxiety to find some kind of validation outside the parameters of the ordinary. But the desire to be 'deliverid of this world and of this life', whilst it similarly incorporates a sense of dissatisfaction, does seem to register a shift in Julian's attitude to embodiment. The implication is that bodily life is a process of gestation. This is confirmed in Chapter 64 by Julian's vision of a new-born child symbolizing death-as-birth (significantly, this vision is not recorded in the Short Text):

> And in this tyme I sawe a body lyand on the erth, which body shewid hevy and ogyley, withoute shappe and forme as it were a bolned quave of styngand myre. And sodenly out of this body sprang a ful faire creature, a little childe full shapen and formid, [CW: swyft] and lively, whiter than lilly, which sharpely glode up onto hevyn. And the bolnehede of the body betokenith gret wretchidnes of our dedly flesh, and the littlehede of the child betokenith the clenes of purity in the soule. (64.105)[23]

[22] See Glasscoe, *English Medieval Mystics*, pp. 240–1, and p. 261; also Glasscoe, Time of Passion', pp. 154–8.

[23] The Middle English poem *Pearl*, with its dream-maiden image of celestial youthful innocence, is readable as pointing to the spiritual perfection (the pearl of great price) to which life in this world is orientated (the world's your oyster, so to speak). Julian might say that the making of that pearl is helped along by the grit of 'behovabil' sin.

As readable from this passage, Julian's estimate of bodily life looks at first glance extremely negative, and it is probably true that she does not entirely free herself from the powerful, religious dualistic impulses which traditionally privilege spirit over matter, soul over body. Indeed it would be astonishing if traces of such dualism were completely absent given that Julian is heir to a Christian mystical tradition strongly shaped by the neo-Platonism of figures such as Augustine and the Pseudo-Dionysius, both of whom, throughout the Middle Ages, carried an *auctoritas* little short of biblical in weight.[24] But the passage has an imagistic suggestiveness that works to disrupt the apparent dualism. The language Julian uses to describe the discarded human body from which the small child springs may well seem uncompromisingly derogatory: 'hevy', 'ogyley', 'withoute shappe and forme as it were a bolned quave [ie. a swollen bog] of styngand myre'. The idiom is clearly intended to evoke disgust. Yet there are some scriptural echoes here which, when recognized, put another, and essentially positive, gloss on the description. The phrase 'without shappe and forme' recalls the formless void described in the second verse of the Bible:

> And the earth was void and empty, and darkness was upon the face of the deep. And the spirit of God moved over the waters.[25]

Earth and water; a formless 'bolned quave of styngand myre'. Yet this swampy, unpromising mess is the very condition of God's creative act. It is 'behovabil' (27.38). The image of the lily, which Julian introduces in order to approximate the whiteness (freshness, purity, innocence) of the child, affirms the principle that life and form emerge out of darkness and formlessness. A lily cannot be considered in isolation from the earth which nourishes it and which it needs. The image of the new-born child makes this explicit. This terrestrial, bodily life, for all its pains and misery – and these cannot be denied – is the gestation period of the life of the world to come. Creation needs chaos; the lily needs the mud; the child needs the womb; 'Synne is behovabil, but al shal be wel' (27.38). All the particularities of growth, of the 'encresing' that the operation of mercy and grace generate within the dialectic of sin and forgiveness, are written into the very flesh of the 'child' who emerges from the 'womb' of this world and of this body. This life can seem on the face of it so chaotic and

---

[24] The pre-eminence of Augustine hardly needs noting. For the importance to the scholastic Middle Ages of Pseudo-Dionysius, see Louth, *Origins*, especially pp. 159–60. For discussion of *auctoritas*, scriptural and literary, see A. J. Minnis, *Medieval Theory of Authorship: Scholastic literary attitudes in the later Middle Ages*, second edition (Aldershot, 1988). Also on *auctoritas* and *auctores*, consult index of Ernst Robert Curtius, *European Literature and the Latin Middle Ages*, trans. Willard R. Trask, paperback reprint (London, 1979).

[25] Genesis 1:2. See also CW 622, n. to line 31.

unpromising, yet in the end nothing is lost. Even what is evil has a crucial part in nurturing what it good.

Christ the Mother

The central theological discourse of the Long Text culminates in a remarkably bold and rigorously thought-through notion of divine motherhood,[26] which gives expression to Julian's concern with the paradoxes of humanity's union with and separation from God; and also affirms the intrinsic spiritual value of contingent human experience within the womb of bodiliness and space-time. In both these respects the theme of the divine motherhood can be understood as expressing in a special and demonstrative way Julian's over-arching concern to establish credible grounds for a radically theological estimate of the person as such; and so for an equally radical theological interpretation of personal experience, with the obvious payback this might secure both for herself and her prophetic mission. That is, the serious and sustained theological use to which Julian puts the distinctly human, organic and personalizing language of motherhood, together with the way in which this language mediates between natural and supernatural dimensions of reality, can be understood as pointing, at least in part, to theological priorities and preoccupations born of her own contingent personal need.

In Julian's scheme the image of the divine mother properly applies to Christ since, in quite specific ways, it symbolizes creation and incarnation, and all that these imply for the relationship between God and human beings. The image of Christ the mother is itself not original and antecedents might be cited from Anselm, from the early Cistercians and no doubt from many other sources.[27] Additionally, the Johannine-Pauline theme of Christ as the Wisdom of God (wisdom as both creative and illuminating, life and light) naturally implies the feminine sophia-figure of Old Testament Wisdom literature. In more general terms, the Hebrew and Christian scriptures both make use of maternal imagery in describing

---

[26] Julian's image of Christ the mother has inevitably elicited much comment. The following are useful: Baker, Julian of Norwich's *Showings*, especially Chapter 5, pp. 107–41; Paula S. Datsko Barker, 'The Motherhood of God in Julian of Norwich', *Downside Review*, 100 (1982), pp. 290–304; Ritamary Bradley, 'Patristic Background of the Motherhood Similitude in Julian of Norwich', *Christian Scholar's Review*, 8 (1978), pp. 101–13; Jennifer Heimmel, *'God Is Our Mother': Julian of Norwich and the Medieval Image of Christian Feminine Deity* (Salzburg, 1982); Jantzen, *Julian of Norwich*, pp. 115–24; Maisonneuve, *L'univers visionnaire*, pp. 224–34; Nuth, *Wisdom's Daughter*, pp. 65–9.

[27] On early Cistercian use of maternal imagery, see Walker Bynum, *Jesus as Mother*, pp. 110–69.

the relationship between God and humanity.[28] It is important, however, to recognize that in the Christian era up to (and indeed beyond) Julian's time the use of a 'feminine' language of religion is exceptional rather than normal, private rather than public, being found more in poetical and devotional contexts than in the formal discourse of ecclesiastically-accredited preachers, teachers and commentators. In particular, the post-Aquinas scholastic world, with its gender-theory derived from Aristotle, coupled with a neo-Platonist/Augustinian setting of reason-as-masculine above sensuality-as-feminine, was hardly the natural environment for the development of an integral, generic, sexually-inclusive concept of human nature.[29] The actual details of the theories in question are perhaps less significant for us than the simple fact that distinction of gender was confidently taken to imply distinction of moral and spiritual capacity; and this despite pressures to the contrary within Christian tradition, and even within the writing and thought of the proponents of a strongly gendered Christianity.[30] In such a cultural context, the theological extent and consistency of Julian's maternal imagery represents a quite special achievement. In her hand, the image of Christ the mother, which is given considerable weight within the text, becomes a powerful, alternative and feminine symbol of the incarnation, a corrective to the tendency of traditional christologies (despite the cross-currents) to attach prestige to the masculine as distinct from the human.

Julian proposes that the whole Trinity works in the motherhood of Christ, but that only Christ has a human nature and so is the locus of mediation:

[28] On biblical and patristic precedents, see Bradley, 'Patristic Background', and also Bradley, *Julian's Way*, pp. 135–51; and Barbara Newman, 'Some Medieval Theologians and the Sophia Tradition', *Downside Review*, 108 (1990), pp. 111–30. Newman's article is especially recommended. Surprisingly, neither Newman nor Bradley makes a connection between the female Sophia-figure and the creative Logos of St John's gospel.

[29] For insight into classical/medieval gender theories (Aristotle, Jerome, Augustine, Thomas Aquinas and others), see relevant sections of *Woman Defamed and Woman Defended: An Anthology of Medieval Texts*, ed. Alcuin Blamires (Oxford, 1992). See also Baker, *Showings of Julian of Norwich*, especially pp. 123–34; Ritamary Bradley, 'Perception of Self in Julian of Norwich's Showings', *Downside Review*, 104 (1986), pp. 227–39, and especially pp. 238–9; also, Robertson, 'Medieval Medical Views'. More obliquely, see Michael Sells, 'The Pseudo-Woman and the Meister: "Unsaying" and Essentialism', in ed. Bernard McGinn, *Meister Eckhart and the Beguine Mystics: Hadewijch of Brabant, Mechtild of Magdeburg and Marguerite Porete* (New York, 1994), pp. 114–46 – an interesting discussion of Marguerite Porete's deployment of *apophasis* against gender-essentialism (and see pp. 140–46 for a warning against gender-stereotyping of medieval writers).

[30] The most obvious example is St Paul. He famously subordinates the woman to the man (I Corinthians 11:2–9), but also asserts that in Christ 'there is neither male nor female' (Galations 3:28).

126

> I saw that the second person, which is our moder substantial, that same
> derworthy person is become our moder sensual . . . And thus our moder
> is to us dyvers manner werkyng, in whom our parties are kepid
> ondepartid . . . (58.94)

In the image of Christ the mother Julian focuses three aspects of her vision
of humanity as it relates to God: the ontological, the existential and the
eschatological. To put it another way, she employs the image *variously*
(the word is important) to express what human beings are and where they
are from (ontology); where they are going (eschatology); and the process
by which they will get to where they are going ('the existential'). The
image of the mother has three modulations, each pertaining to the
operations of a distinct person of the Trinity, though it is crucial to bear
in mind that the image is always primarily christological and that
whatever significances it assumes come within that definition. This is to
say that the mother as such is Christ, not the Father and not the Holy
Spirit; though the operations of Father and Spirit through the mediation of
Christ the mother are, by virtue of that christological mediation, describ-
able as motherly activities. The following passage, with the particular
relation it adduces between Trinity-Christ-humanity, condenses much of
what Julian seems to be trying to express through the language of divine
motherhood. Note especially the three 'manner of beholdyng of moderhede in God' – motherhood of 'kinde', motherhood of mercy, motherhood
of grace – which we shall discuss in greater detail below:

> And thus is Iesus our very moder in kynde, of our first makyng, and he
> is our very moder in grace be takyng of our kynde made. All the fair
> werkyng and all the swete kindly office of dereworthy moderhede is
> impropried to the second person; for in him we have this godly will hole
> and save withoute ende, both in kinde and grace, of his owne proper
> goodnes. I vnderstode iii manner of beholdyng of moderhede in God:
> the first is groundid of our kinde makeying; the second is taken of our
> kinde, and there begynnyth the moderhede of grace; the thrid is
> moderhede of werkyng, and therein is a forth-spreadyng, be the same
> grace, of length and bredth and of heyth and of depenes withouten end,
> and al his own luf. (59.96–7)

Julian's language both here and in subsequent developments of the
motherhood theme achieves three important objectives. First, she gives
due weight to the distinction of persons within the Trinity. Second, the
integral image of the mother affirms the theological truth of trinitarian
coinherence, that the whole Trinity is implicated in any discrete operation
formally attributed to one particular divine person. Third, Julian stresses
Christ's unique role as mediator of the divine life to human beings.

(i) Motherhood of kind

The first mode of the divine motherhood refers to creation in the primary sense, humanity's 'first makyng' (59.96, see quotation immediately above) in the image and likeness of God. Creation in this sense is referred to as 'kinde makeying'. The word 'kinde' can be translated as 'nature' as long as we retain the crucial theological resonance the word has for Julian. God himself is 'kynde', uncreated nature, uncreated being, whereas human life (indeed, all being) is derived from him:

> God is kynde in his being: that is to sey, that goodnes that is kind, it is God. He is the ground, he is the substance, he is the same thing that is kindhede, and he is very fader and moder of kynde. And all kindes that he hath made to flowen out of him to werkyn his will, it shall be restorid and browte ageyn into him be the salvation of man throw the werking of grace . . . (62.101–2)

There is implicit in Julian's understanding of humanity's 'first makyng' a model of creation along the lines of sexual generation. The Father, as male priniciple and source of form and potency, impregnates the receptive, 'feminine' Son (Christ the mother) who brings forth children in the divine likeness;[31] these children are engendered all at once in eternity, but 'delivered' variously into space-time from the womb of the divine mother. From a theological point of view each member of the Trinity is equal in dignity, therefore Julian's image of Christ as female pro-genitor might be said to imply a critique of traditional assumptions about the ontological inferiority of women to men, especially since a standard, Aristotle-derived 'proof' of this inferiority is precisely a woman's passive role in conception (as understood, of course, in terms of medieval and pre-medieval biology).[32]

Through the implied image of sexual generation between Father and feminized Son, Julian affirms what is for her the prime truth about humanity in general, and the individual person in particular. This truth is articulated in Chapter 53 as follows: 'and thus is mans soule made of God and in the same poynts knitt to God' (53.85); and again in Chapter 55, as we have seen: 'I saw no difference atwix God and our substance, but as

---

[31] Fitting the Holy Spirit into this scheme would appear to require a bit of jesuitical cunning (is the Spirit that with which the Father impregnates the Son? Then what of the Nicene Creed's, 'qui ex patre *filioque* procedit', the Spirit's procession from the Father *and the Son*?) But the point so far as the text is concerned is surely not whether the implied metaphor of sexual generation is subsumable into a watertight trinitarian theological paradigm, but what the metaphoricity permits in terms of Julian's characterization of Christ's functions as mother in creation, incarnation and passion.

[32] See Blamires (ed.), *Woman Defamed*, pp. 39–41; Robertson, 'Medieval Medical Views', pp. 144–50; and Baker, *Showings of Julian of Norwich*, pp. 122–9.

it were al God' (55.87). We have already considered something of the significance of humanity's substantial union with God in Christ. What is important about the generation/motherhood theme is that it reinforces the intrinsic nature of that substantial union. Whatever happens to the child, whatever deformations are incurred by sin, the family origin and identity remain ineradicable. Such a notion is not peculiar to Julian and is really another way of talking of talking about the *imago dei*. But the obvious riskiness of Julian's seeming, however obliquely, to implicate Father and Son in a sex-act that generates humanity reflects the strength of her commitment to asserting the reality and non-negotiable primacy of the bond between God and human beings. This is first of all the bond of 'kinde'; it is strong, indeed unbreakable; it 'grounds' human substance (if not sensuality) in its ontological divine origin, its 'kyndly stede'; it is associated with the Father who is both the fountainhead of being itself and, as we have noted, the active, 'male' principle of generation. Yet it is only through Christ that this bond of 'kinde' achieves expression, both in the incarnation of Christ himself and in the creation of humanity.

(ii) Motherhood of grace

The second mode of divine motherhood is 'moderhede of grace' (59.96), initiated, as Julian says, in Christ's 'takyng of oure *kynde made*' (created nature). Having been born into space-time, a sphere of growth-through-freedom in which sin is possible in theory and inevitable in practice, humanity suffers a deficiency in what we might call ontological integrity. This is to say that, whilst human beings remain united to God in substance by virtue of their 'kynde makyng' in Christ, their sensuality has become corrupted, dissociated, a law unto itself, and to that extent incapable of engagement with God. The fallen-sensual self is trying to keep itself on the road, but in an inappropriate manner, like driving in the wrong gear, or with the wrong kind of fuel. The result is a flagging half-existence, bereft of the divine energy needed for full, vigorous and expansive life: 'in our substance we arn full, and in our sensualite we faylyn' (57.91). The divine energy that is needed is the Holy Spirit, taking the form of grace.

According to Thomas Aquinas, the grace of God has two functions: it redeems and sanctifies.[33] In Julian's largely conventional scheme, redemption is attributed specially to Christ, sanctification (as the fullness

---

[33] 'The grace of the sacraments seems to have two functions: it removes defects left by past sins, which though finished as actions leave behind liability to penalties; and it disposes and strengthens the soul to worship God through the religion of a Christian life', *Summa Theologiae* (ed. McDermott), p. 553. For a comment on Aquinas' sacramental theology, see Davies, *Thomas Aquinas*, pp. 343–76.

of redemption) to the Holy Spirit.[34] But the axiom of coinherence applies here as elsewhere. It is through the Holy Spirit-as-grace that redemption is made effective; and it is through Christ's redeeming work that the Holy Spirit-as-sanctifying-grace is offered. It is the Spirit who impregnates the Virgin,[35] thus sowing the seed (Christ) of the new creation of grace, of which the Church is the earthly sacrament but which looks towards a heavenly fulfilment. Christ's life and death both figure and achieve the gestation of this humanity:

> We wetyn that all our moders beryng is us to peyne and to deyeng . . . but our very moder Iesus, he, al love beryth us to ioye and to endles lyving; blissid mot he be! Thus he susteynith us within himselfe in love, and traveled into the full tyme that he wolde suffre the sharpist throwes and the grevousest peynes that ever were or ever shall be, and dyed at the last . . . and so born us to bliss . . . (60.97)

This passage is suffused with the language of pregancy and childbirth: 'beryng', 'beryth us', 'susteynith us within himselfe', 'traveled into the full tyme', the sharpist throwes', 'the grevousest peynes', 'born us to bliss'. It clearly echoes the following passage from St John's gospel, in which Christ, speaking at the Last Supper, refers to his impending death as ultimately bringing *joy* to himself and his followers ('and so born us to bliss'):

> A woman, when she is in labour, hath sorrow, because her hour is come; but, when she hath brought forth the child, she remembreth no more the anguish, for joy that a man is born into the world.[36]

We might also remember in this context an earlier episode from the same gospel, where Christ says to Nicodemus: 'unless a man be born again of water and the Holy Ghost, he cannot enter the Kingdom of God'.[37] In Julian's scheme, as in John's, the death of Christ wins for humanity the grace of the Holy Spirit by which they might be born again and live a new life.

There is also, and perhaps even more significantly, a good deal of deeply absorbed Pauline christology, ecclesiology and soteriology glimmering through the prism of Julian's language and imagery in this part of

---

[34] For example, Walter Hilton writes: 'The redemption is ascribed and appropriated to the Son . . . But the justifying and full salvation of a soul by the forgiveness of sins is appropriated to the third person, that is, the Holy Spirit . . .', *Scale* 1, ch. 34, p. 265.

[35] Or we could say that the Father impregnates the Virgin *with* the Holy Spirit. The language here is better understood in a category of the poetical rather than of the philosophical-technical. See also n. 31, above.

[36] See John 16:21.

[37] John 3:5.

the text. Christ is the first-born from the dead, the new Adam. To be implicated in the resurrection, to be reborn as Christ, one must first participate in Christ's death. This notion of participating in Christ's death is related by St Paul to *baptism* (something implicit also in John – 'of *water* and the Holy Ghost'), a relationship which can be confidently taken as being implicit in Julian's writing.[38] The motherhood of grace refers to the gift of eternal life, sown in baptism as a seed, nurtured sacramentally in the context of the Church, especially in the eucharist, and achieving fulfilment in the eschatological future. The grace of the Holy Spirit is transcendence now, eschatology anticipated and already in part operative. The Spirit, though transformative in the present,[39] is a downpayment on future glory, a pledge of future fulfilment[40] – 'and by yelding and [gevyng] in grace of the Holy Gost we arn fulfilled' (58.95). In the following passage Julian fuses christology, ecclesiology and a theology of grace in the image of Christ the mother, who, having brought forth children, feeds and cares for them:

> He myte not ne more dyen, but he wold not stynten of werkyng. Wherfore than him behovyth to fedyn us, for the dereworthy love of moderhede hath made him dettor to us. The moder may geven hir child soken her mylke, but our pretious moder Iesus, he may fedyn us with himselfe; and doith full curtesly and full tenderly with the blissid sacrament that is pretious fode of very lif. And with al the swete sacraments he susteynith us ful mercifully and graciously. (60.97–8)

Here, Jesus himself is Holy Mother Church, source of the Spirit-as grace. The practical and pastoral implications of this imaginative synthesis of christology, ecclesiology and a theology of grace are considered in greater detail below (iii.b).

---

[38] Within medieval Catholic culture baptism represented the sine qua non of accredited social and religious identity, especially in view of the intimate relation between religious and secular realities. Without baptism, according to Aquinas, one could not be saved (see Summa *Theologiae*, ed. McDermott, p. 564). It will be remembered that Dante puts the unbaptised in the first circle of Hell – *Inferno* Canto IV, lines 31–42, *The Divine Comedy*, trans. Charles S. Singleton, *Inferno 1: Text*, paperback reprint (Princeton, 1989), pp. 36–7; and there is no evidence to suggest that Julian dissents in any way from the theological positions implied in either Dante or Aquinas. She does not, of course, understand baptism in itself to be an absolute guarantee of salvation: 'I vnderstode that al creatures that arn of the devils condition in this life and therin enden, there is no more mention made of hem aforn God and al his holy than of the devil, notwithstondyng that thei be of mankynd, *whether they have be cristenyd or not*' (33.46–7, my emphasis).

[39] See Ephesians 3:16–19.

[40] See Romans 8:23.

(iii) Motherhood of working

The third mode of divine motherhood is 'moderhede of werkyng' (59.96). This is not so much a discrete category of maternal activity as a formula by which Julian denotes the forms – biological, soteriological, sacramental, mystical – taken by the motherhoods of kind and grace. As already indicated, all the operations of motherhood are coinherently operations of the whole Trinity focused through Christ the mother. We have noted that Julian attributes motherhood of kind in a special way to the Father; and motherhood of grace to the Spirit. The motherhood of working, then, denotes Christ's mediation of these operations within the sphere of human experience in space-time. This 'earthedness' is implicit linguistically: whereas 'kinde' and 'grace' are culturally-privileged, propositional terms with an abstract force, the more distinctively Julianic term 'werkyng' is suggestive, both referentially and grammatically,[41] of dynamism, tension and effort. It specifically implies embodied life and temporality. This, in the final analysis, is Julian's most characteristic emphasis and points to the essentially practical import of her text. Fascinated as she is by the more speculative questions of ontology and eschatology, Julian continually looks to the visible and the knowable, to a sphere of incarnation where life is coextensive with the body. We shall go on to consider the motherhood of working according to its two modalities: first kind, and then grace.

a. Motherhood of working: *kind*   Christ's role in 'conceiving' humanity through his 'impregnation' by the Father is knowable in space-time only through the role of the natural mother who (with the natural father) is a secondary efficient cause of the child's production, to use the Aristotle-derived language of the medieval schools.[42] Christ (with the Father and the Spirit) is the first cause, and in this sense the 'true' mother':

> for thow it be so that our bodily forthbrynging be but littil, low and semple in regard of our gostly forthbringing, yet it is he that doth it in the creatures be whom that it is done. (60.98)

Furthermore, all the functions which maternity imposes are the work of Christ acting through the natural mother, the secondary agent:

> The kynde, loveand moder that wote and knowith the nede of hir child, she kepith it ful tenderly as the kind and condition of moderhede will. And as it wexith in age she chongith her werking, but not hir love. And

---

[41] That is to say, the word 'werkyng' might be read (according to context) as a present participle or a verbal substantive.

[42] I have borrowed the phrase 'secondary efficient cause' from Minnis, *Medieval Theory of Authorship*, which discusses the impact of Aristotelian theory of causality on exegetical and literary questions. See especially pp. 73–105.

whan it is waxin of more age, she suffrid that it be bristnid in brekyng
downe of vices to makyn the child to receivyn vertues and graces. This
werkyng, with al that be fair and good, our lord doith it in hem be whom
it is done. (60.98)

The concept of motherhood of kind denotes the power of an indivisible
love operating *variously*, altering its form according to the particular
needs of the child's psychosomatic development at any given stage.
Julian's implication of Christ not only in the dynamics of conception,
gestation and childbirth but in the parental works of nourishment, care
and discipline represents a powerful statement of her belief in the
contingently human as a locus of divine engagement. This fragile,
physical life, if looked at with the eyes of faith, is a true 'revelation of
love' (1.1); as is, more specifically, the relationship of love between parent
and child.

In affirming the christological basis of human parenthood Julian is
careful not to obliterate the proper role and integrity of the natural
mother, or to relegate her to the status of a mere cipher for Christ. Julian
does this nicely by showing the natural mother to be implicated in the
promotion of the proper conditions for the sowing and flourishing of the
child's *supernatural* life. In all the ordinary care and discipline adminis-
tered to the child, the natural mother is preparing him or her 'to receivyn
vertues and graces' (60.98). Natural parenthood involves a co-operation
with God in performing the proper natural functions; but since human
nature is destined to share in the divinity of Christ, these natural functions
of conception, gestation, childbirth, nourishment, care and discipline have
as their ultimate orientation the accommodation of divine life.

b. Motherhood of working: *grace*   Grace is the principle of that divine
life to which human nature is orientated, which brings us back to the
other form of motherhood mediated through the working of Christ: the
motherhood of grace. Our emphasis is now less on the dogmatic and
theological import of a concept of grace, but on how the mediation of
grace is made operative existentially, incarnationally.

As we have noted, the conception of Christ within the womb of the
Virgin Mary constitutes also the inception of the new creation of grace, the
beginning in space-time of the redemption and transformation of a
human nature defiled by sin. The creation (according to kind) and re-
creation (according to grace) of humanity are presented as a movement of
emanation from God and return to God. The movement of return is not
merely the emanation in reverse, not just a rewinding of the tape: grace
both redeems *and* sanctifies, it restores the integrity of wounded kind *and*
raises it to a higher spiritual level:

> for kinde is al good and faire in the selfe, and grace was sent out to saven
> kind and destroyen synne and b[r]yngen ageyn fair kinde to the blissid
> poynt fro whens it came, that is God, *with mor noble and worshipp* be the
> vertuous werkeyng of grace . . . (63.102, my emphasis)

Here the concepts of kind and grace seem to be discretely reified, as
though the latter is acting upon the former, each a distinct entity. This
'billiard ball' scenario represents a trap characteristic of propositional
theology where abstract terms are presented as self-contained units of
calculable value governed by logical necessity.[43] Nevertheless, Julian
displays an awareness of the danger of allowing analytical language to
obscure a necessary sense of the integral unity of God's being and his
works:

> Thus is kind and grace of an accord; for grace is God as kind is God. He
> is in ii manner werkyng and one in love, and neyther of hem werkyth
> without the other, non be departid. (63.102–3)

But we have seen before that Julian, though interested in theological
speculation, is fundamentally concerned with the practical implications
of the processes of redemption and transformation within the sphere of
human experience, and with making the relation between theology and
experience evident to her audience.[44] A correct theological interpretation
of experience can make all the difference for the individual who wishes to
give an appropriate response in co-operation with the grace of God;
whereas an interpretation made on other and less reliable grounds might
lead to inappropriate behaviour, and perhaps even to moral and spiritual
peril. The concept of kind flowing from God and being restored to him
with greater glory through the working of grace is a crucial one for Julian,
but it is not intended merely as a beautiful intellectual abstraction to
delight her audience, remaining otherwise unconnected to them and their
experience. In fact, the concept itself weighs rather lighter in the rhetorical
balance than the image of the mother through which Julian communicates
the intrinsic applicability to real human beings of the emanation-return
paradigm. The idea of the motherhood of grace might seem to suggest
something intangible and unknowable, a divine activity unavailable to
human consciousness, and in a sense this is not untrue. Grace does denote
in a particular way the divine as distinct from the human. But the whole

---

[43] For an illuminating and eloquent discussion of the difference between 'linear'
(i.e. logical, propositional) theology and 'spatial' (i.e. poetical, paradoxical)
theology, see Maggie Ross, *Pillars of Flame* (London, 1987), especially
pp. xxxv–xl.

[44] Marion Glasscoe notes that, for Julian, salvation 'is not a matter of intellectually
formulated theology'; theology 'can only point to a reality known through the
dynamic of faith', *English Medieval Writers*, p. 254.

point of grace in the context of soteriology is that it has been 'sent out to saven *kind*' (63.102) and to effect its transformation 'be proces of tyme' (63.103).

Just as Christ is 'our kynd moder' (60.97), so he is 'our gracious moder'. As 'kynd moder' he is implicated in the natural production of human beings, their 'bodily forthbrynging' (60.98); as 'gracious moder' he is the agent of their 'gostly forthbringing':

> And in our gostly forthbringyng he usith mor tendernesse of keping,
> without ony likenes, be as much as our soule is of more price in his syte.
>
> (61.99)

Two images of motherhood are employed in Chapter 61, one pre- the other post-natal. The image of the 'gostly forthbringyng' implies that life in the sphere of space-time is to be understood as Christ's act of giving birth to his redeemed children. But this is a theological truth perceptible to the eyes of faith, not deducible from sense-experience. Within the perspectives of the mundane, death looks like death and not like birth. In order to focus her audience on the actual lived-through dynamics of the growth towards death signalled by the image of life-as-childbirth, Julian takes the image of the natural mother used in Chapter 60 and recasts it to convey the ups and downs of life in this world, but with a difference. She is not here concerned with the nourishing, care and discipline provided by the natural mother, but adduces these ordinary maternal functions as images through which to interpret in spiritual terms – that is, according to the motherhood of grace and in the perspective of eternity – experiences that are common among those trying to live a religious life (in both the special and the general sense) within the context of the Church. This is to say that the image of the mother has here a distinctly pastoral modulation whereby Julian is concerned to impress upon her audience God's implication in the actual processes of redemption and transformation. The context is existential.

In Chapter 61 Julian conveys an integral sense of life lived in the body according to the dynamics of grace, and she does this by enunciating certain themes which are recognizably key elements in the broad contemplative/monastic spiritual tradition. For ease of reference the following quotations are numbered 1–6:

(1) he ky[n]delyth our vnderstondyng, he directith our weys, he esith our consciens, he comfortith our soule, he lightith our herte and gevith us, in parte, knowyng and lovyng in his blisful Godhede, with gracious mynd in his swete manhood and his blissid passion
(2) And we fallen, hastily he reysith us be his lovely clepyng and gracious touchyng . . .

135

(3) we wilfully chesyn him, be his swete grace, to be his servants and his lovers lestingly without end.

(4) it nedith us to fallen, and it nedith us to sen it; for if we felle nowte we should not knowen how febil and wretchid we arn of ourselfe . . .

(5) And be the assay of this failyng we shall have an hey mervelous knoweing of love in God without ende . . . And this is one vnderstonding of profite. Another is the lownes and mekenes that we shall gettyn be the syte of our fallyng; for therby we shal heyly ben raysid in hevyn; to which reysing we might never a come withoute that mekeness.

(6) And he will than that we usen the propertie of a child that evermor kindly trosteth to the love of the moder in wele and in wo. (61.99–100)

An inventory of contemplative/monastic spiritual attitudes and practices as discernible in these passages would look something like this (the numbers correspond to those used above):

(1) an emphasis on the Holy Spirit as interior guide and giver of contemplative, experiential knowledge of God;[45] meditation on the life and death of Christ;[46]

(2) repentance and forgiveness;[47]

(3) desire for God; union of wills;[48] dependance on grace;[49]

(4) self-knowledge obtained through moral failure;[50]

(5) the spiritual efficacy of trials;[51] humility;[52] hope for heaven;[53]

---

[45] See *Hilton*, Scale 2, ch. 34, p. 266; and also Gilson, *Mystical Theology*, pp. 101–15.

[46] See generally Chapter 2 of this book, and notes 3, 4, 17, and 18 to the same chapter.

[47] Clearly the idea of repentance is proper to Christian religion as such, but it is particularly emphasized in monastic tradition. See *Rule of St Benedict*, ch. 4, line 57: 'Every day with tears and sighs confess your past sins to God in prayer', pp. 184–5; also, ch. 20, line 3: 'We must know that God regards our purity of heart and tears of compunction, not our many words', pp. 216–17.

[48] An emphasis on longing for God, and so for a union of wills with him, is to be found especially in the hugely influential Gregory the Great and in Bernard of Clairvaux, and no doubt in many other lesser monastic luminaries. For Gregory, see Leclercq, *Love of Learning*, pp. 31–44; and for Bernard, see generally, Gilson, *Mystical Theology*.

[49] See *Rule of St Benedict*, Prologue, line 41: 'What is not possible to us by nature, let us ask the Lord to supply by the help of his grace', pp. 164–5; for the Holy Spirit-as-grace in Bernard of Clairvaux, see Gilson, *Mystical Theology*, especially pp. 210–11.

[50] Self-knowledge is a great theme of Bernard of Clairvaux (developed largely out of Augustine). He is concerned with a positive as well as a negative aspect, the dignity (*imago dei*) as well as the frailty and egoism of human beings. See Gilson, *Mystical Theology*, especially, pp. 69–73.

[51] The *Rule of St Benedict* is strongly influenced by Old Testament wisdom-literature in this area, notably Sirach (or Ecclesiasticus) and the Book of Proverbs. For an index of direct citations from these texts, see *Rule*, p. 588.

[52] See *Rule of St Benedict*, Ch. 7, pp. 190–203, on the twelve steps of humility. Inspired

(6)   trust in God;[54] perseverance.[55]

The image of the mother provides the context of this description of the spiritual life.[56] In fact, it is not the image of the mother in isolation that is most important here but the image of the mother-child *relationship*. When individual believers find themselves at the mercy of their own sins and weaknesses, and are afflicted by the spiritual blindness that prevents them from understanding what is going on, it is important for them to maintain – through faith – a proper sense of context. They are, that is, always *within* the sphere of the mother's care, unless they choose not to be. Conscientious believers might feel overwhelmed by the apparent disastrousness of their experience, but a shift in self-image might make all the difference. If people maintain the self-image of the fully respon-sible, capable adult, they will be inclined to despair when experience thwarts their moral and spiritual efforts; but if they reimagine themselves as dependant children of Christ the mother, things can look more positive:

> But oftentymes whan our fallyn and our wretchidnes is shewid us, we arn so sore adred and so gretly ashamid of ourselfe that onethys we wettyn where that we may holden us. But then will not our curtes moder that we fle awey, for him wer nothing lother. But he will than that we usen the condition of a child; for whan it is disesid or dred it rennith hastely to our moder for helpe with al the myte . . . (61.100)

The imagery in Chapter 61 of the mother-child relationship focuses more on the distressed child than on the figure of the mother; and the mother's presence is largely left to be inferred from the behaviour of the child rather than being presented by means of direct portrayal. When Julian does shift her focus onto the mother herself she presents the image

by this chapter, Bernard of Clairvaux wrote his *De Gradibus Humilitatis*, cited frequently in Gilson, *Mystical Theology* (see, for example, p. 232, n. 92). See also *Cloud of Unknowing*, Chs. 13–14, pp. 22–3, where imperfect meekness (or humility) involves facing up to personal sinfulness; and perfect meekness is attained through a self-forgetful contemplation of God's superabundant love and worthiness.

[53] See Leclercq, *Love of Learning*, pp. 65–86.

[54] On *fiducia* (confidence, trust) in Bernard, see Gilson, *Mystical Theology*, espe-cially p. 138, n. 207, and p. 143. See also, J. P. H. Clark, '*Fiducia* in Julian of Norwich, I', *Downside Review*, 99 (1981), pp. 97–108; and '*Fiducia* in Julian of Norwich, II' *DR*, 99 (1981), pp. 214–29.

[55] *The Rule of St Benedict* urges the monk to persevere in the monastic way 'usque ad mortem', until death. Prologue, line 50, pp. 166–7.

[56] In the second section of Chapter 5 I discuss the pastoral thrust of Julian's text in greater detail. In this present chapter, however, I have been principally concerned with the way the image of Christ the mother modulates from an ontological to a soteriological and finally into a pastoral signification.

with the minimum of detail, seeming reluctant to paint too naturalistic a picture. There are at least two possible reasons why this could be so. First, as with any image, that of the mother is only provisional. Images are theologically and devotionally useful. They can free the mind from being in thrall to the phenomenal surface of things and so from seeking God only there and on those terms. But if clung to excessively or interpreted literalistically, images can hijack the mind and freeze it in precisely the superficial mode of perception from which, when used appropriately, they ought to deliver it. The wide open spaces of poetry give way to the literalist's prison.

The second possible reason why Julian might wish to avoid too naturalistic a portrayal of the mother in Chapter 61, and the more directly relevant one, is that she wishes to propose an identification of the mother not merely with Christ, but Christ qualified as 'Church' (as we have to some extent already seen):

> And he will than that we usen the propertie of a child that evermor kindly trosteth to the love of the moder in wele and wo. And he will that we taken us mytyly to the feith of holy church and fyndyn there our dereworthy moder in solace of trew vnderstondyng with al the blissid common . . . (61.100)

The sinner's recourse to Christ the mother represents the claiming of access to the grace of God, a birthright derived from the sacrament of baptism and belonging to his or her identity as a member of the Church:

> And therfore a sekir thing it is, a good and a gracious, to willen mekely and mytyly be susteyned and onyd to our moder, holy church, that is Crist Iesus; for the [P: flode] of his mercy that is his dereworthy blode and pretious water is plentious to make us faire and clene. (61.101)

We have noted in the second chapter of this book that the blood and water flowing from the side of Christ signify in traditional exegesis the founding of the Church; and it is through baptism that the Church is inwardly and personally 'founded' within each individual Christian. This passage, however, is probably more about the individual believer's ecclesiological identity as a baptised person, together with all that flows from that, than about baptism itself. This ecclesiological identity is actualized through the recourse individuals have to the sacraments of the Church. Such recourse is never once-for-all, but part of a continuous and dynamic situation in which, whatever the ups and downs, the mother's hands are always 'redy and diligently aboute us' (61.101).

So the interpretation of religious experience in terms of a mother-child relationship is not based on an arbitrary choice of imagery. This imagery classically denotes the eccelsiological/sacramental context within which grace heals and transforms human nature; and within which certain validly performed ritual acts – the sacraments – both signify and objectively guarantee the religious meanings attachable to contingent personal experience. The visibility of this is very much to the point. The motherhood of grace (or the *grace* aspect of the motherhood of *working*) operates within space-time, a sphere of development rather than of stasis; a sphere of bodiliness and of the dialectics of growth; of ascesis, desire, sin-repentance-mercy; and of the coinherence-through-sacrament of the personal and the ecclesiological. The image of Christ the mother might be suggestive of the conventional idea of Christ as Church, but the nature of the image itself also serves Julian's purpose in special sense. It is employed to indicate all the diverse modes and moods of a relationship that is actualized in the form of nurturing and growth. Through this intrinsically fluid imagery, with its dynamic potentialities, Julian is able to imply, and sometimes more than just imply, the attaching of spiritual and eternal value to all in human experience that might seem merely contingent, random, uninterpretable in terms of any larger divine scheme.

Incarnation and Autobiography

The whole point of Julian's sacramental and mystical theology is that it is understood precisely to affect real people in the particularities of their experience. It is axiomatic for Julian that theology seeks incarnation. Grace has not been sent out to obliterate kind but to heal and transform it, and though the fulfilment of this motherhood of grace is only attained upon birth into the next world, there are anticipatory signs of it even now. As grace finds progressively more unhindered scope within human nature, so the distinction between kind and grace breaks down. Kind becomes the matter, so to speak, of which grace is the form, so that Julian can evoke the perfection of the mother-child relationship through a concept of kind now transposed into the register of grace:

> Faire and swete is our hevenly moder in the syte of our soule; precious and lovely arn the gracious children in the syte of our hevinly moder, with myldhede and mekeness and all the fair vertues that long to children in *kynde*; for *kindly* the child dispeirith not of the moder love; *kindly* the child presumith not of the selfe; *kindly* the child lovith the moder and ilke on of the othe[r]; these arn the fair vertues, with all other that ben like, wherwith our hevenly moder is servid and plesyd.
>
> (63.103, my emphases)

Grace so fully disposes the child in love towards the mother that humility and trust, as well as other virtues, are natural, 'kindly'.

It is appropriate to complete our 'incarnation diptych' with this notion of theology incarnated as virtue. This points to the practical import of Julian's theology and to its answerability within the sphere of lived religious experience. We have seen in the example of the lord and the servant, and in the chapters immediately following it, that Julian affirms the real bond, in Christ, between God and humanity, first at the general level and then, crucially, at the personal level. The theme of Christ as mother gives yet more bold and rigorous expression to the reality of that bond, affirming its ontological character vis-à-vis the individual person; and also relating it in particular to the ups and downs of lived experience. One crucial effect of Julian's rigorously-pursued emphasis on the incarnation, and on all this implies both for humanity as a whole and for the individual, is to create certain intellectual and imaginative conditions in which a *theological* interpretation of contingent personal experience might credibly be made. It creates, that is, the conditions for *shareable religious autobiography*, whereby a given person (Julian; anyone) might project his or her own experience via an authoritative christological paradigm, and that for the specific spiritual benefit of their fellow Christians. The word 'authoritative' is important here. By ensuring that her perceptions and reflections both about the role of Christ and about the nature of the person are deeply folded into a specific ecclesiology, Julian implicitly proposes a legitimization of that religious-autobiographical manoeuvre whereby she presents herself – like the Church in its magisterial function – as mediator and authoritative interpreter of divine truth. She may address the Church authoritatively because, at the microcosmic level, she *is* the Church, and as such is in union of charity with all Christians:

> the charite of God makyth in us such a unite that whan it is trewly seyn, no man can parten himse[l]fe from other. (65.106)

She may speak on behalf of Christ because, in common with all the baptised of whatever rank or degree, she shares Christ's nature by virtue both of kind and grace. The seamless unity adduced here – between Julian and Christ, and in Christ between Julian and her fellow Christians – is, in an important sense, Julian's mature answer to the loneliness and risk implicit in her prophetic vocation.

5

Interiority and the Pastoral Dimension

IF THE previous two chapters have been especially concerned with Julian's theological estimate of the person and of personal experience, and with the implicit defence she makes of the possibility of authoritative and credible religious autobiography, the present chapter, which is divided into two contrasting sections, explores at two particular rhetorical levels the text's implicit preoccupation with these questions.

The first section considers what might be called Julian's idiom of interiority and explores how her distinctly theological and mystical appraisal of the humanly contingent is facilitated, rhetorically speaking, by the peculiar metaphorical character of this idiom. The second section focuses on Julian's concern, both stated and implied, for the practicalities of a dedicated Christian life as lived by specific devout individuals. It concerns itself largely with a discernible rhetoric of spiritual counsel that runs through the text, and which links Julian – despite her double handicap of being a woman and a non-cleric – to a certain religious-literary tradition. We can infer from the distinctly pastoral intention that is evidently operative within the text Julian's conviction of theology's answerability – and of her own text's answerability – to the *personal*.

I. INTERIORITY

As we have seen, Julian's central concern in the chapters following the example of the lord and the servant[1] is to explicate the bond of nature and supernature that unites God and humanity, as implied in the identification of the servant with both Adam and Christ. But she does not rely merely on formal theological statements in order to secure rhetorically a sense of this relationship and of its implications for the relations between human beings. The text as a whole is suffused with an idiom of interiority that gives rhetorical form and force to the mystical axiom that the apparently separate worlds of God, humanity, Julian and the reader are

[1] That is, Chapters 52–64.

in reality coinherent. The notion of interiority as a defining feature of Julian's conceptual world is both formally proposed and linguistically enacted.[2]

This section will begin by considering interiority in separate thematic compartments: first, the archetypal inwardness of God; followed by a briefer look at the inwardness attributed to creation; and then a fuller consideration of the privileged inwardness of Adam, God's 'most lovyd creatur' (51.76) and chosen 'wonyng place' (54.86). After considering the idiom of interiority as applied to the human individual, the focus will shift to Julian's treatment of the Virgin Mary as exemplar of human interiority. It is hoped to show that Julian's concern with the enactment of the total Christian mystery within each individual soul – something of which both the Virgin Mary and Julian herself are, in contrasting ways, presented as paradigmatic – simultaneously works to underline the intrinsic nature of the bond between God and humanity; and to answer, at least in part, Julian's rhetorical need to attach credible religious value to her own personal experience. In considering the idiom/notion of interiority as Julian applies it to human beings, a certain emphasis will be given to the importance of a distinct sacramental culture as the implicit (and sometimes explicit) context of Julian's discourse. It is a culture in which the sacraments, especially the eucharist, constitute the officially-accredited source of grace, of inner spiritual dynamism; and any discussion of the question of interiority really misses a key point if this aspect of Julian's world is not acknowledged. Indeed, to acknowledge it also enables us to take cognizance of the fact that the sacramental theology of the medieval Church, as well as giving ritualized public expression to the self-understanding of a hugely powerful religious and political institution, also has intrinsically mystical potentialities.[3] The sacraments can therefore be understood as signifying a relation between, as well as a possible integration of, interior and exterior, private and public, personal spirituality and ecclesiological communion. In recognizing this we can legitimately suggest that Julian does not propose an anti-ecclesiological personal mysticism over against communal Catholic orthodoxy,[4] but is

---

[2] I have been greatly stimulated by Janet Martin Soskice, *Metaphor and Religious Language*, paperback reprint (Oxford, 1992). Soskice is especially illuminating on metaphoricity as an antidote to literalism, as well as on the provisionality of metaphor itself in the sphere of theological discourse. In the scriptural and literary examples she cites, metaphor has both a 'cataphatic' and an 'apophatic' force; it has a power of positive signification, but also resists hermeneutic closure. See especially pp. 142–61.

[3] On the relationship between eucharistic devotion and the mystical experience of certain medieval (mainly thirteenth century) women, see Walker Bynum, *Jesus as Mother*, especially pp. 256–62; also, Rubin, *Corpus Christi*, especially pp. 316–19.

[4] Walker Bynum makes the point that the eucharistic spirituality associated with

looking (whether always wholly conscious of this or not) to the realization of possibilities already implicit in the sacramental culture of the official Church.

The Interiority of God

The distinction between outward and inward that Julian makes with regard to the figures of the lord and the servant in Chapter 51 provides perhaps the best starting-point for an examination of the idiom of interiority. Just as Augustine sees a reflection of God's trinitarian nature in the psychological triad of memory, intellect and will,[5] so in Julian's text the inward/outward paradigm which is adduced to interpret the structure of all reality and all relationships is understood to be archetypally figured in God. Both the lord and the servant are portrayed, as we have seen, in a certain iconic mode; but, as with the vision of the wounded side of Christ in Chapter 24, Julian creates an illusion of three-dimensionality. Outwardly the servant suffers the pain of his fall; inwardly 'he was as onlothful and as good . . . as whan he stode afor his lord redy to don his wille' (51.73). Outwardly the lord regards the servant with a look of 'grete ruth and pety'; inwardly he rejoices on account of 'the worshipful resting and nobleth that he will and shall bryng his servant to be his plentevous grace'. The lord and the servant are inwardly united in that 'ground of love' by which 'the love he [the servant] had to the lord was even like to the love that the lord had to hym' (51.77). The interiority of Father and Son in their relation to one another finds expression in the 'Holy Gost [the] even love which is in them both' (51.78). In addition, the Holy Spirit is the link between divine and human interiority, as the identification of the Spirit with grace would suggest. The inwardness of the lord is particularly vividly evoked as 'an hey ward, long and brode, all full of endles hevyns' (51.75), while even his outward appearance is understood to indicate the inner fullness of divinity:

> The larghede of his clothyng, which were fair, flamand abowten, betokenith that he beclesid in hym a[ll] hevyns and al ioy and blis.
>
> (51.76)

This characterization of the lord/Father in terms of inner fullness stands in contrast to the evocation of the servant/Son whose inwardness is referred to but barely characterized.

We might be justified in drawing the inference that whereas the Father

the monastery of Helfta partly represented, in effect, an affirmation of clerical prestige.

[5] See Chapter 4, n. 15, above.

is depicted in terms of fullness, the conspicuous failure to attribute a similar divine fullness to the Son expresses a theological truth. Julian's Christ, as Rowan Williams points out, manifests 'the essentially "kenotic" character of the divine'.[6] Among the persons of the Trinity, it is Christ who uniquely empties himself of all the prerogatives – all the *fullness* – of divinity and takes the form of a servant.[7] His divine substance remains intact, but it cannot 'fill' his created human nature until the work of redemption has been completed. Julian's image of the gardener illustrates this. His job is to dig vigorously in order to 'sekyn the depnes' (51.77) and 'make swete flods to rennen'. These 'swete flods' can be understood as representing the Holy Spirit, the 'rivers of living water'[8] which Christ says shall flow from the believer's heart. The image of the gardener implies that there is some kind of blockage preventing this stream of divine life communicating itself. The production of 'noble and plenteous fruits' is thereby thwarted. The notion of fruit, of course, suggests the realization of potential, an achieved *fullness*. The kenotic Christ – Christ in the form of a servant – experiences humanity's fruitlessness, its unfulfilledness, precisely in order to remedy it. His divine consciousness is put in abeyance so that 'almost he had forgotten his owne luf' (51.73). The completion of his work will not only bear fruit in the salvation of humanity but will bring about his own glorification as a man, the untrammelled suffusion of his created human nature with the fullness of divinity. It is this glorification that is expressed towards the end of Chapter 51 where Christ ascends to the Father's right hand, having exchanged 'Adams old kirtle' (51.80) for a robe of unparalleled splendour which represents his human nature divinely transfigured:

> and our foule dedly flesh, which was Adams old kirtle, steyte, bare and short, than be our saviour was made fair now, white and bryte and of endles cleness, wyde and syde, fairer and richer than was than the clothyng which I saw on the Fadir; for that clothyng was blew, and Christs clothyng is now of a fair, semely medlur which is so mervelous that I can it not discrien; for it is al of very worshipps. (51.80)

Christ's robe is 'richer' than that of the Father precisely because, in the Trinity, Christ is the unique possessor of a created human nature. As Julian says in Chapter 52, human life contains 'a mervelous medlur bothen of wele and woe' (52.81) and Christ's personal human experience is not discarded in his glorification but, as the above quotation indicates,

---

[6] See Williams, *Wound of Knowledge*, p. 143.

[7] '[Christ] emptied himself, taking the form of a servant, being made in the likeness of men', Philippians 2:7.

[8] John 7:38.

is woven into the 'fair, semely medlur' of his clothing, which Julian finds indescribably 'mervelous'.

The image of Christ in his glorified body represents the redemption won for humanity in general. Julian points out in Chapter 23 that 'Al the Trinite wroute in the passion of Criste' (23.34) but it was only Christ, 'the mayden son', who suffered; so the title of 'saviour' belongs to him in a way that it does not belong either to the Father or the Holy Spirit. On the strength of this, and incurring a hefty debt to St Paul,[9] Julian attributes to Christ a unique inwardness which pertains to his distinct identity as a person within the Trinity. This inwardness is characterized imagistically as an enclosing space in which redeemed humanity, the fruit of his redemptive work, is given access to the inner life of the Godhead:

> Criste in his body mytyly berith [CW: vs] up into hevyn; for I saw that Christ, us al havand in him that shal be savid in him, worshipfully presentith his Fader in hevyn with us . . . (55.87–8)

The reference to Christ's body here has a strong ecclesiological resonance, as with St Paul.[10] The Church is the sacrament of Christ's salvific spaciousness; his wounded side is the door to that 'faire delectabil place . . . large enow for al mankynd that shal be save' (24.35). The enclosure of redeemed humanity in Christ is expressed later in a particularly surreal, even playful, modulation of Julian's notion of the divine motherhood. In its refusal of the natural progression from gestation to childbirth the following image might raise a few post-Freudian eyebrows:

> our saviour is our very moder in whom we be endlessly borne and neve[r] shall come out of him. (57.93)

Humanity-that-is-to-be-saved is, by definition, eternally 'in Christ'. He is the one 'out of whom we be al cum, in whom we be all inclosid, into whome we shall all wydnyn' (53.85).

There is another sense in which it is possible to speak of humanity as being inescapably enclosed in God, and therefore of another mode of the divine inwardness, and that is in respect of humanity's creaturely dependence on God for existence itself. Each individual shares this fundamental dependence on God with all creatures, animate and inanimate, but in the peculiar and pre-eminent way that belongs to the unique dignity of human nature. Humanity's dependence on the sustaining power of God's goodness is expressed in Chapter 5 by the image of

---

[9] I am thinking of St Paul's characteristic phrase 'in Christ', which has soteriological, ecclesiological and mystical resonances.

[10] Ephesians 5:23.

clothing, which has a resonance of intimacy that is reinforced by the anthopomorphic language suggestive of God's personal solicitude for human beings:[11]

> In this same time our lord shewid me a ghostly sight of his homely loveing, I saw that he is to us everything that is good and comfortable for us. He is our clotheing that for love wrappith us, [G: halseth] us and all beclosyth us for tender love, that hee may never leave us, being to us althing that is gode, as to myne understondyng. (5.7)

Immediately after these words Julian relates her vision of a 'littil thing, the quantitye of an hesil nutt in the palme of my hande', a generalization to all creation of what has been said first in relation to human beings. As the 'littil thing' is held in the palm of Julian's hand, so the whole of the created order is enclosed in the hand of God who is 'the maker, the keper and the lover'.[12]

In Chapter 6 Julian brings this vision to bear on the peculiarly human experience of dependance on God. Her earlier image of God as 'our clothing' now seems inadequate. A naked person is still a person, but creation would lose its very being and 'fallen to nowte' if God were to withdraw his love. But in Chapter 6, although Julian does take up again the image of clothing, it is only the first in a sequence of images which together recreate an imaginative journey penetrating progressively deeper into the human body:

> for as the body is cladde in the cloth, and the flesh in the skynne, and the bonys in the flesh, and the herte in the bouke, so arn we, soule and body, cladde in the goodnes of God and inclosyd; ya, and more homely, for all these may wasten and weren away; the godenes of God is ever hole, and more nere to us withoute any likenes . . . (6.9)

Humanity's enclosure within the goodness of God is wholly other than the kinds of enclosure observable in nature. To emphasize this, Julian sets up the metaphorical sequence only in order to subvert it: 'the godenes of God is ever hole, and more nere to us withoute any likenes'.[13]

Julian's metaphors of enclosure in God logically invite the inference that God is, or contains, an enclosing space. Such an inference is supported also by the notion of humanity as a 'tresor . . . ground[dy]d in the lord' (51.77), and in another way through the language of

---

[11] This anthropomorphic language conveying God's personal solicitude for human beings has echoes of Genesis 3:21: 'And the Lord God made for Adam and his wife garments of skins, and clothed them.'

[12] See Chapter 3, n. 1, above.

[13] On this part of Chapter 6, see Gillespie and Ross, 'Apophatic Image', pp. 66–7.

hiddenness and secrecy applied to the divine: 'I saw a mervelous hey privitye hid in God' (27.39).[14]

In the following two sections we shall consider how Julian uses this language of enclosure in reverse so that creation in general and humanity in particular are evoked, explicitly and implicitly, in terms of an interiority in which God is somehow accommodated. The image sequence from Chapter 6 suggests itself as a convenient bridge. Ostensibly, the physical layers – cloth, body, skin, flesh, bones, trunk, heart – denote by analogy both the strength and intimacy of God's goodness, in which humanity is enclosed. But the penetration to the physical extremity of inwardness anticipates Julian's conception of the primacy of personal interiority in the enactment of Christian mystery, a spiritual interiority represented (as traditionally) by the *heart*.

Before looking at the specific question of human interiority we shall briefly examine the language of inwardness as Julian applies it to God's indwelling of creation in general.

The Interiority of Creation

One of the ways in which Julian conveys the dependence of creation on its creator is through the language of divine immanence. She speaks of God's presence within created reality as that which causes and sustains its being, and of his active power as its inward source of dynamism. This sense of the immanence of God in creation is present from the first revelation. Julian is there concerned with how the fragile creation, the 'littil thing, the quantitye of an hesil nutt'(5.7), relates to God. Perhaps with an eye to Genesis 1 – 'God saw all that he had made and indeed it was very good' – Julian comes to focus especially on the goodness of God as the defining attribute of his immanence in creation.[15] It is a goodness that belongs to creation from the beginning and according to its very nature:

> for his goodness fulfilleth all his creatures and all his blessed workes (and) ouer passeth without end. (CW 303.42–3)

Taking this reading based on P, what is of particular interest is the invocation of a metaphor of fulfilment, together with the implied

---

[14] The very notion of revelation implies the existence of things that are normally inaccessible; and Julian's sense of the inexhaustibility of revelation (the *begynnyng* of an ABC', 51.79) implies that there will always be things *still hidden*.

[15] See Chapter 3, n. 2, above.

metaphor of capacity. The goodness of God fills creation; therefore, according to the logic of the metaphor, creation can be understood, wholly and in its discrete parts, as a kind of vessel containing that goodness. These complementary metaphors are so familiar, having countless antecedents in Christian and other religious traditions, that it would be all too easy to skim over them without taking sufficient account of the extent to which, and the peculiar ways in which, Julian's textual world is structured through them.

It is in the third revelation that the concept of God's immanence in creation is most clearly stated:

> And after this I saw God in a poynte, that is to sey in myn vnder-stondyng, be which sight I saw that he is in al things . . . for I saw truly that God doth althing be it never so litil. (11.17)

Julian says that she did not see the activity of creatures as such, but 'of our lord God in the creature; for he is in the mydde poynte of allthyng and all he doith' (11.18). A little further on she asserts that 'ther is no doer but he' and confirms this by putting in God's mouth the words, 'Se I am God. Se I am in al thing. Se I doe althyng' (11.18–19). Again, what can be inferred from statements such as these is a metaphorical understanding of creation as a space (and discrete spaces) inhabited by God, in which he can act. The metaphorical construction of Julian's text through reversible images of filling and containment implies a particular kind of universe; a universe that 'contains' the infinity of God and also shrinks to the size of a hazelnut in the palm of a hand; and a universe, as the following section will make clear, in which the individual person is both enfolded in God and fully a sphere of active divine mystery.

Human Interiority: Christ and Sacrament

According to Julian, humanity belongs inalienably to 'kynde', taking its proper place within a natural order sustained by God's presence and power. But Adam, as Julian says in Chapter 51, is God's 'most lovyd creatur' (51.76) and is privileged from the beginning by virtue of his being made in the image and likeness of God. All other creatures in the material universe, whether animate or inanimate, exist unreflectingly in a state of necessary 'obedience' to the creator. Man, on the other hand, has a unique capacity for personal union with God. The mode of God's presence in man, therefore, while at one level identical to, at another level is qualitatively different from the mode of God's presence in the rest of creation. In the first place, man is dependent on God for his material being just like any other member of the animal kingdom. But man is also rational and spiritual, and this means that a special kind of interiority is posited for him that is not merely the place of God's sustaining presence and power but the scene of a dynamic process through which the human potential for union with God is realized.

Julian understands the inner source of this dynamism to be Christ himself. It is essential to recognize the ecclesiological context and reference of Julian's account of the way the power of Christ operates within individual believers. We have considered this to some extent in the discussion of the motherhood of grace, a concept predicated on sacramental orthodoxy, but it is worth focusing on this in a slightly different perspective, with an eye to Julian's affirmation of the human person as ecclesiological subject.

There is no evidence that Julian is a charismatic illuminist proposing a private, mystical alternative to the medieval Church. On the contrary, when she writes about the nature of Christ's inner presence and activity the discussion, as mentioned above, is dependant on an uncriticized sacramental culture which, through ritual, dramatizes and interprets personal experience according to a christological paradigm within the larger context of the Church. Julian's explicit references to the sacraments, notably baptism, confession and the eucharist, have not been spatchcocked into the text as a sop to authority; rather, they disclose the instinctive orthodoxy that conditions and informs both Julian's visionary experience and her authorial task (even if that orthodoxy does not entirely govern either of these). Julian's Catholic contemporaries would certainly realize that it was precisely, and only, their implication in the sacramental life of the Church that would enable them to read the text as being directly relevant to their own spiritual condition. The inner Christ Julian presents as the measure of human inwardness is not, in such a context, understood merely as a subjectively-experienced interior phenomenon, but primarily, though without prejudice to the subjective dimension, as an objective theological reality susceptible of juridical authentification.[16]

Thomas Aquinas speaks of 'the glory that is to come in which every truth will be unveiled and made perfectly clear and in which *there will be*

---

[16] Scholastic debates about the sacraments (especially the eucharist) feed into a broader ecclesiastical anxiety about defining a territory of *rightness* which might be controlled juridically. Whatever theological value they might have, arguments about definition and language in relation to the sacraments bear directly on questions of social order, and of political and religious power. See Rubin, *Corpus Christi*, pp. 12–82. It is worth bearing in mind that the Fourth Lateran Council of 1215 (under Pope Innocent III, 1198–1216), at which the eucharistic dogma of transubstantiation was promulgated, represented the culmination of a process whereby the papacy asserted its divine authority above the merely secular powers. This process had been begun in earnest by Pope Gregory VII (1073–85), hence the 'Gregorian Reforms' – see Ozment, *Age of Reform*, pp. 141–4.

no sacraments' (my emphasis).[17] The sacraments, of which the eucharist would be the most prominent in the life of a medieval Catholic,[18] pertain by definition to the terrestrial sphere, offering a means of access to spiritual realities for Christians making their journey to heaven through the vicissitudes of a fallen world. The continued existence of the sacraments depends on their answering to this specific need, and when the need has been answered definitively, in heaven, they will cease to be. The Latin term *viaticum*, meaning literally 'money for a journey', came to be applied to the reception of the eucharist by a dying person. The consecrated host was their provision for the final journey through death and into the next world.[19] But the term could also be applied to the eucharist in general which provided every Christian with the necessary means of spiritual sustenance on the pilgrimage through life.

As we have already noted, Aquinas identifies the two principal functions of the sacraments as being to remedy the effects of sin, and to 'dispose and strengthen' a person to worship God: redemption and sanctification[20] If we remember that the sacraments are understood to effect an inward union between Christ and the believer, we can infer that these functions are precisely the functions of the indwelling Christ. This inner Christ is both medicine and food. He is in the first place the active, inner remedy of the effects of sin, a source of mercy and healing, the one Augustine addresses as 'tu, medice meus intime'.[21] But he also operates as a dynamic principle of life in co-operation with which the individual can become spiritually mature, growing progressively stronger and more perfectly disposed to the worship of God. The exigencies of theological controversy and ecclesiastical politics from the eleventh to the thirteenth century led to the development of a conceptual framework within which a sacramental theology emerged through scholastic processes of categorization and definition.[22] The language of that theology can obscure for us

---

[17] See *Summa Theologiae* (ed. McDermott), p. 550.

[18] Eamon Duffy points out that 'the reception of communion was not the primary mode of lay encounter with the [eucharistic] Host. Everyone received at Easter, and one's final communion, the viaticum or "journey money" given on the deathbed, was crucially important to medieval people . . . But for most people, most of the time the Host was something to be seen, not to be consumed', *Stripping of the Altars*, p. 95. Of course, the fact that reception of communion among lay people was so rare points precisely to the overwhelming significance and sacredness of the sacrament, as does its association with the deathbed. Furthermore, *looking* at the consecrated bread was clearly in itself understood as a real participation in the sacramental event, as Duffy's research makes clear (pp. 95–102).

[19] See Duffy, *Stripping of the Altars*, p. 95.

[20] See McDermott, pp. 555–7; and Chapter 4, n. 21, above.

[21] *Confessions*, X.iii (4), Skutella, p. 211, line 7; Chadwick, p. 180.

[22] See Chapter 2, n. 19, above.

what is clearly understood by Julian: that the Christ of the sacraments is above all a personal reality, saving and perfecting believers from within. Medieval popular piety and traditions of affective religion attest to this understanding. More significantly here, Julian's use of the image of Christ the mother for expressing the realities of Church and sacrament reinforces a sense of the personal as against the merely juridical or 'technological' (sacrament as dispensing-machine of grace-as-commodity).

The text contains diverse images of Christ's habitation of the human soul which can be read as indices of the individual's inner experience of Christ's saving and perfecting activity. The particular quality of inward experience Julian wishes to evoke must be inferred from the kind of image she uses. For convenience we shall take Aquinas as a guide, considering Julian's presentation of Christ first as the believer's inner source of mercy and healing; and then as the principle of life, growth and virtue.

Christ as inward source of mercy

Towards the end of the text Julian returns explicitly to the stubbornly persuasive theme of sin, although this time she is less interested in a rational comprehension of the nature of sin in itself than in its practical significance for the individual. From this point of view the important thing is not to come to some sort of philosophical definition of sin but to an understanding of the dynamics of sin within the process of one's personal salvation and sanctification. This inevitably takes sin out of conceptual isolation and places it in relation to traditional Christian notions of repentance and the mercy of God for sinners. Furthermore, for Julian it is not enough simply to set these concepts alongside one another as separate realities. If experience has taught her anything it is that God is 'our ground of whom we have all our life and our being' (78.125). In the light of this she is particularly concerned to show that God's union with a given individual persists through all modes of that individual's experience, notably in sinning, repenting and receiving mercy. More than this, God's presence is not static. He actively works to bring the sinner into complete and willing union with himself.

In Chapters 79 and 80 the themes of sin, repentance and mercy coalesce in an image of Christ lamenting in solitude:

> he stondyth al [P: aloone] and abideth us swemefully and moningly till whan we come, and hath haste to have us to him; for we arn his ioy and deligte, and he is our salve and our life. (79.128)

This image is largely derived from the example in Chapter 51 where both the lord and the servant are depicted in respective states of temporary isolation, the servant languishing alone after his fall into the slade (see 51.73), and the lord sitting 'on the erth barren and desert, alone in

151

wildernes' (51.75). With respect to the image in Chapter 79, it is helpful to draw a distinction between Christ himself and the place of his solitude, which is identified in Chapter 80 as the individual soul (80.128–9, see below). The fact that Christ finds himself alone in the soul suggests the individual's separation from God. We are expected to transfer the image of isolation to the sinner, understanding that it is humanity's sinful self-alienation that is registered here (similarly to the way Julian's spiritual condition is registered in her evocation of the crucifix at the end of her bed[23]). A person's moral and spiritual condition can be inferred from the particular degree of Christ's solitude. The sinner reinforces that solitude – abandons Christ the more – by deliberately continuing in sin; by apathy (not to be confused with *apatheia* in the ancient monastic sense[24]); or even by morbid self-accusation. On the other hand, Christ's solitude is nullified to the extent that these patterns of behaviour are rejected. This is made explicit in Chapter 80:

> And what tyme I am strange to hym be synne, dispeir or slawth, than I let my lord stonden alone, in as mekill as [P: he] is in me; and thus it farith with us all which ben synners. (80.129)

But the figure of the solitary Christ is not merely a rhetorical expedient for presenting an indirect account of human sinfulness. The image equally signifies the larger context within which sin must be understood, a context which Christ himself orders and defines. His very presence in the soul points to one of Julian's central theological themes, that of Christ's union with the sinner prior to any movement of repentance. The fact that Christ is alone is an effect of human choice and therefore signifies sin, but the fact of his presence per se, regardless of how the individual acts or does not act, signifies God's unbroken and unbreakable love for the sinner: 'his goodnes suffrith us never to be alone' (80.129). Humanity's sinfulness does not alter the fact that 'ere God made us he lovid us; which love was never slakid, ne never shall' (86.135).

In Chapter 37 God brings to Julian's mind the fact that, despite the extraordinary revelation she has received, she will inevitably remain prone to sin. But he consoles her with the words, 'I kepe the ful sekirly' (37.51). The notion of 'suernesse of kepyng' (CW 443.13) is central in the dynamics of sin-repentance-mercy. It provides the assurance that at every stage the process of salvation is rooted in the omnipotence and dependability of God rather than the moral fickleness of the individual:

[23] See generally Chapter 2 of this book.
[24] For the immensely influential Evagrius of Pontus (349–99), *apatheia* denotes that state of bodily and psychological tranquillity which is a prerequisite for supple responsiveness to God. See Louth, *Origins*, pp. 103–10.

Our lord shewid that a dede shall be done and hymsef shal don it; and I shal do nothyng but synne, and my synne shal not lettyn his goodnes werkyng. (36.49)

Even as the individual commits sin, the presence of Christ within the soul – albeit a solitary Christ – is a token of 'his grace inwardly keping' (79.127). When individuals abandon their own best spiritual interests through sin, he alone continues to bear responsibility for them:

And what tyme that we fallen into synne and leve the mynd of him and the keping of our own soule, than kepith Criste alone al the charge of us ... (80.129)

When Julian says of Christ that he 'abideth us swemefully and moningly till whan we come' (79.128) she conflates two ideas. The first is that of the continual availability of mercy which Christ's presence in the soul guarantees. Like the father in the parable of the Prodigal Son, Christ is always waiting for the sinner to return home,[25] to that Augustinian interior 'home' which is the integrated self in communion with God[26] (integrated, of course, precisely by virtue of that communion). The second idea is that the journey home is itself the work of Christ, who waits in the soul 'swemefully and moningly'. It is when the sinner 'hears' and positively identifies with Christ's sorrow that the homeward journey begins. This willing identification with Christ's sorrow, by which Julian denotes repentance, is itself a work of grace, of Christ-in-the-Spirit. In fact, Julian's initial prayer for the 'wound of very contrition' (2.3) clearly suggests that even at a relatively early stage in her life she understood repentance itself to be in God's own gift, and to be his own work. This is confirmed for her in the fourteenth revelation when God says to her, 'I am ground of thi besekyng' (41.56), from which she deduces that 'it is most impossible that we shuld besekyn mercy and grace and not have it' (41.57). For those who are to be saved, sin, repentance and mercy are experienced within a continuum of divine love mediated to the individual through the sacramental and mystical agency of the indwelling Christ.

Christ as inward principle of growth

As food is necessary for growth in the natural order, so there is a kind of food that is necessary for bringing human beings to a spiritual maturity which will subsume the natural in a supernatural fulfilment. In the eucharist Christ is simultaneously the one who feeds and the food

---

[25] Luke 15:11–32.
[26] This is implicit, for example, in *Confessions*, X.xvii (38). See Chapter 1, n. 19, above.

itself. The extrinsic functions of natural motherhood are, in one sense, a mere reflection of the intrinsic operations of the sacramental Christ (Christ-in-the-Spirit) by which grace is mediated to and within the soul:

> The moder may geven hir child soken her mylke, but our pretious moder Iesus, he may fedyn us with himselfe; and doith ful curtesly and full tenderly with the blissid sacrament that is pretious fode of very life.
> (60. 98)

It is probably true, as Colledge and Walsh point out, that we have here an allusion to the traditional eucharistic symbol of the mythical pelican that feeds its young on its own blood.[27] Christ feeds souls at the ultimate cost to himself; and it is by virtue of this interiorized motherly activity of feeding and nurturing that Christ is a principle of increase.

The inner work of Christ is intended to bring individuals to a maturity in which they attain, each in their own unique way, the fullness of that human nature, redeemed and transfigured by grace, which God first created for his own Son:

> And all the gefts that God may geve to cretures he hath geven to his Son Iesus for us; which gefts he, wonand in us, hath beclosid in him into the time that we be waxen and growne, our soule with our body and our body with our soule [CW: . Eyther] of hem takeing help of other, till we be browte up into stature as kynd werkyth; and than, in the ground of kind with werkyng of mercy, the Holy Gost graciously inspirith into us gifts ledand to endless life. (55.88)

It is probably correct to identify the gifts which 'the Holy Gost graciously inspirith . . . ledand to endless life' with those gifts described as being 'beclosid' within the indwelling Christ. The word 'ledand' suggests a gradual process of maturation. It is precisely through the gifts of the Holy Spirit, made available through the inner Christ, that the believer attains full maturity. Christ, who already contains all these gifts in himself, is 'perfit man' (57.92), the source and image of human completeness. Every human being, made in the image of God, has a potential for this completeness. Each person has a natural and a supernatural potential to grow towards maturity-in-Christ; a maturity which, as the next section shows, Julian evokes by means of an image markedly different from that of Christ weeping in solitude.

The mature Christ

As we have noted, Julian's descriptions of Christ weeping in the desert of the human soul are, at least partly, metaphorical indices of the individual's experience of sin and repentance. These two kinds of experience

---

[27] See CW 596–7, note to line 30.

necessarily imply a disjunction between God and the person in question. The lonely anguish of Christ is the measure of that person's alienation. By contrast, the sixteenth revelation, which Julian regards as having been 'conclusion and confirmation to all xv' (66.105), consists in a serene vision of the inner Christ, a picture of the individual's achieved union with God. In looking at the sixteenth showing it will be useful once again to distinguish between Julian's description of the soul as the place Christ inhabits spiritually and her description of Christ himself.

The showing begins with Julian's perception of her own soul, realized in spatial terms:

> And than our lord opened my gostly eye and shewid me my soul in midds of my herte. I saw the soule so large as it were an endles world and as it were a blisfull kyngdom; and be the conditions I saw therin I understode that it is a worshipful syte [i.e. city]. (67.109)

The soul here is not the blank, uncharacterized landscape of Chapters 79 and 80, the indifferent setting of Christ's solitary and sorrowing presence. The triad of images – world, kingdom, city – suggest through their own mutual consonance an ordered universe accommodating diversity within a comprehending structural unity. The order of the city is sustained within the order of the kingdom, and both in turn are sustained within the order of the world. The fact that the world is described as 'endles' indicates that the whole concentrically-layered structure is held in being by God, the source of all order, of whom Julian says in Chapter 5, 'he is the *endles*hede' (5.8). Unlike the lawless desert which is a lonely and threatening place,[28] the kingdom and the city are images of civilization, political stability and the warmth of human society. In a specifically religious perspective they call to mind the biblical 'kingdom of God' or 'kingdom of heaven'; the mystical and eschatological 'Jerusalem'; and perhaps also Augustine's 'city of God'.[29]

The sequence of images culminates in a picture of Christ residing in the city, an image contrasting sharply with that of his anguished solitude, and one which conjures something of the grave serenity of medieval sculptures of Christ in majesty (such as, for a particularly breathtaking example, the sculpture set centrally above the west door of Chartres Cathedral[30]):

[28] See Chapter 3, n. 35, above.
[29] The 'city' must be primarily interpreted in this context as the anagogical 'Jerusalem', the soul united mystically with God. See Hilton, *Scale* 2, ch. 25: 'This city [Jerusalem] signifies the perfect love of God set on the hill of contemplation', p. 239. On the monastic development of the theme of Jerusalem, both anagogical and eschatological, see Leclercq, *Love of Learning*, pp. 65–86.
[30] Illustrations of this sculpture are readily available in many books. I have before

> In the midds of that syte sitts our lord Iesus, God and man, a faire person
> and of large stature, heyest bishopp, solemnest king, worshipfulliest
> lord . . . (67.109)

The image of Christ in majesty, ruling and governing, as P has it,
'withoutyn ony instrument or besynesse' (CW 640.11–12), and in a state
of 'peace and rest' (67.109), is directly related to the image in Chapter 51 of
the lord who 'sittith solemnly in rest and in peace' (51.72). In that chapter
Julian positively identifies this figure of the lord as 'the Fadir, God'
(51.78), but at the end of the same chapter the servant/Son is described
similarly, sitting 'on his Fadirs ryte hand in endles rest and peace' (51.81).
Here and in Chapter 68 the portrayal of Christ in terms that have already
been used for the Father expresses the divine consubstantiality of Father
and Son, a theological truth which could not be deduced from the crucifix
alone, or from the figure of the suffering/labouring servant. As the
incarnate Word, however, Christ is alone among the persons of the Trinity
in sharing a natural bond with humanity, and so with the whole created
order. The three-fold jurisdiction of Christ indicated here – bishop, king,
lord – expresses in terms of ecclesiastical, political and divine power the
union of uncreated divinity with a created human nature by means of
which Christ functions as Logos in creating, sustaining and ordering the
world.

The inward movement suggested by the sequence of images – world,
kingdom, city, Christ – points to a special logic of interiority which
dictates that the closer one gets to the centre the fuller one's experience
of the whole. In terms of this logic each successive image comprehends
and subsumes the one it follows, so that Julian's picture of Christ as a
specific person occupying a clearly demarcated space, the city, is paradoxically the most inclusive of all.

As 'God and man' (67.109), Christ is 'perfit man' (57.92), the cosmic
person who contains within himself the fullness of all creatures. In
Chapter 53, echoing Ephesians and Colossians,[31] Julian says that

> ilke kind that hevyn shall be fulfillid with behoveth nedes, of Gods
> rythfulhede, so to be knitt and onyd to him that therin were kept a
> substance which myte never, ne shuld be, partid from him . . . (53.85)

me Whitney S. Stoddard's, *Art and Architecture in Medieval France* (New York,
1966) b/w illustration p. 160 (indifferent quality).

[31] See Ephesians 1:9–10: 'That he might make known to us the mystery of his will,
according to his good pleasure, which he hath purposed in him/In the
dispensation of the fullness of times, to re-establish all things in Christ, that
are in heaven and on earth, in him' and also Colossians 1:16–17: 'For in him
were all things created in heaven and on earth, visible and invisible, whether
thrones or dominations, or principalities, or powers. All things were created by
him and in him/And he is before all; and by him all things consist.'

This knitting of all created natures into Christ is understood by Julian to be accomplished through the incarnation, on the grounds that all modes of being in the natural order – material, animate, spiritual (as a potentiality) – are fully and uniquely appropriated to human nature. Human nature is creation's heart, its inwardness, the centre that comprehends and subsumes the whole:

> for of all kyndes that he hath set in dyvers creatures be parte, in man is all the hole in fulhede, in vertue, in fairhede and in goodhede, in rialtie and nobley, in al manner of solemnite of pretioushede and worshipp.
> (62.102)

Because the whole created order is united with Christ in creation and incarnation, the redemption of creation as a whole is achieved in the redemption of humanity:

> And all the kindes that he hath made to flowen out of hym to werkyn his will, it shall be restorid and browte ageyn into hym be the salvation of man throw the werking of grace . . .
> (62.101–2)

The sixteenth showing affirms that the mystery of salvation – the redemption of the cosmos through the incarnation and passion of Christ, and all that flows from this in ecclesiological terms – is enacted within the soul of each individual Christian. In a passage from Chapter 62 that defies visual representation the individual's relation to the rest of creation, to the Church and to Christ are, as it were, folded inwards and effectively conflated:

> us nedith not gretly to seken fer out to knowen sundry kindes, but to holy church, into our moder brest; that is to sey, into our owen soule, wher our lord wonnyth. And ther shall we fynde all; now in feith and in vnderstondyng; and after, verily in himselfe, clerely, in blisse.
> (62.102)

If Christ dwells in the soul – and in him is all – the soul itself must be in some way commensurable with that reality. The human soul is understood to have a privileged status above all other creatures; as Christ's 'homliest home and endles wonyng' (67.110) it is the 'heghest of al his werkes':

> For I saw in the same shewing that if the blisfull Trinite myte have made manys soule ony better, ony fairer, ony noblyer tha[n] it was made, he shuld not have be full plesid with the makyng of manys soule. [CW: But for he made mannes soule as feyer, as good, as precious as he myght make it a creature, therfore þe blessyd trynyte is fulle plesyd withoute ende in þe makyng of mannes soule.] (67.110; CW 644.41–3)

Although Julian does frequently invoke the traditional body-soul paradigm of human structure, her preference, as will already be clear, is for the substance-sensuality paradigm. In Chapter 56[32] she briefly and perhaps rather self-consciously suggests that the one might be accounted for in terms of the other:

> and as anemptis oure substance it may ryghtly be callyd our soule, and anemptis oure sensualite it may rightly be callyd oure soule, and that is by the onyng that it hath in god. (CW 572.20–22)

Julian seems at least mildly anxious that the unusual, though certainly not original, language of substance-sensuality should be harmonized, even protected by, a religious idiom accredited by mainstream Christian tradition and of more general currency.[33] But this is not to say that textual references to the soul are merely ancillary. While Julian does seem here to invoke the concept in a slightly defensive way, the quotation suggests nevertheless that she assigns a distinct and positive function to this traditional language. Substance and sensuality are referred to as 'oure soule' individually and in their own right, without Julian committing the outrageous solecism of positing two souls in one person. It is worth pointing out Julian's awareness of the provisionality of such language, as instanced in her use of the qualifying phrase 'it may ryghtly be callyd'. The phrase indicates both the possibility of saying something true – 'ryghtly' – and a sense that terms are deployed in order to construct, in Eliot's phrase, 'a ways of putting it' – 'it may . . . be callyd'. Definitions, that is, are not absolute. Strikingly, this self-consciousness about language glimmers precisely at a point in the text where Julian appears to be concerned with the soul as such, as distinct from the many occasions when she uses the term with an unreflecting briskness. It seems that when she comes to consider it, there is not really an 'it' there. Despite appropriating the definite article, the soul is not conceived of simply as an entity, a thing among all the various other things that go to make up a human being. It would be wrong to say that Julian thinks of the soul as a

---

[32] Following S1, Glasscoe here reads: 'And anempts our substan[c]e and sensu-alite, it may rytely be clepid our soule' (56.90). CW's reading based on P, which I use here, produces a quite different effect, as will be clear. To my mind, both versions have merits and neither of them is demonstrably superior to the other. I prefer CW because it suggests that whilst substance and sensuality are conceptually discrete, they are really integral to one another, 'soule' being a term of synthesis – this strikes me as harmonizing with Julian's general instinct for the integral unity of things.

[33] Joan M. Nuth writes: 'As far as I can tell, the pairing of the words "substance and sensuality" in this context is unique to Julian' but also notes (without citing examples) that 'the soul was generally called a "spiritual substance"', pp. 109–10.

'spiritual component' lurking in the individual's unconscious depths. Perhaps the modern sense of the word 'person' can be adduced in order to convey something of the meaning Julian attaches to the concept of the soul, although it cannot be taken as an uncomplicated equivalent. Julian uses 'soule' as a term of synthesis, to signify the integral unity of a human being – the person, the subject. Just as an individual is characterized as person in all conditions and functions proper to himself as a human subject, so, in Julian's view, the individual is characterized as soul. She is close to Aristotle and Thomas Aquinas in using the notion of soul to convey 'that by virtue of which [a person] is the kind of thing he is'.[34]

But we must bear very much in mind that, for Julian, the person, or the soul, is not identical to the secularized, atomized subject postulated by post-Enlightenment philosophy. In Julian's theological universe the potential for willing, personal union with God, whether or not that potential is activated or to any extent realized, is the defining attribute of the human being as such; and Julian's characterization of the individual as 'soule' expresses this distinctive potential of human beings. The realization of this potential, in whatever degree, is a fulfilling of nature that makes it possible to speak of the individual becoming more and more himself. The dynamic reality of the individual's growth as 'soule' in Julian's sense is indivisible from and constituted by his evolving relationship with the creator. The soul thereby becomes more and more capacious for the indwelling Christ, an 'endless world' (67.109) of order and peace rather than a threatening, faceless, uncultivated desert.

Altering the image slightly, Julian also pictures the soul as the pinnacle of creation. In order to come 'into the self' (67.110) the soul must go 'aboven all creatures' but the journey does not end there since it is not the soul's function to contemplate itself:

> yet it may not abyden in the beholdyng of the selfe, but all the beholding is blisfully sett in God that is the makar wonand therinn; for in manys soule is his very wonyng . . . (67.110)[35]

Julian could be accused of creating the impression here that the soul arrives at the contemplation of itself and then moves on to the contemplation of God, but another and more satisfactory reading suggests itself. It is not that the soul is morally obliged to prefer the contemplation of God to the contemplation of self, or even to use the latter as a stepping-stone to the former. Rather, the soul does not contemplate itself at all, because it

---

[34] I have relied here on Davies, *Thomas Aquinas*, pp. 207–20. Apart from providing ample reference to Aquinas, Davies quotes from Aristotle, *De Anima*, 412 (b) 6. See also Hugh Lawson-Tancred's translation of *De Anima* (Harmondsworth, 1986), p. 157.

[35] See Chapter 4, n. 16, above.

cannot. To suppose such a thing would be to make a category-mistake in the terms of Julian's peculiar mystical logic. The soul no more beholds itself than the eye beholds itself: it is not a self-contemplating type of thing. As we can infer from the vision of Christ in the sixteenth revelation, the conscious realization of the soul is experienced indivisibly as a conscious realization of the indwelling Christ. Whilst Julian does describe the soul in spatial terms – world, kingdom, city – these images, like that of Christ weeping in solitude, are indices of various conditions of the engaged human subject in its relation to God. Her fundamental point seems to be about that relationship, and the fact that God is not 'out there' but 'in here'.

As the locus not merely of certain private and discrete 'experiences' but of the total Christian mystery, each individual 'soule' has a dignity that is at once eternal and unique, and in an important sense paradigmatic. Our discussion of interiority concludes, appropriately, with a consideration of the way Julian evokes the figure of the Virgin Mary as the paradigm of paradigms. The Mother of God, simultaneously a particular individual and the pre-eminent type of the Church,[36] is the model for an interiorized religion that is nevertheless interpretable ecclesiologically. Even more significantly, as conceiver and bearer of the Word of God she becomes an implied model for Julian herself as Christian, visionary and author.

The Virgin Mary

The Virgin Mary's privileged status as the mother of Christ sets her apart from the rest of humanity (under Christ), but this very separation means that she uniquely represents the acme of human inwardness in its accommodation of divine reality. Her special inward relation to Christ, that of natural motherhood, also puts her in a unique relation to all those with whom Christ is involved, a relation of *spiritual* motherhood:

> Thus our lady is our moder in whome we are all beclosid and of hir borne in Christe; for she that is moder of our savior is moder of all that shall be savid in our savior. (57.92–3)

Mary's bearing of the divine child is not a private matter but a central aspect and requirement of God's plan of salvation. Her physical womb is adopted as an image of the 'womb' of Mother Church in which all believers are spiritually, and in a certain sense physically, enclosed and nurtured until they are delivered into the next world. Thus, to be 'in

---

[36] See Louth, *Origins*, pp. 200–1.

Christ' is to be 'in Mary', not withstanding that motherhood, whether spiritual or natural, is derived from Christ.[37]

Mary is an archetype, but she is such by being a specific individual and this very specificity is instructive. She is the only person apart from Christ who is shown to Julian 'in special' (25.37), in particular. Although at several points in the revelation Julian is discouraged from concerning herself with specific applications and particular people, she is invited to pay special attention to the Virgin Mary. Two things become clear as we look at how Julian presents this figure. First, Mary is evoked not so much corporeally as in terms of inner qualities. Second, she is presented as an instrument of Julian's self-understanding, an idealized picture of the perfect inward dispositions and spiritual fulfilment to which Julian aspires.[38] We shall take these in turn.

Julian's descriptions of the animated crucifix contrast utterly with her barely visualized recollection of Mary as

> a simple mayde and a meke, young of age and little waxen above a child, in the stature that she was wan she conceived with child. (4.6)

This is as vivid as it gets. Much more important to Julian than the details of Mary's appearance are 'the wisedam and the trueth of hir soule', her 'reverend beholding' of God, and her humble 'mervelyng with greate reverence' that the creator would be 'borne of hir that was a simple creature of his makeyng'. These inward dispositions are what really matter. This sense of the priority of the inner over the outer in relation to the Virgin is reinforced linguistically through an idiom of filling and fulfilment. Mary is described in Chapter 4 (following P here) as being 'more then all that god made beneth her in wordines and in *fullhead*' (CW.298.38–9). In Chapter 7 Julian says that Mary was '*fulfilled* . . . of reverend drede' (7.10) in her beholding of God; that this 'reverend drede *fulfillid* hir of mekenes'; and that 'she was *fulfillid* of grace and of al manner of vertues'. Mary is physically capacious for the Christ-child, and spiritually capacious for the fullness of grace, a plenitude traditionally ascribed to her in the Vulgate translation of Gabriel's salutation, 'Ave Maria, gratia plena'; and in the prayer into which these words were absorbed. The phrase 'fulfillid of grace' is clearly a vernacular rendering

---

[37] 'And thus is Iesus our very moder in kynde of our first makyng, and he is our very moder in grace be takyng of our kynde made. All the fair werkyng and all the swete kindly office of dereworthy moderhede is impropried to the second person', 59.96.

[38] Tarjei Park gives a suggestive account of the way Julian narrates her own experience as resonating with the experience of the Virgin Mary in her conceiving and giving birth to Christ, and of Christ the mother in his conceiving and giving birth to redeemed humanity. See 'Reflecting Christ', pp. 32–7.

of 'gratia plena', though with a nice additional suggestion of realized potential – Mary's conception of Christ was that for which she was created from the beginning, and does not therefore represent merely an extrinsic or arbitrary operation of divine power. Again, in Chapter 18 Julian says that the natural love that exists between creatures and the creator was 'most *fulsomely* shewyd in his swete moder' (18.27). In Chapter 25 (following P again) Julian combines the idiom of fullness ('*blyssydfulle* soule', see below) with a concern to stress the Virgin's inner qualities and asserts that a bodily sight of the Virgin is not her concern in this life but to have some perception of the quality of her inner life of union with God:

> But here of am I nott lernyd to long to see her bodely presens whyle I am here, but the vertues of her blyssydfulle soule, her truth, her wysdam, her cheryte, wher by I am leern(yd) to know my self, and reuerently drede my god. (CW 399.19.22)

The last part of the above quotation points to the figure of Mary as a visionary/imaginative instrument of Julian's self-understanding, that 'wher by I am leern(yd) to know my self, and reuerently drede my god'. In Chapter 4 Julian presents her first response to the revelation in these terms:

> And I said: 'Benedicite domine!' This I said, for reverence in my meneing, with a mighty voice; and full gretly was astonyed for wonder and mervel that I had that he that is so reverend and dredfull will be so homely with a synfull creture living in wretched flesh. (4.6)

Julian's description of her first vision of Mary, which comes only a few lines later, and to which we have already in part referred, echoes this passage both verbally and thematically. Julian's unexpected and sudden experience of revelation inspires the two main responses – reverence and humility – that are then attributed in their ideal form to Mary in the context of the annunciation:

> I understood the reverend beholding that she beheld hir God and maker, mervelyng with greate reverence that he would be borne of hir that was a simple creature of his makeyng. (4.6)

Mary is characterized in terms of the perfect consonance of her self-knowledge and her knowledge of God; her perception, that is, of 'the gretenes of [G: her] maker' (4.6) on the one hand, and of the 'littlehede of hirselfe' on the other. Julian also has these perceptions, but in her own degree. She, after all, is 'synfull' where Mary is 'simple'; and while Mary replies 'full mekely' to Gabriel, Julian's immediate reaction to her own experience is to cry out 'with a mighty voice'. There may be nothing intrinsically wrong with crying out, but Julian is deliberately contrasting the pre-eminently modest *ethos* of the Virgin with her own noisy uncouthness. Julian, being sinful in way that Mary is not, necessarily registers a greater degree of shock when sacred realities intrude directly.

Just as Julian places her own responses and dispositions in the light of Mary's, so she is brought to perceive her own destiny in her, and by extension the destiny of all her fellow believers. In her spiritual glory Mary is a vision of achieved possibility, of a perfectly realized union with God that awaits all who will be saved:

> And for the hey, mervelous, singular love that he hath to this swete mayden, his blissid moder, Seyt Mary, he shewid hir heyly enioyng, as be the menyng of these swete words, as if he seyd: 'Wil thou se how I love hir, that thou myte ioy with me in the love that I have in her and she in me?' And also to more vnderstondyng this swete word our lord God spekyth to al mankynde that shal be save as it were al to one person, as if he seyd: 'Wilt thou seen in hir how thou art lovid?' (25.36)

The interpenetration here of the universal and the particular is characteristic of Julian, underlining that sense of the spiritual capaciousness of the individual which her overall idiom of interiority works to secure within the text. The Virgin is a true and universal paradigm of God's love for everyone, but that love is not a generalized thing. It is as intimately personal in respect of each individual as it is in respect of the Virgin herself as an actual person. When Julian imagines God placing the Virgin before mankind as an example of his universal love, she also imagines him speaking to humanity 'as it were al to one person', employing the singular and familiar pronoun, 'thou': 'Wilt thou seen in hir how thou art lovid?' And of course what this ultimately implies is that the life and experience of any Christian person might likewise be read as offering a paradigm of the irreducibly personal character of God's love, something which clearly has crucial implications for Julian herself:[39]

> It is God will that I se myselfe as mekil bounden to him in love as if he had don for me al that he hath don. And thus should every soule

[39] In Tarjei Park's terms, Julian's reported experience, in that it reflects and resonates with the experience both of Christ and the Virgin, itself takes on something of the paradigmatic quality attaching to those religious figures: 'In the Passion we encounter a birthing sequence that connotes Christ, Mary and Julian giving birth. Julian's body acts as a signifier', 'Reflecting Christ', p. 37. Of course, Julian's body is a signifier only by virtue of its literary representation as such. The figure of the Virgin Mary also paradigmatically represents the possibility of *any* particular Christian standing for the Church as a whole. See Louth, *Origins*, p. 201 for citation of Hans Urs von Balthasar, who says that the Magnificat (Luke 1:46–55) is both the song of the individual – Mary/the Christian – and of the Church. See also Chapter 3, n. 34, above.

thinkyn inward of his lover; that is to seyn, the charite of God makyth in
us such a unite that whan it is trely sen no man can parten himse[l]fe fro
other. And thus oweth our soule to thinken that God hath don for him al
that he hath don . . . (65.106–7)

Paradoxically, the union-in-charity of all believers is only authentically
experienced and grasped to the extent that the individual realizes the
divine charity inwardly and personally. As we have seen, in Julian's
peculiar logic of interiority any movement inwards implies a fuller rather
than a lesser experience of the whole; which further implies that inwardness as such is for Julian a measure of reality. This principle is strikingly
illustrated in Chapter 25 by the fact that no further bodily sight of the
Virgin Mary is granted her in addition to what she received in the first
revelation: 'I wend a seen hir bodily presens, but I saw hir not so' (25.36).
Instead she is here given a 'gostly sigte of her' that defies visual location.
As previously, Julian is enabled to perceive Mary in terms of certain
qualities, although the qualities now perceived are no longer those of a
creature humble and reverent before God, but of a creature transfigured
in heavenly glory: 'he shewid hir than hey and noble and glorious and
plesyng to hym above al creatures'. The enigmatic, non-visual evocation
of the Virgin reflects Julian's instinct that this supremely paradigmatic
figure should not be wholly objectified, an image 'out there', something to
be admired from a distance. Rather, the inwardness of this person must be
inwardly apprehended and engaged. What is outward can be a distrac-
tion; it is the inward that is truest, and most real.

II. THE PASTORAL DIMENSION

The Authority of Experience

Julian's idiom of interiority serves to underline her affirmation of the
capacity of human beings for personal relationship with God, and also to
secure a sense of the potentially paradigmatic nature of a given person's
life and experience in the context of theology and ecclesiology. But
characteristically, Julian's concern for the interiorizability of Christian
dogma does not remain at the level of argument or symbol. If the text is
pervaded by an idiom of interiority it is also pervaded by what can be
called a pastoral tone, and an idiom of spiritual counsel, at certain points
more evident than at others. The writing is governed by a sense of
answerability to the demands of practical experience within the sphere
of religion-as-lived. To this extent the text does bear some significant
relation to that body of distinctly practical spiritual treatises which is

perhaps best represented by the works of the *Cloud*-author and Walter Hilton. In England in the high and late Middle Ages there was evidently a significant number of devout individuals, both alone and in communities, who provided ready audience for the kind of ascetical and contemplative teaching associated with these and other writers; and although Julian's text does not fit neatly into a specific genre of medieval devotional treatise, it certainly does address itself to the kind of people who would be looking for bread and butter advice on the pursuit of a contemplative religious ideal. But unlike Hilton, Julian does not set out a systematic account of the stages of spiritual development; and unlike the *Cloud*-author, she does not give detailed instructions on exactly how to conduct oneself in the time of prayer.

The assumption of religious authority implicit in the writing of a formal book of instruction would have been precluded by Julian's non-clerical status and her gender (notwithstanding that, as an anchorite, her informal, orally-given advice was evidently in demand[40]). Julian, therefore, admits her didactic and pastoral agenda under cover of the visionary. She proffers her thoughts on prayer and on the vicissitudes of the spiritual life by folding them into her account of the showings themselves, such that, as so often, the distinction is fuzzily drawn between what is presented as being from God and what from Julian by way of amplification. In the visionary mode she can rhetorically efface herself by claiming to be merely an instrument of the divine, a transmitter of God's own teaching. This is conveyed through a pedagogic idiom by which God is implicitly characterized as a teacher, the one who provides a 'lesson of love' (6.10) and 'blissid teching' (73.117).[41] Julian's authority, we are to understand, is derived neither from self nor from office but from God. Nevertheless, there is an irony here since, as should be clear by now, Julian's claim to be merely an instrument seeks justification precisely through an implicit, and sometimes explicit, assertion of the intrinsic religious value of personal experience, her own in particular. Visionary authority is by definition a form of the authority of experience. But under cover of the visionary it is as much the authority of experience in the ordinary sense that seems to come through.[42] Though uncertificated and

---

[40] Margery Kempe's reported visit to Julian provides evidence that Julian's advice was more generally sought. Margery calls the 'ankres' an 'expert' in the matter of discerning supposed 'wondirful reuelacyons', and says that she could give 'good cownsel' in such things. See *Book of Margery Kempe*, ch. 18, p. 42, lines 7–16.

[41] See Chapter 3, n. 31, above.

[42] In referring to 'the authority of experience in the ordinary sense' I mean to suggest that the text is suffused with and expresses all that Julian has achieved as a human being – emotionally, intellectually – quite apart from whatever authority she might be said to claim, even indirectly, on the strength of the supernatural.

ecclesiastically unenfranchised, Julian stands shoulder to shoulder with the accredited male *magistri*, at once a praxis-orientated theorist of the spiritual life, an acute diagnostician of psycho-spiritual ills, and something of a strategist. This should become evident as we explore Julian's pastoral intention under the following three headings: 'prayer'; 'contemplative praxis and discretion'; 'fear and love'.

Prayer[43]

Julian's formal discussion of prayer is to be found in Chapters 41 to 43 inclusive, which substantially constitute her presentation of the fourteenth showing:[44]

> After this our lord shewid for prayers; in which shewing I se ii conditions in our lordis menyng: on is rytfulnes, another is sekir troste. (41.56)

Within the general structure of the text this revelation 'for prayers' follows a number of chapters in which Julian has been specifically concerned with the problem of sin, and that not merely in an abstract sense but in direct relation to the experience of the devout: 'Synne is the

---

[43] The most substantial discussion of Julian as belonging to a literary sub-set of 'writers on the spiritual life' remains Paul Molinari, Julian of Norwich: *The Teaching of a 14th Century Mystic* (London, 1958). The book is very illuminating in parts, but the author's preoccupation seems to be with seeing how Julian measures up to John of the Cross (1542–91) and Teresa of Avila (1515–82), the great Carmelite mystics of the Spanish Counter-Reformation. John in particular is taken as authoritative and technically accurate in the field of mystical experience. Molinari's approach is not untypical of its time, but now seems very dated indeed.

[44] Colledge and Walsh argue that the 14th revelation lasts from Chapter 41 to Chapter 63 inclusive. They claim that these chapters cover thematically all that pertains to God's union with individuals, and that this simply represents a development of the theme of prayer (for discussion, see introduction to CW, pp. 113–62). Ritamary Bradley agrees with them – see her article, 'Julian on Prayer', in *Medieval Religious Women 2, Peaceweavers*, ed. Lillian Thomas Shank and John A. Nichols (Kalamazoo, Michigan, 1987), p. 299. I am sympathetic to this view, especially since it underlines my own sense of the importance for Julian of a *lived* theology. Nevertheless, the example of the lord and the servant (Ch. 51) does seem to mark a distinct and new impetus, and subsequent chapters relate quite explicitly to the example, as I have tried to show in my own Chapters 3 and 4. Marion Glasscoe believes that the 14th revelation lasts from Chapter 41 to Chapter 50 inclusive (see *English Medieval Mystics*, pp. 242–6). In fact, I would suggest that Chapters 41–3 ought to be regarded as the revelation proper (if such a designation can ever really be satisfactory given the fluidity of Julian's text). Chapter 44 marks a recognizable shift away from the theme of prayer as such.

sharpest scorge that any chousyn soule may be smyten with' (39.53). The believer's continuing experience of sin exposes human weakness and in this way, through the grace of God, motivates prayer:

> But whan we seen ourselfe so foule, than wene we that God were wroth with us for our synne, and than aren we steryd of the Holy Gost be contrition into prayers and desire to amendyng of our life . . . (40.54–5)

Prayer, therefore, is an activity of fallen human beings, a mark of their distance from the creator.

Just as any act of communication implies a disjunction between two parties, a gulf across which the message must arc, so prayer arcs across an ontological abyss; and often prayer itself seems only to bring the reality of that abyss all the more clearly into focus.[45] Julian's discussion of prayer moves swiftly away from the question of ideal dispositions ('rytfulnes', 'sekir trost', 41.56) to consider the exigent conditions within which prayer is experienced, and how it often feels to the one who prays:

> But yet oftentymes our troste is not full, for we arn not sekir that God herith us, as us thynkith, for our unworthynes and for we felyn ryth nowte; for we arn as barren and dry oftentymes after our prayors as we wer aforn; and this, in our felyng our foly, is cause of our wekenes; for thus have I felt in myself. (41.56, punctuation slightly altered)

Julian is addressing herself to devout individuals, people like herself ('for thus have I felte'), who face demoralization as prayer brings their own weakness and spiritual impotence into focus. It is against this background of religious anxiety and frustrated aspiration that Julian sets out her understanding of prayer, as derived from the fourteenth showing. Where the individual feels that the effort of praying is futile, or even that the prayer is somehow not worthy or valid, Julian affirms that God himself, substantially united with each person, is the source of the prayer:

> And al this browte our lord sodenly to my mend and s[h]ewid these words and seid: 'I am ground of thi besekyng; first it is my wille that thou have it, and sythen I make the to willen it, and sithen I make the

---

[45] For the *Cloud*-author, painful self-knowledge is both an inevitable concomitant and a motivator of prayer. For example, see *Cloud of Unknowing*, Ch. 40, p. 43, lines 23–36. The sense of sin is a crucial negative charge in the spiritual quest. This is implicit in the 13th revelation. There, Christ's 'ghostly thirst' for the salvation of sinful humanity is a mirror-image of crucified (i.e. by sin) humanity's thirst for salvation. The implication of this is that a sense of sin (humanity's moral aridity) is convertible into desire (thirst) for salvation; and in this it meets, and is empowered by, Christ's own thirst which is also a 'luflongyng'. See 31.4–3. Self-knowledge, though painful, is necessary and a sign of hope.

besekyn it and thou besekyst it; how shuld it than be that thou shuld not have thyn besekyng?' (41.56)

The 'godly wil that never assentid to synne' (37.51) is the very power and agent of prayer. Despite appearances, true prayer must by definition achieve its object since God cannot deny himself:

> for it is most impossible that we shuld besekyn mercy and grace and not have it; for of all thyng that our good lord makyth us to besekyn, hymselfe hath ordeynid it to us from withoute begynnyng. (41.57)

Julian's theorizing about prayer has the very practical purpose of firming-up the wavering spirit. She insists upon the theological reality of prayer against the contrary evidence of day-to-day experience. Her intention is to inspire her readers to perseverance, arming them with solid theology against the demons of discouragement.

If the general tenor of Chapters 41–3 is one of reassurance, the source of any such reassurance, according to Julian, must be a sure conviction that the whole enterprise of prayer is rooted in and guaranteed by the unbreakable love of God. It is through 'onknoweing of love' (73.117, my emphasis) that trust fails, so that the one who prays becomes less and less wholehearted, less confident, giving way to lassitude and other forms of negative emotion. In the following passage from Chapter 43 Julian expresses concisely the intimate connection she sees between prayer, trust and knowledge of love:

> For this is our lords will, that our prayors and our troste ben both alyk large; for if we trost not as mekyl as we preyen, we doe not ful worship to our lord in our prayors and also we taryen and peyn ourself; and the cause is, as I leve, for we *know not* truly that our lord is ground on whom our prayors springith, and also that we *know not* that it is goven us be the grace of his love; for *if we knew* this it would maken us to trosten to have, of our lords gyfte, al that we desire. (42.58–9, my emphases)

Knowledge of the love of God, as presented here, is not of the order of intellectual concepts, something for the mind to contemplate as a thing of beauty. Rather, this knowledge (appropriated, of course, through *faith*) is presented as being subordinate to the practical imperatives of a life of devotion. It inspires confidence and trust, and so motivates perseverance. This is not to say that Julian is uninterested in what can be described as contemplative, experiential knowledge of God, in 'mystical experience' as commonly understood. In Chapter 43 she writes of a 'hey, onperc[ey]v-able prayor' (43.61) when God 'of his grace shewith hymse[l]fe to our soule'. In this 'syte and beholdyng of hym to whome we prayen' love and knowledge are so fused that particular acts of prayer are layed aside:

and then we se not for the tyme what we shuld pray, but al our entent
with al our myte is sett holy to the beholdyng of hym . . . (43.61)

But as with the *Cloud*-author, who speaks of a 'beme of goostly liʒt'
piercing the cloud of unknowing,[46] the sense here in Julian's text is very
much of a rare and fleeting kind of experience, the result of what is called
in P a 'speciall grace' (CW 477.18). It is striking that she does not greatly
detain her audience at this point in the text with descriptions of felt
mystical union, or with theories about it.[47] She certainly takes appropriate
account of the possibility of this special form of experience, but within the
text as a whole, and certainly within the chapters specifically concerned
with prayer, it is not her main focus. Extraordinary experiences cannot
represent any kind of norm and Julian's overwhelming preoccupation is
with what will actually be pertinent to most of her devout audience most
of the time. Descriptions of felt mystical union are pertinent in the same
sense as theological statements about prayer. They serve to reassure and
encourage, and in this sense are brought within the sphere of the
mundane.

Contemplative Praxis and Discretion

The mundane context of space-time is that of contingent bodiliness, of 'the
dede [of redemption and sanctification through mercy and grace] that is
now in doyng' (42.59); the time of 'werkyng' and growth, in which the
individual is configured with the incarnate, suffering Christ as he brings
the new creation to birth. For each one (and, of course, for the Church), the
'tyme of this life' is mystically readable as 'the time of his passion' (4.5),
and Julian presents her own illness as signifying this in an exemplary
way: 'my body was fulfillid of feling and mynd of Crysts passion and
deth' (55.89).[48] The 'tyme of this life' is an extended moment of crisis, of
moral and spiritual 'peril' (78.152), when 'our enemies . . . arn full fel upon
us'. This is made graphically clear by Julian's descriptions both of her
momentary loss of faith in the showings (Chapter 66) and of her
subsequent demonic visitations (Chapters 67, 69 and 70). This sense of
precariousness and unresolvedness has also been suggested in Chapter 15

---

[46] See *Cloud of Unknowing*, ch. 26, p. 34, lines 31–2.

[47] Despite the religious and rhetorical complexity of Julian's text, much of
Molinari, *Julian of Norwich* (especially pp. 94–139), seems like an attempt to
conjure out of it the white rabbit of a full-blown systematic mystical theology. I
can only hope that my own attempt to identify Julian's concern for 'the spiritual
life' will be judged more circumspect, and more willing to take Julian on her
own terms.

[48] See n. 39, above.

where Julian is tossed 'I suppose about xx tymes' (15.23) between a feeling of 'everlasting sekirnes' on the one hand and of 'hevynes and werines of my life and irkenes of myselfe' on the other. In God and in God's eternity there is peace and rest,[49] but in space-time and for the embodied creature peace is intermittent, part of a dynamic rhythm that also, and necessarily, includes unrest. Julian is attentive throughout the text, more or less explicitly, to the exigencies of the mundane, and this attention exercises something of a downward gravitational pull on her more speculative theological passages. But it is especially towards the end of the text that she focuses on the practical question of the individual's religious dispositions, on what ought to be aimed for in terms of attitude to God, and what resisted or repudiated.

The question of how one ought to conduct oneself in relation to an unseen God may seem quite a rarefied one, more or less removed from practical considerations as we tend to think of them. What we can call the movement from action to contemplation looks, on the face of it, like a movement away from the practical and towards the abstract. But in drawing such a conclusion we would be in serious danger of misconstruing the context within which Julian is writing, and forgetting that it is an audience of devout people that she has in mind. For people who have set themselves to live an intensely focused life of religious introversion – a life that will absorb much of their energy – characteristically 'introvert' questions of thought, feeling, aspiration and motivation become questions of the most practical import. We should bear in mind that, according to the *Cloud*-author, the higher part of the *active* life lies in 'good goostly meditacions'[50] on one's own sinfulness, as well as on the passion of Christ and other related religious themes. The higher part of the active life as understood by the *Cloud*-author is also the lower part of the *contemplative* life, and the contemplative life is intrinsically the superior of the two (though only to be assumed by those specially called to it).[51] Within the broad spiritual tradition out of which Julian writes, the shift from outward, bodily acts of mercy and charity to the more introverted acts of

---

[49] 'For this is the cause why we be not all in ese of herte and soule; for we sekyn here rest in these things that is so littil, wherin is no rest, and know not our God that is almighty, al wise, alle gode; for he is the very rest', 5.7; 'Now sittith the Son, very God and very man, in his cety in rest and peace, which his Fadir hath adyte to him of endless purpose', 51.81.

[50] See *Cloud of Unknowing*, ch. 8, p. 17, lines 25–30.

[51] On the importance of being personally called by God to contemplative union see, for example, *Cloud of Unknowing*, Prologue, p. 2, lines 1–13, and ch. 75, pp. 73–4. The *Cloud*-author allows that this call might be given by God to a person living an active life, but the general tenor of his works suggests that a certain withdrawal from society (whether by resort to a monastery, an anchorhold or a hermitage) is taken to be a normal prerequisite for a life of contemplation.

pious meditation and contemplation is understood to be a move towards a truer and intenser engagement with God and with reality, not a lesser one – a mystical principle we have already discussed in the section on interiority. Of course the traditional commonplace of the superiority of Mary's contemplative vocation over Martha's active vocation is adduced by writers such as the *Cloud*-author at least partly as a pre-emptive salvo against those unreconstructedly materialist souls who must have existed even in a society saturated with Catholic religion, and no doubt even in monasteries.[52] Against such unspiritual brutes *The Cloud of Unknowing* as a whole implicitly asserts that far from being a retreat into a state of complete vacuousness where the individual need have no concern with particulars of any kind whatsoever, the pursuit of contemplative perfection involves a finely-tuned praxis of its own.

The grace of God is understood by Julian to work during 'the tyme of this life' (52.81) in the soul, effecting the individual's redemption and sanctification. But she also understands that there is a work of co-operation on the part of the individual whereby the work of God is facilitated. Prayer and good living constitute the form this co-operation takes: 'it plesyth hym that we werkyn and in our prayors . . . and good levyng' (41.57). The stipulation here – 'prayors . . . and good levyng' – seems quite general, and could be taken as referring to Christians in any walk of life. There is certainly a sense in which the text does intend such a general application. But the intensely and self-consciously devotional tone of the text, quite apart from its demanding theological loftiness, seems to indicate a more immediate, and more commitedly devout audience: individuals for whom, whether or not because of formal religious commitment, the practice of prayer and the (self-)conscious search for God would be a dominant feature of their life. Whilst, as we have already mentioned, Julian's text is not a formal treatise on the spiritual life, it is clear that for her and for her immediate audience, as for the *Cloud*-author, the matter of how best to dispose oneself in the search for God is very much a practical question.

One perenially significant aspect of spiritual praxis as derived from the ascetical-monastic tradition, and very much implicit in Julian, is the question of discretion. We have already considered something of the nature of discretion in relation to the function of practical reasoning in the spiritual life.[53] Discretion is practical reason put at the service of faith, and as such it needs to be correctly informed by true knowledge of good and evil. It can be said to have two forms, diagnostic and strategic.

---

[52] On Martha and Mary as representing active life and contemplative life respectively, see *Cloud of Unknowing*, chs. 17–23, pp. 26–32; and also *Ancrene Wisse*, ed. J. R. R. Tolkien with an introduction by N. R. Ker, EETS, o.s., 249 (London, 1962), Part VIII, pp. 211–12.

[53] See Chapter 1, n. 39, above.

In its diagnostic form it involves the individual's being alert to all influences (emotional, intellectual, moral, spiritual, and others) that impinge on his or her sensibility and assessing them as to their admissibility in view of the desired end of complete union with God. In the strategic form, discretion marshals the resources of practical reason to respond in an appropriate manner to all influences, especially temptations to sin. Both these forms of discretion are evident, for example, in Julian's advice concerning how best to deal with thoughts of other people's sins as these arise during time given to prayer. She not only asserts the spiritual undesirability of this state of affairs but recommends practical strategy by which these importunate thoughts might themselves be assimilated to the act of prayer:

> The soule that will be in rest , whan other mannys synne commith [G: to mynde], he shall fleen it as the peyne of helle, seking into God for remedy, for helpe [G: agayne] it; for the beholdyng of mannys synnes, it makith as it were a thick myst aforne the eye of the soule, and we may not for the tyme se the fairhede of God, but if we may beholden hem with contrition with him, with compassion on him and with holy desire to God for hem; for withouten this it noyeth and tempestith and lettith the soule that beholdith hem . . . (76.122)

Proper discretion operates through practical reason enlightened by sound moral and spiritual principles, and the sphere and cause of its operation is precisely a consciousness darkened by sin. This is what makes it necessary:

> The heyest bliss that is, is to have him in cleerty of endless life, him verily seand, him swetely feland, all perfectly haveand in fulhede of ioy . . . I saw that synne is most contrarie so ferforth that as long as we be medled with ony part of synne we shall never see cleerly the blissfull cheere of our lord. And the horibler and the greivouser that our synnes bene, the deeper are we for that time fro this blisfull syte. (72.115)

Towards the end of the text, after she has narrated her own lapse of faith and subsequent confirmation in the truth of all she has seen, Julian turns to the question of how those who are to be saved should deal with the inevitable problem of continuing sin and temptation:

> But now behovith me to tellen in what manner I saw synne in the creatures which shall not dyen for synne, but liven in the ioy of God without end. (72.115)

The fact that this particular focus on the practicalities of a devout life comes at the end of the text when the showings themselves have all been narrated suggests strongly that Julian understands the revelation as a whole to be orientated to this practical and pastoral end.

The obscurity caused by sin is the premise of Julian's concern for the vicissitudes of the spiritual life, as the immediately subsequent chapters show (subsequent to Chapter 72, quoted above). This obscurity has been represented by that of the servant in the slade who 'cowde not turne his face to loke upon his loving lorde, which was to hym ful nere' (51.72). Significantly, Julian describes the blindness of the servant as a 'faylyng of comforte', and refers to the lord whom the servant cannot see as the one 'in whom is ful comfort'. She has said in Chapter 8 that the showings were given 'in comfort of vs al' (8.13) and that those who encounter the text should be 'truly taught', with the aim that they might 'love God the better' (9.13). When we recall that the revelation/text is given 'for ese and comfort', we can all the more read the servant in the slade as a figure for the reader who, with a mind obscured by sin, is in need of just the kind of energizing reassurance that the servant lacks. In its rhetorical and provisional way, the text seeks to dispel the cognitive darkness by providing theological grounds for hope and confidence. Julian's conviction of the certainty of this comfort informs the pastoral thrust of the latter part of the text, so that whatever she says about the vicissitudes and temptations afflicting the devout person, there is always the implicit assurance of 'suernesse of kepyng' (CW 443.13). In this context of the unbreakable love of God for each individual, and for the Church as a whole, she is able to broach freely some of the more negative aspects of the life of faith.

Fear and Love

We have noted that, according to Julian, the fundamental debilitating factor in a person's relationship with God is the obfuscation of the divine light by sin and its effects. This induces a degree of cognitive failure which Julian defines quite specifically as 'onknoweing of love' (73.117). In considering the actual effects of this 'onknoweing' as experienced by individuals, it is striking that Julian does not share with other religious writers of the period a relish for taxonomies of sin and virtue (though her taxonomy of types of dread, given in Chapter 74 and discussed below, should be cited here as the exception). Just to give one example, there is no mention of the seven deadly sins as a distinct category of offence, and certainly no didactic trawling through each of these sins in turn such as we find in many late medieval devotional works.[54] Although Julian does

---

[54] For example, the seven deadly sins are considered at length by Walter Hilton in *Scale* I, chs. 52–76, pp. 123–49; and by the *Cloud*-author in *Cloud of Unknowing*,

speak of 'synne dedly' (72.115), the phrase seems intended in a general sense, self-consciously so in view of the fact that she does not adduce the technical connotations attachable to the phrase in the context of contemporary moral and penitential theory.[55] The phrase here seems more to denote 'al that is not good' (27.38). If there are discrete 'deadly sins', they proceed from a prior condition of sinfulness, of separation from God and 'onknoweing of love'.

Despite this, Julian is too much of a realist, and too pastorally-orientated, not to give concrete, particularized expression to the matter of sin. She avoids a multiplication of distinctions and definitions by focusing the whole universe of potential temptations and sins through her description of just two fundamentally deleterious attitudes:

> God shewid ii manner of sekenes that we have: that on is impatience or slaith, for we bere our trevell and our pey[n]es hevily; that other is despeir or doubtfull drede, as I shall seyen after. Generally he shewid synne wherin that all is comprehendid, but in special he shewid not but thes two. (73.117)

As the whole law, according to the gospels, is summed up in the love of God and neighbour,[56] so for Julian the whole problem of sin, practically speaking, can be summed up in 'ii manner of sekenes': impatience and doubtful dread. Furthermore, as Chapter 73 continues, the problem of impatience is elided into that of doubtful dread so that the latter is identified by implication as the primary sickness, the former deriving from it. The 'onknoweing of love' spawns doubtful dread. This in turn demoralizes the individual, especially when dredged-up memories of 'synnes aforn don' (73.118) make him or her so 'sorry and . . . hevy' that 'listiness', the supple and eager responsiveness of spirit regarded as so important by the *Cloud*-author, becomes impossible.[57] Doubtful dread does not supply energy, it saps it. This dread, which is synonymous for Julian with despair, is the fear that plagues one who is not assured of grounds for hope and confidence in God, but feels only God's judgement or his absence. Since this kind of fear attacks the very root of the spiritual life in that it calls the love of God into question, Julian devotes a substantial chapter to a consideration of different kinds of fear in an attempt to give her audience clear, concise guidance in a crucial (the *most*

---

ch. 10, p. 20, lines 13–36. See also the 'confession' of the (personified) deadly sins in *Piers Plowman*, Passus V, pp. 58–60.

[55] Eamon Duffy gives an account of a fifteenth century manual of instruction about confession (aimed at parish clergy); the manual focuses especially on the seven deadly sins. See *Stripping of the Altars*, pp. 58–60.

[56] Matthew 22:37–40.

[57] See *Cloud of Unknowing*, Prologue, p. 5, line 11.

crucial) area. The taxonomic character of Chapter 74 introduces an overtly didactic note that jars somewhat with the immediate context at this point in the text, and this inevitably draws our attention to the fact that the chapter has been substantially lifted from the concluding chapter of the Short Text.[58] This strongly suggests that Julian herself regards her identification of the 'iiii maner dreds' (74.118) as being close to the heart of the essential message of the revelation as such, and therefore of considerable pastoral significance. The didactic tone also confirms in our minds Julian's belief in the importance of precise and true knowledge as an effective antidote to the obfuscations of sinfulness.

The four dreads are as follows: 'drede of afray' (74.118); 'drede of peyne'; doubtfull drede' (74.119) and 'reverent drede'. The first two forms of dread Julian takes to be admissible, indeed beneficial, in appropriate circumstances. Dread of 'afray' (loosely speaking, of attack) 'helpith to purge man' (78.118). We might say it keeps people on their toes, alert to danger, and thus is quite proper to their vulnerable, sensual condition. The second dread, of 'peyne', includes fear of bodily suffering, fear of death and fear of 'gostly enemyes' (74.119). In the Short Text this dread also includes a fear of 'the fyre of purgatory' (CW 276.8). Surprisingly, Julian does not explicitly include the fear of *hell* in this category, despite the fact that convention would unblushingly affirm this fear as a legitimate and salutary goad to good living, indeed the most obvious goad of all.[59] This suggests that she understands herself to be preaching to the converted, to devout people who are sufficiently rooted in their religious commitment no longer to require threats of hell-fire as their motivation. Such tactics might be saved for the retrograde, the half-hearted and the downright impious. In fact Julian seems to draw attention in Chapter 76 to her omission from Chapter 74 of any reference to the fear of hell, and in such a way as to confirm the impression that she is writing more to inspire the devout than to put the wind up the unreconstructed. She states that the soul despises the 'vilehede and horribilite' (76.122) of sin more than 'all the peyne that is in hell' and indeed accounts sin itself as the true hell: ' the soule that beholdith the kindenes of our lord Iesus, it hatith non helle but synne' (76.122). It is surely only the assumption of a devout, spiritually 'advanced' readership – souls 'that beholdith the kindenes of our lord Iesus' – that allows Julian the liberty of a distinctly spiritual, as opposed to a more or less material, understanding of hell.

Julian has already dealt with 'doubtfulle drede' (74.119), which is her third category. Of the four dreads, this alone is never appropriate in a Christian context and is to be unequivocally rejected, since 'it may never

---

[58] ST chapter xxv, CW 276–8.
[59] On the torments of hell, see, for example, *Orcherd of Syon*, pp. 88–90; and on the fear of purgatory, see Duffy, *Stripping of the Altars*, pp. 343–57.

plesyn our lord that his servants douten his goodnes'. The fourth category, 'reverent drede', is the equivalent of the biblical 'fear of the Lord', *timor domini*:

> The fear of the lord is the beginning of wisdom ... To fear God is the fulness of wisdom ... The fear of the Lord is a crown of wisdom, filling up peace and the fruit of salvation.[60]

The *timor domini* theme is central to the primitive monastic tradition that finds expression in the *Rule of St Benedict*;[61] and is subsequently of great importance to the later monastic tradition represented most clearly by the twelfth century Cistercians, notably Bernard of Clairvaux[62] and William of St Thierry.[63] In the fourteenth century it is taken up by the *Cloud-author*, among others, in his treatise, *The Epistle of Prayer*, which shows the strong influence of Bernard.[64] In her own identification of 'reverent drede' (74.119) as the only kind of dread 'that fully plesith God in us', Julian affirms her conscious connection with a particular spiritual tradition. This becomes even clearer when we consider the relation she adduces between dread and *love*. According to the Bernardine paradigm, servile fear of God, which is proper to the fallen creature, is transmuted through love (in the form of God's grace) into filial awe, which is really a mingling of reverence and love.[65] All this is found in Chapter 74, if we think of doubtful dread as servile fear:

> Doutfull drede, in as mech as it drawith to dispeir, God will have it turnyd in us into love be the knowyng of love; that is to sey, that the bitternes of doubt be turnyd in us into sweteness of kinde love be grace ... (74.119)

In its coupling with dread in this chapter, love denotes homeliness and familiarity, and all that goes with these – trust, informality, ease, playfulness. Reverent dread on the other hand denotes awe and courtesy.

---

[60] Sirach [Ecclesiasticus] 1:16, 20 and 22.
[61] Benedict's first step of humility is 'that a man keeps the fear of God always before his eyes' ['primus itaque humilitatis gradus est si, *timorem Dei* sibi *ante oculos* semper ponens', italics as given in text, denoting scriptural allusion], *Rule*, ch. 7, pp. 192–3.
[62] On the *timor domini* theme in Bernard, see Gilson, *Mystical Theology*, especially pp. 65–6 and 136–7.
[63] See *Golden Epistle*, p. 29, paras. 50–1.
[64] See *The Epistle of Prayer* in *Cloud of Unknowing*, pp. 101–7; and for more on Bernard's influence, see Hodgson's remarks on this treatise, pp. 182–4.
[65] Gilson writes (with Bernard in mind): 'Transfiguring fear and cupidity, it [love] leaves the soul free to pass beyond them. Fear is then no longer terror, but rather this profound reverence for the thing that it loves, which accords the loved object all its worth and makes it only the more desirable', *Mystical Theology*, pp. 112–13.

It partly suggests the creature's 'tremeland and quakand' (75.121) in the presence of the divine Other. But it is also the instinctive courtesy of love taken to the nth power. It involves an acute sensitivity by which the individual literally *dreads* to cause injury to God; and so, as we have seen, the soul 'hatith more synne . . . than it doth all the peyne that is in hell' (76.122). Such courtesy respects precisely the otherness of the beloved, and does not casually presume on the relationship.

> And thus we shall in love be homley and nere to God; and we shall in drede be gentil and curtes to God

In a medieval context, courtesy is specifically associated with high social status. It is not courtesy that inferiors owe to their superiors but obeisance; and yet superiors retain a right of gratuitous condescension whereby they might show courtesy to an inferior as a mark of particular honour.[66] So, in saying here that human beings ought to be 'gentil and curtes' to God, Julian is placing them in a sense on his level, and maybe higher; and putting him, in a sense, at their mercy. In this way she seems implicitly to characterize God not so much as omnipotent and majestic, and therefore to be feared on that account; but as strangely vulnerable, and needful of consideration (is this not what the crucifix has taught her?).

Dread (awe/courtesy) and love (homeliness/familiarity) are both finally subsumed into *caritas*, love in its deepest and widest religious sense. Julian, therefore, is not describing the potentially conflicting operations of differing attitudes within one individual, as though an individual might constantly be switching from familiarity with God to reverence towards him. Rather, these attitudes can be said to coinhere in the integral, mature love of the spiritual subject. As we have seen, the Virgin Mary is the model of human interiority and spiritual maturity. Being the biological mother of Christ she is the embodiment par excellence of 'homely loveing' (5.7), yet Julian notes specifically, and with emphasis, Mary's 'reverend beholding' (4.6) of God and her 'mervelyng with greate reverence that he would be borne of hir'.

Julian's pastoral intention is discreet but unmistakeable. Her concern for interiorized religion finally and crucially expresses itself as a concern for the ups and downs – and the quite special practicalities – of the spiritual life as experienced by actual individuals. Prayer is a real activity that takes up time and energy. It expresses precisely the longing for God of one who is separated from him through sin. Because of sin the individual can become disheartened and enervated, so that reassurance is needed that the whole enterprise is worthwhile. In Julian's text this reassurance takes

---

[66] See Julian's Chapter 24 (p. 35) for her experience of Christ's particular courtesy towards herself.

the form of an emphatic confirmation of that knowledge of the love of God which the individual is understood to possess already by virtue of his or her assent to Christian doctrine. More specifically, there is the reassurance that prayer itself is the work of God in the soul.

Nevertheless, despite such reassurances, the obfuscations of sinfulness are inescapable in this life. The individual is in need of help to make the appropriate response. Here rationality is crucial, but rationality in the form of discretion. Discretion, as we have noted, is both diagnostic and strategic. It enables sound interpretation of all the data being presented to the individual, whether from within or without, and knows what to accept and what to reject. A clear sense of the divinely underwritten shape of the spiritual quest and of the goal to which its whole praxis is orientated is the touchstone of discretion, as well as being an indispensable source of confidence. It is this clear sense of shape and goal, this teleology uniting the practical and the transcendent, that defines the intrinsically pastoral character of Julian's text. Her final chapter confirms this:

> and in the swete words wher he seith full merrily 'I am ground of thi beseking' . . . trewly I saw and vnderstode in our lords mening that he shewid it for he will have it knowen more than it is, in which he will give us grace to loven him and clevyn to him . . .

> Thus was I lerid that love was our lords meaning. And I saw full sekirly in this and in all, that ere God made us he lovid us; which love was never slakid, no never shall. And in this love he hath done all his werke; and in this love he hath made all things profitable to us; and in this love our life is everlastand. In our making we had beginning; but the love wherin he made us was in him from withoute begynnyng; in which love we have our beginning. And all this shall be seen in God without end; which Ihesus mot grant us. Amen. (86.134–5)

In the 'slade' of this world and the 'tyme of this life', this is exactly what the Christian needs to know. Furthermore, and crucially, in the light of this knowledge anyone's experience of the actualities and practicalities of faith might organize itself into a potentially shareable, paradigmatic theological narrative. A belief in the possibility of making a theological interpretation of actual experience is the informing dynamic of Julian's text in its pastoral dimension; and in a larger sense, of her total religious and authorial project.

CONCLUSION

In the course of this book we have examined Julian and her writing under a number of ostensibly quite diverse aspects.

We have considered Julian as a narrator of her personal experience, as one who makes a coherent story out of her own past and proposes that story to her presumed audience of fellow Christians as a medium of authentic and compelling religious truth. In the central two chapters of the book we have examined what is central to Julian both humanly and authorially: a distinctively incarnational theology that comes in a striking way to posit the individual person, by virtue of his or her participation in the primary humanity of Christ, as irreducibly and integrally a sphere of active divine mystery. The theme of Christ the mother, in its intricacy and subtlety, and not least in its consistency, gives remarkably bold expression to the intimate reality of that christological bond – understood at the natural as well as the supernatural level – which unites human beings with God. And Julian's alertness to the ecclesiological implications of her incarnational theology testifies to her concern not for the human subject as private and solitary, but for the person as mystically united in and through Christ with the entire communion of saints living and dead – 'al the blissid common' (61.100), as she puts it. In the last chapter we examined the way a certain idiom of interiority ultimately works to secure a sense of the individual's real union with God, or capaciousness for God, with the Virgin Mary, conceiver and bearer of the Word of God both physically and spiritually, as the paradigm par excellence both for the individual Christian and for the Church as a whole. Finally, we have considered the text's pastoral dimension, and the manner in which Julian's large-scale theological vision is brought to bear on the peculiar and practical needs of the devout in their day to day engagement with the divine.

It is a principal claim of this book that there is a discernible and significant continuity between each of the textual levels indicated above. There is a continuity, that is, between Julian's predicament as a visionary/autobiographical writer; the precise character of her theology as it exfoliates in response to the pressures of that predicament; and the quite practical ends to which her text as a whole directs itself. This continuity is hard to define, but it clearly involves a preoccupation with the value attachable to the person as such, and to personal experience; and in a more specific sense, with the possibility and legitimacy of making a theological and potentially shareable interpretation of experience in a

179

religio-political context where grace and truth are taken as being authoritatively and definitively mediated by the clergy.

This sends us straight back to the beginning, to the observation made in Chapter 1 of this book that in Julian's text we hear a distinct personal voice crackling down to us from the early fifteenth century; and in particular to the notion of intrinsic autobiographicality as discussed in the same chapter. Intrinsic autobiographicality implies precisely a real continuity between life and text, however uncapturable either of these might finally be in philosophical or critical terms. Authors are real people under real pressure and their DNA, so to speak, is all over their texts. This goes for Julian as for any other writer, but with a special pertinence since she has a particularly heightened concern for the irreducible reality and worth of the person as such.

The whole of Julian's text, in whatever register it is written at any given point – anecdotal, didactic, descriptive, theological, analytical, advisory – is rooted in the vulnerable soil of the author's contingent personal experience. This is most obviously the case when Julian reconstructs specific experiences by means of anecdote, but the premise of the whole text, even at its most speculative, is that the author is speaking out of the exigencies of her own real-life situation. The very range of literary skill and intellectual acumen evidenced in Julian's writing testifies to the intellectual and emotional expansion she has attained, with great effort, by 'proces of tyme' (63.103). This is, of course, especially seen in the progression from Short Text to Long Text. It seems that, as apparently with Langland, Julian has just one literary project that grows organically with her, something that becomes more or less impossible to finish and close off. The Long Text confirms this impression in its comparative freedom vis-à-vis the expected behaviour of logical discourse. Certainly Julian does pursue a precise logic in much of the text, and with a degree of subtlety which can seem at times almost to obscure its own purpose. But in amongst her carefully plotted articulations of careful thought we find an extraordinary degree of rhetorical playfulness, of a serious kind. She repeats, amplifies and alters phrases and words. She undermines the linearity of her narratives, something that can be seen particularly in the way that the anecdotal parts of the text get swamped by theological speculation. Many of her terms (such as 'kinde', 'werkyng', 'kepeing', 'fullhede', 'conceived', 'deliverid') accumulate meaning and implication as the text proceeds, so that the text's conceptual and imaginative space is expanded from within. This process is evident in what can otherwise, and certainly at first reading, seem like repetitiousness or mere wordiness. Roland Maisonneuve is right to speak of Julian's 'universe' (the 'univers visionnaire') of his title, suggestive as this is of expanding space, and of order evolving unendingly out of creative chaos. And this metaphor of expanding space emerging out of chaos might stand here as a metaphor for Julian's own life in its contiguity with the text that is her life's work.

If Julian's text might justly be considered autobiographical in the sense outlined above and in the early part of this book, it might also be understood as implying an apologia for the autobiographical, and specifically for the autobiographical as a potential sub-category of the theological. Julian not only writes about her life and proffers reflections on her experience, she does so in a specific religio-political context, as we have already noted. Such a gesture in such a context is hardly neutral or unproblematical. Julian's very attempt at communication implies, and is continuous with, a defence both of a certain estimate of the personal, and of the legitimacy of presenting personal experience and its meditated fruits as being of authentic religious significance and value to others. This book has claimed that Julian's theology unfolds substantially in response to this felt pressure. Her emphasis on the individual's ontological union with Christ as the basis of the ecclesiological union of all Christians in him has the effect of assigning real religious value to persons and to their experience whilst giving due weight to the Church. Church and individual are mystically coinherent. Thus she affirms, in the context of a distinctly mystical ecclesiology, that the person as such, in the very particularity of his or her particular life and experience, is capable of assuming a true and integral sacramentality: that is, of making Christ really present in the world. We can see this notion as symbolically expressed in the text by the image of Christ, 'a faire person and of large stature' (67.109), sitting in the soul 'even ryte in peace and rest'. From there he 'ruleth and gemeth hevyn and erth and all that is'. The image has the specific effect of affirming that the individual person, the 'soul' (meaning Julian herself in the immediate context; but by extension anyone), has an intrinsic and objective religious value that cannot be denied with impunity. Julian's own conviction in this regard is expressed in the form of the text itself. Here the potential of contingent personal experience for bearing, and indeed generating, shareable religious meanings – its potential, that is, for attaining the status of significant autobiography in a religious context – is realized in specimen form; and presented in terms of a theological vision that seeks to legitimize and underwrite the exercise. To this extent, Julian's theology contributes to, if it does not entirely define, an apologia for autobiography.

The term 'apologia' suggests a certain defensiveness, the determination to affirm something in a potentially, or an actually, hostile situation. In the earlier part of this book we noted that Julian's attempt to communicate her own experiences to fellow Christians implies a peculiar predicament that is both religious and, in the broadest sense, political. She achieves troubled singularity as the subject both of religious experience and of autobiography. Her assumption of the autobiographical 'I' is thinkable in terms of a wound sustained by her own consciousness, a consciousness that becomes, in a special and heightened way, split between 'self' and 'other(s)'. It is a wound of self-consciousness, of self-differentiation. Paradoxically, the text itself becomes an attempt to assuage this wound, to link up 'self' and 'other(s)' and so achieve some kind of reintegration.

The image exile is perhaps even more expressive in this regard. In order to achieve authorial self-consciousness Julian has to depart from the homeland of undifferentiated, communally determined and supervised identity. This experience is accompanied by a sense of loss and isolation, by grief and by a yearning for return. As an oblique but telling illustration of this we may cite Julian's own images of isolation and yearning: the servant in the slade (Chapter 51) and the abandoned Christ weeping in the human soul (Chapters 79 and 80); and also Julian's deep sense of *home*: of God as humanity's 'kindly stede' (60.97) and of God's making in human being 'his homeliest home and his endles wonyng' (67.110). The fundamental dynamism out of which the text is generated seems to derive from the tension between her yearning for home and the interior imperative not to deny her own visionary and religious integrity. So the tension between self and other(s) is also readable as a tension within or of the self.

But the images of woundedness and exile suggest precariousness and vulnerability, and we should be wary about regarding Julian's yearning for healing and homecoming as being uncomplicatedly fulfilled by the text. In concluding this book, certain important qualifications must be made of its broad claims, specifically with reference to some of the implications of writing as such, and of Julian's aspirations and anxieties precisely as a writer. The very act of literary communication implies the persistence of a gap between writer and audience, between self and other. The separateness implicit in Julian's authorial subjectivity means that she cannot obliterate the gap between herself and her audience. Her writing points to and, in an important sense, sustains this gap. But she can and does seek to engage the other through the text. This attempted engagement is at once exercise of her achieved subjectivity; a summons to the latent subjectivity of the reader; and a plea for the plausibility of a conceptual world in which this kind of achieved subjectivity, this self-awareness in relationship, is viable without admixture of guilt.

Julian's mode of engagement is rhetorical, in the broad sense (and arguably also in the technical sense). In making her private experience public, Julian is subject to the exigencies of rhetoric, to its liabilities as well as its possibilities. On the positive side, she can use language to persuade her audience to a particular response, namely the acceptance of the real link her text proposes between the theological and the personal; and she might be more or less successful in this respect. But on the negative side, rhetoric cannot securely underwrite such a link between the theological and the personal, nor can it in any sense necessitate the desired response in the reader. The relation between Julian and her audience, of which her text is the occasion and the sign, has this intrinsic insecurity.

The theological rationale Julian adduces to affirm simultaneously the unique value and the genuinely paradigmatic nature of her personal experience is, like 'thought' in an untitled poem by R. S. Thomas, 'held fast by the horns,/a sacrifice to language'. To quote the relevant verse in full:

> The way the brain resembles
> a wood, impenetrable thicket
> in which thought is held fast by the horns,
> a sacrifice to language.[1]

Thomas clearly has in mind here the story of Abraham's near-sacrificing of his son Isaac as told in Genesis 22. At the last moment, as the knife is being raised, the angel of the Lord commands Abraham instead to slay a ram that is caught in a thicket nearby.[2] Abraham, of course, is the Old Testament type of faith.[3] It is only faith, the poet implies, that delivers thought (the mind, the self) from its slavery to language; but the price is of thought's immolation as sacrifice to God. Similarly, we might say that readers cannot disentangle Julian's theological apologia for autobiography from its own rhetoric, except perhaps by a movement analogous to faith that does not itself depend on the rhetorical, and which therefore transcends the text. This movement of 'faith', this decision to accept and trust Julian, and the link she makes between theology and the personal, might be inspired by rhetoric, but rhetoric does not produce or secure it. Julian's whole project is therefore fraught with the risk that the hoped-for response will not be given, that the home-comer will be neither recognized nor welcomed. It seems fitting that a text so concerned for the personal should hang for acceptance on the contingency of a personal decision.

Such contingency is intrinsic to rhetoric, and to the relationships engendered and signified, whether actually or presumptively, by rhetorical acts. This is because contingency is intrinsic to the kind of world in which rhetoric must operate. The finished literary product may seem in one sense unassailably an artefact: fixed, dead. But this 'deadness' might be reimagined as the silence that follows the asking of a question: the givenness of a text, of a work of art, is readable as its silent expectation of a

---

[1] R. S. Thomas, *Counterpoint* (Newcastle upon Tyne, 1990), p. 43.
[2] Genesis 22:1–3.
[3] See Galations 3:6–9; and Hebrews 11:8–12.

response. This orientation of the rhetorical and the artistic to the hoped-for response of the irreducible human other implies a world both fractured and dynamic. It is a world in which relations between human beings – not least between writer/artist and audience – are both haunted and motivated by a sense of the incommensurability of persons. With the writer this is further complicated by an acute, but potentially creative, anxiety about the incommensurability of experience and language.

As a creative but uncertain exercise, the making of a text can thought of as belonging very much in the kind of conceptual universe constructed and proposed by Julian herself. Whilst her text seeks to adduce a credible theological rationale for its own would-be status as religiously-significant autobiography, in the process of doing so it puts forward, as we have seen, a peculiarly dynamic vision of life lived by ordinary mortals in space-time. This embodied life in space-time is a womb; it is provisional, but creatively so. The dynamics of growth are conveyed in terms of a dialectical tension rooted in certain disjunctions. The fundamental disjunction is that experienced within the structure of human nature itself: the alienation of sensuality from substance. Various other disjunctions and tensions are implied by this primal bifurcation and can be expressed in binary terms, thus: sin and mercy, 'wele and wo' (52.81), dying and rising, death and birth, desert and city, isolation and union. Yet it would be wrong to speak of binary *oppositions* here; indeed that would be to miss the point completely. All the negative terms can be understood as being comprehended in the term 'sin': 'in this nakid word "synne" our lord browte to my mynd generally al that is not good' (27.38). Yet sin is 'behovabil'. It has been converted into a dialectical term, the negative charge of the divine energy operative within the processes of human growth towards spiritual maturity:

> for wickidnes hath ben suffrid to rysen contrarye to the goodnes, and the goodnes of mercy and grace contraried ageyn the wickednes, and turnyd al to goodness and to worship to al these that shal be savid; for it is the properte in God which doith good agen evil. (59.95)

For the 'time of this life' the process of growth continues apace and any apparent achievement of settled virtue, insight, self-awareness or even identity is an illusion. Wickedness, or pain, will always in some form 'be suffrid to rysen contrarye to the goodnes'; and, more positively, beholding will always stimulate further seeking.

Like prayer, the text is a 'wittnes' (43.60). It testifies to Julian's desire for completeness of union between God, herself and her fellow Christians. As with prayer, the fulfilment of this desire is deferred to a transcendent, eschatological future:

yet may we never stint of morning nor of weeping ne of longyng til whan we see him cleerly in his blissful chere; for in that pretious, blisful syte [sight? city? both?] there may no wo abiden ne no wele faillen.

(72.116)

Both rhetoric and prayer express a tension towards the 'other' that never definitively resolves itself within space-time. Julian's sense of the dynamism of the mundane and human context perhaps explains why we can detect a certain restlessness in the fact, as noted, previously, that she seems to have a deep resistance to closure.[4] Not only do we have the witness of the relation between Long Text and Short Text, there is also the tantalizing suggestion that Julian envisaged – perhaps was already undertaking – further revision:

This book is begunne be Gods gift and his grace, but it is not yet performid, as to my syte. (86.134)

Julian's apparent reluctance to claim finality for this version of her text has further implications. If it is suggestive of the provisionality of the text as a literary artefact (quite apart from its vulnerability in relation to an audience, as discussed above), it also indicates the provisional nature of any theological interpretations which might be made of personal experience; that is, the provisional nature of precisely the kind of interpretations we have understood as being implicitly pleaded for by the text. In Julian's world, 'achieved subjectivity' is not an attainment of stasis, an apotheosis of the controlling ego. Rather, it implies a mature freedom for dynamic relationship, for an authentically personal communion with God and others which would itself necessarily preclude closure in any sense. In view of this it is easy to see why images of pregnancy and childbirth come so readily to her mind. They suggest openings and possibilities, the freedom of the children of God always to begin again without end:

And than shall the bliss of our moder in Criste be new to begynnen in the ioyes of our God; which new begynnyng shal lesten without end, new begynnand. (63.104)

---

[4] On Julian's resistance to textual closure, see Nolan, *Cry Out and Write*, pp. 137–203.

BIBLIOGRAPHY

Unless otherwise stated, all biblical quotations in English are from the Douay/Rheims version of the Bible, reprint (London, 1956). I have occasionally used the Revised Standard Version [RSV], as given in *The New Oxford Annotated Bible with the Apocrypha*, expanded edition (New York, 1977). The Latin Vulgate is cited from *Biblia Sacra Juxta Vulgatam Clementinam* (Rome, 1947).

PRIMARY SOURCES

(a) Julian of Norwich

Julian of Norwich, *A Revelation of Love*, ed. Marion Glasscoe, revised edition (Exeter, 1993).
A Book of Showings to the Anchoress Julian of Norwich, ed. Edmund Colledge and James Walsh, 2 volumes (Toronto, 1978).
The Shewings of Julian of Norwich, ed. Georgina Ronan Crampton (Kalamazoo, Michigan, 1993).

(b) Primary Sources Other than Julian of Norwich

Aelred of Rievaulx's De Institutione Inclusarum, ed. John Ayto and Alexandra Barratt, EETS, o.s., 287 (Oxford, 1984).
——*Mirror of Charity [Speculum Caritatis]*, trans. Elizabeth Connor, with introduction and notes by Charles Dumont (Kalamazoo, Michigan, 1990).
Ancrene Wisse, ed. J. R. R. Tolkien, with an introduction by N. R. Ker, EETS o.s., 249 (London, 1962)
——*Ancrene Wisse: Parts Six and Seven* ed. Geoffrey Shepherd, revised edition (Exeter, 1985).
Aquinas, Thomas, *Summa Theolgiae*, condensed and trans. Timothy McDermott, paperback edition (London, 1992).
Aristotle, *De Anima*, trans. Hugh Lawson-Tancred (Harmondsworth, 1986).
Augustine, *Confessiones* [critical Latin text], ed. Martin Skutella (Stuttgart, 1981).
——*Confessions*, trans. Henry Chadwick (Oxford, 1991).
——*Enchiridion*, trans. Ernest Evans (London, 1953).
——*Augustine: Later Writings*, trans. John Burnaby (London, 1955).
Bernard of Clairvaux, *S. Bernardi Opera I, Sermones Super Cantica Canticorum*, ed. J. Leclercq, C. H. Talbot and H. M. Rochais (Rome, 1957).
——*On the Song of Songs I, 2*, trans. Kilian Walsh (Kalamazoo, Michigan, 1981).

Bernard of Clairvaux, *On the Song of Songs III*, trans. Kilian Walsh and Irene M. Edmonds (Kalamazoo, Michigan, 1979).

Boethius, *The Consolation of Philosophy*, trans. V. E. Watts (Harmondsworth, 1969).

The Liber Celestis of Bridget of Sweden I, ed. Roger Ellis, EETS, o.s., 291 (Oxford, 1987).

Chaucer, Geoffrey, *The Riverside Chaucer*, ed. Larry D. Benson et al., third edition (Boston, 1987).

The Cloud of Unknowing and related treatises, ed. Phyllis Hodgson (Salzburg, 1982).

Deonise Hid Diuinite, ed. Phyllis Hodgson, EETS, o.s., 231 (London, 1955).

Dante Alighieri, *The Divine Comedy* [Italian text with facing translation] ed. Charles S. Singleton, 6 volumes including commentary, paperback reprint (Princeton, New Jersey, 1989).

Dickens, Charles, *David Copperfield*, ed. Trevor Blount, reprint (Harmondsworth, 1985).

Eliot, George, *Middlemarch*, ed. W. J. Harvey, reprint (Harmondsworth, 1983).

English Medieval Religious Lyrics, ed. Douglas Gray, revised edition (Exter, 1992).

English Mystery Plays, ed. Peter Happé, reprint (Harmonsdworth, 1985).

Geoffrey of Vinsauf, *Poetria Nova*, trans. M. F. Nims (Toronto, 1967).

Hilton, Walter, *The Scale of Perfection*, ed. and trans. John P. H. Clark and Rosemary Dorward (Mahwah, New Jersey, 1991).

The Book of Margery Kempe, ed. Sanford Brown Meech, with prefatory note by Hope Emily Allen, EETS, o.s., 212 (London, 1940).

Søren Kierkegaard, *The Sickness Unto Death*, trans. Alastair Hannay (Harmondsworth, 1989).

Langland, William, *The Vision of Piers Plowman*, ed. A. V. C. Schmidt, corrected and revised reprint (London, 1984).

Medieval English Prose for Women: Selections from the Katherine Group and Ancrene Wisse, ed. Bella Millett and Jocelyn Wogan-Browne, paperback edition (Oxford, 1992).

The Orcherd of Syon I, ed. Phyllis Hodgson and Gabriel M. Leigey, EETS, o.s., 258 (London, 1966).

Pearl, Cleanness, Patience and Sir Gawain and the Green Knight, ed. A. C. Cawley and J. J. Anderson (London, 1976).

Richard of St Victor, *The Twelve Patriarchs, the Mystical Ark, Book Three of the Trinity* [respectively, *Benjamin minor*, *Benjamin major* and *De Trinitate*], trans. Grover A. Zinn (New York and London, 1979).

Rolle, Richard, *Prose and Verse*, ed. S. J. Ogilvie-Thomson, EETS, o.s., 293 (Oxford, 1988).

The Rule of St Benedict, ed. Timothy Fry et al. (Collegeville, Minnesota, 1981).

Selections from English Wycliffite Writings, ed. Anne Hudson (Cambridge, 1978).

Thomas, R. S., *Counterpoint* (Newcastle upon Tyne, 1990).

William of St Thierry, *The Golden Epistle*, trans. Theodore Berkeley with an introduction by J. M. Déchanet (Kalamazoo, Michigan, 1980).

Women Defamed and Women Defended: An Anthology of Medieval Texts, ed. Alcuin Blamires (Oxford, 1992).

II. SECONDARY SOURCES

(a) *Julian of Norwich*

Abbott, Christopher, 'Piety and Egoism in Julian of Norwich: A Reading of Long Text Chapters 2 and 3', *Downside Review*, 114 (1996), pp. 267–82.

——— 'His Body, the Church: Julian of Norwich's Vision of Christ Crucified', *Downside Review*, 115 (1997), pp. 1–22.

Baker, Denise Nowakowski, *Julian of Norwich's Showings: From Vision to Book* (Princeton, New Jersey, 1994).

——— 'Julian of Norwich and Anchoritic Literature', *Mystics Quarterly*, 19 (1993), pp. 148–60.

Barker, Paula S. Datsko, 'The Motherhood of God in Julian of Norwich's Theology', *Downside Review*, 100 (1982), pp. 290–304.

Baldwin, Anna P., 'The Triumph of Patience in Julian of Norwich and Langland', in ed. Helen Phillips, *Langland, the Mystics and the Medieval Religious Tradition: Essays in Honour of S. S. Hussey* (Cambridge, 1990), pp. 71–83.

Benedicta, Sister, 'Julian the Solitary', in Kenneth Leech and Sister Benedicta, *Julian Reconsidered* (Fairacres, Oxford, 1988), pp. 11–31.

Bradley, Ritamary, *Julian's Way: A Practical Commentary on Julian of Norwich* (London, 1992).

——— 'Patristic Background of the Motherhood Similitude in Julian of Norwich', *Christian Scholar's Review*, 8 (1978), pp. 101–13.

——— 'Christ the Teacher in Julian's *Showings*: the Biblical and Patristic Traditions', in *MMTE* (Exeter, 1982), 127–42.

——— 'Perception of Self in Julian of Norwich's *Showings*', *Downside Review*, 104 (1986), pp. 227–39.

——— 'Julian on Prayer', in ed. Lillian Thomas Shanks and John A. Nichols, *Medieval Religious Women. Volume Two: Peaceweavers* (Kalamazoo, Michigan, 1987), pp. 291–304.

——— 'The Goodness of God: A Julian Study', in ed. Phillips, *Langland, the Mystics and the Medieval Religious Tradition*, pp. 85–95.

Clark, J. P. H., '*Fiducia* in Julian of Norwich, I', *Downside Review*, 99 (1981), pp. 97–108.

——— '*Fiducia* in Julian of Norwich, II', *Downside Review*, 99 (1981), pp. 214–29.

——— 'Predestination in Christ according to Julian of Norwich', *Downside Review*, 100 (1982), pp. 79–91.

——— 'Nature, Grace and the Trinity in Julian of Norwich', *Downside Review*, 100 (1982), pp. 203–20.

——— 'Time and Eternity in Julian of Norwich', *Downside Review*, 109 (1991), pp. 259–76.

Cummings, Charles, 'The Motherhood of God according to Julian of

Norwich', in ed. Shanks and Nichols, *Medieval Religious Women. Vol Two*, pp. 305–14.

Davies, Oliver, 'Transformational Processes in the Work of Julian of Norwich and Mechtild of Magdeburg', in *MMTE: V* (Cambridge, 1992), pp. 39–52.

Gillespie, Vincent and Ross, Maggie, 'The Apophatic Image: The Poetics of Self-Effacement in Julian of Norwich', in *MMTE: V*, pp. 53–77.

Glasscoe, Marion (ed.), *MMTE* (Exeter, 1980).

———(ed.), *MMTE* (Exeter, 1982).

———(ed.), *MMTE: V* (Cambridge, 1992).

———'Visions and Revisions: A Further Look at the Manuscripts of Julian of Norwich', *Studies in Bibliography*, 42 (1989), pp. 103–20.

———'Time of Passion: Latent Relationships between Liturgy and Meditation in Two Middle English Mystics [Julian of Norwich and Richard Rolle]', in ed. Phillips, *Langland, the Mystics and the Medieval Religious Tradition*, pp. 141–60.

Hanshell, Deryck, 'A Crux in the Interpretation of Dame Julian', *Downside Review*, 92 (1974), pp. 77–91.

Heimmel, Jennifer, *'God Is Our Mother': Julian of Norwich and the Medieval Image of Christian Feminine Deity* (Salzburg, 1982).

Jantzen, Grace, *Julian of Norwich: Mystic and Theologian* (London, 1987).

Johnson, Lynn Staley, 'The Trope of the Scribe and the Question of Literary Authority in the Works of Julian of Norwich and Margery Kempe', *Speculum*, 66 (1991), pp. 820–38.

Lagorio, Valerie, 'Variations on the Theme of God's Motherhood in Medieval English Mystical and Devotional Writings', *Studia Mystica*, 8 (1985), pp. 15–37.

Lang, Judith, ' "The Godly Wylle" in Julian of Norwich', *Downside Review*, 102 (1984), pp. 163–73.

Lichtmann, Maria, R., ' "I desyrede a bodylye syght": Julian of Norwich and the Body', *Mystics Quarterly*, 17 (1991), pp. 12–19.

Lorenzo, Bernadette (trans. Yvette Le Guillou), 'The Mystical Experience of Julian of Norwich with reference to the Epistle to the Hebrews (ch. xi): Semiotic and Psychoanalytic Analysis', in *MMTE* (Exeter, 1982), pp. 161–81.

Maisonneuve, Roland, *L'univers visionnaire de Julian of Norwich* (Paris, 1987).

McIlwain, James T., 'The "Bodelye syeknes" of Julian of Norwich', *Journal of Medieval History*, 10 (1984), pp. 167–80.

Molinari, Paul, *Julian of Norwich: The Teaching of a 14th Century English Mystic* (London, 1958).

Nolcken, Christina von, 'Julian of Norwich', in ed. A. S. G. Edwards, *Middle English Prose: A Critical Guide to Major Authors and Genres* (New Brunswick, New Jersey, 1984), pp. 97–108.

Nuth, Joan M., *Wisdom's Daughter: The Theology of Julian of Norwich* (New York, 1991).

Panichelli, Debra Scott, 'Finding God in the Memory: Julian and the Loss of the Visions', *Downside Review*, 104 (1986), pp. 299–317.

Park, Tarjei, 'Reflecting Christ: The Role of the Flesh in Walter Hilton and Julian of Norwich', in *MMTE: V* (Cambridge, 1992), pp. 17–37.

Pelphrey, Brant, *Love Was His Meaning: The Theology and Mysticism of Julian of Norwich* (Salzburg, 1982).

Pezzini, Domenico, 'The Theme of the Passion in Richard Rolle and Julian of Norwich', in ed. Piero Boitani and Anna Torti, *Religion in the Poetry and Drama of the Late Middle Ages* (Cambridge, 1989), pp. 29–66.

Robertson, Elizabeth, 'Medieval Medical Views of Women and Female Spirituality in *Ancrene Wisse* and Julian of Norwich's *Showings*', in ed. Linda Lomperis and Sarah Stanbury, *Feminist Approaches to the Body in Medieval Literature* (Philadelphia, 1993), pp. 142–67.

Peters, Brad, 'The Reality of Evil within the Mystic Vision of Julian of Norwich', *Mystics Quarterly*, 13 (1987), pp. 195–202.

Ryder, Andrew, 'A Note on Julian's Visions', *Downside Review*, 96 (1978), pp. 299–304.

Watson, Nicholas, 'The Trinitarian Hermeneutic in Julian of Norwich's *Revelation of Love*', in *MMTE: V* (Cambridge, 1992), pp. 79–100.

——— 'The Composition of Julian of Norwich's *Revelation of Love*', *Speculum*, 68 (1993), pp. 637–683.

Windeatt, B., 'Julian of Norwich and Her Audience', *Review of English Studies*, New Series, XXVIII (1977), pp. 1–17.

——— 'The Art of Mystical Loving: Julian of Norwich', in *MMTE* (Exeter, 1980), pp. 47–69.

(b) Other Secondary Sources

Adamson, Sylvia, 'From empathetic deixis to empathetic narrative: stylisation and (de-)subjectivisation as processes of language change', *Transactions of the Philological Society*, 92:1 (1994), pp. 55–88.

Aston, Margaret, *Lollards and Reformers: Images and Literacy in Late Medieval Religion* (London, 1984).

Balthasar, Hans Urs von, *Mysterium Paschale* [*Theologie der Drei Tage*], trans. Aidan Nichols (Edinburgh, 1990).

Bennett, J. A. W., *Middle English Literature*, ed. Douglas Gray, paperback reprint (Oxford, 1990).

Blanchard, Marc Eli, 'The Critique of Autobiography', *Comparative Literature*, 34 (1982), pp. 97–115.

Bourquin, Guy, 'The Dynamics of the Signans in the Spiritual Quest (*Piers Plowman*, the Mystics and Religious Drama)', in *MMTE* (Exeter, 1982), pp. 182–98.

Bynum, Caroline Walker, *Jesus as Mother: Studies in the Spirituality of the High Middle Ages*, paperback edition (Los Angeles and London, 1984).

Clément, Olivier, *The Roots of Christian Mysticism: Text and commentary*, trans. Theodore Berkeley and revised by Jeremy Hummerstone (London, 1993).

Curtius, Ernst Robert, *European Literature and the Latin Middle Ages*, trans. Willard R. Trask, paperback reprint (London, 1979).

Davies, Brian, *The Thought of Thomas Aquinas*, paperback edition (Oxford, 1993).

Davies, Oliver, *God Within: The Mystical Tradition of Northern Europe* (London, 1988).

Duffy, Eamon, *The Stripping of the Altars: Traditional Religion in England 1400–1580* (New Haven and London, 1992).

Edmée, Sister, 'Bernard and Abelard', in ed. Sister Benedicta Ward, *The Influence of Saint Bernard: Anglican Essays*, with an introduction by Jean Leclercq (Fairacres, Oxford, 1976).

Edwards, A. S. G. (ed.), *Middle English Prose: A Critical Guide to Major Authors and Genres* (New Brunswick, New Jersey, 1984).

Elliott, Robert C., *The Literary Persona* (Chicago and London, 1982).

Evans, G. R., *Philosophy and Theology in the Middle Ages* (London, 1993).

——— *Augustine on Evil*, paperback edition (Cambridge, 1990).

Gellrich, Jesse M., *The Idea of the Book in the Middle Ages: Language Theory, Mythology, and Fiction*, paperback reprint (Ithaca and London, 1988).

Gillespie, Vincent, 'Postcards from the Edge: Interpreting the Ineffable in the Middle English Mystics', in ed. Piero Boitani and Anna Torti, *Interpretation: Medieval and Modern* (Cambridge, 1993), pp. 137–65.

Gilmore, Leigh, *Autobiographics: A Feminist Theory of Women's Self-Representation* (Ithaca and London, 1994).

Gilson, Etienne, *The Mystical Theology of Saint Bernard*, paperback reprint (Kalamazoo, Michigan, 1990).

Glasscoe, Marion, *English Medieval Mystics: Games of Faith* (London, 1993).

Hudson, Anne, *Lollards and Their Books* (London, 1985).

——— *The Premature Reformation: Wycliffite Texts and Lollard History* (Oxford, 1988).

Kuryluk, Ewa, *Veronica and Her Cloth* (Oxford, 1991).

Knowles, David, *The Evolution of Medieval Thought*, second edition, ed. D. E. Luscombe and C. N. L. Brooke (London, 1988).

Lambert, Malcolm, *Medieval Heresy: Popular Movements from the Gregorian Reform to the Reformation*, revised second edition with new sub-title (Oxford, 1992).

Leclercq, Jean, *The Love of Learning and the Desire for God: A Study of Monastic Culture*, trans. Catharine Misrahi, revised second edition (London, 1978).

——— *Bernard of Clairvaux and the Cistercian Spirit* (Kalamazoo, Michigan, 1976).

Le Goff, Jacques, *The Medieval Imagination* [*L'imaginaire médiéval*], trans. Arthur Goldhammer, paperback edition (Chicago and London, 1992).

Lewis, C. S., *The Discarded Image: An Introduction to Medieval and Renaissance Literature*, paperback reprint (Cambridge, 1985).

Lomperis, Linda, and Stanbury, Sarah, *Feminist Approaches to the Body in Medieval Literature* (Philadelphia, 1993).

Lossky, Vladimir, *The Mystical Theology of the Eastern Church*, paperback edition (Cambridge, 1991).

Louf, André, 'Solitudo Pluralis', in *Solitude and Communion: Papers on the Hermit Life*, ed. A. M. Allchin (Fairacres, Oxford, 1977).

Louth, Andrew, *The Origins of the Christian Mystical Tradition: From Plato to Denys*, paperback edition (Oxford, 1990).

McGinn, Bernard (ed.), *Meister Eckhart and the Beguine Mystics* (New York, 1994).

Mâle, Emile, *The Gothic Image: Religious Art in France of the Thirteenth Century*, trans. Dora Hussey, paperback reprint (New York, 1972).

Meale, Carol M. (ed.), *Women and Literature in Britain, 1150–1500* (Cambridge, 1993).

Minnis, A. J., *Medieval Theory of Authorship*, second edition (Aldershot, 1988).

Minnis, A. J. and Scott, A. B. (eds.) with the assistance of David Wallace, *Medieval Literary Theory and Criticism c.1100–c.1375: The Commentary Tradition*, revised edition (Oxford, 1991).

Moore, Sebastian, *The Crucified Jesus is No Stranger* (New York, 1977).

Morse, Ruth, *Truth and Convention in the Middle Ages: Rhetoric, Representation and Reality* (Cambridge, 1991).

Newman, Barbara, 'Some Medieval Theologians and the Sophia Tradition', *Downside Review*, 108 (1990), pp. 111–30.

Nolan, Edward Peter, *Cry Out and Write: A Feminine* [sic] *Poetics of Revelation* (New York, 1994).

Osborn, James M., *The Beginning of Autobiography in England* (Los Angeles, 1959).

Ozment, Steven, *The Age of Reform 1250–1550: An Intellectual and Religious History of Late Medieval and Renaissance Europe* (New Haven and London, 1980).

Pacey, J. W., *The Mystical Economy* (London, 1995).

Phillips, Helen (ed.), *Langland, the Mystics and the Medieval English Religious Tradition: Essays in Honour of S. S. Hussey* (Cambridge, 1991).

Porter Abbot, H., 'Autobiography, Autography, Fiction: Groundwork for a Taxonomy of Textual Categories', *New Literary History*, 19 (1988), pp. 597–615.

Riddy, Felicity, ' "Women talking about the things of God": a late medieval sub-culture', in ed. Meale, *Women and Literature*, pp. 104–27.

Riehle, Wolfgang, *The Middle English Mystics*, trans. Bernard Standring, reprint (London, 1981).

Ross, Maggie, *Pillars of Flame* (London, 1987).

Rubin, Miri, *Corpus Christi: The Eucharist in Late Medieval Culture* (Cambridge, 1991).

Schmidt, A. V. C., 'Langland and the Mystical Tradition', in *MMTE* (Exeter, 1980).

Sells, Michael, 'The Pseudo-Woman and the Meister: "Unsaying" and Essentialism', in ed. McGinn, *Meister Eckhart*, pp. 114–46.

Smith, Robert, *Derrida and Autobiography* (Cambridge, 1995).

Soskice, Janet Martin, *Metaphor and Religious Language* (Oxford, 1985).

Southern, R. W., *The Making of the Middle Ages*, paperback reprint (London, 1993).

Steiner, George, *Real Presences* (London, 1989).

Stock, Brian, *The Implications of Literacy: Written Language and Models of Interpretation in the Eleventh and Twelfth Centuries* (Princeton, New Jersey, 1983).

Stoddard, Whitney S., *Art and Architecture in Medieval France* (New York, 1966).

Swanson, R. N., *Church and Society in Late Medieval England*, paperback edition (Oxford, 1993).

Tanner, Norman P., *The Church in Late Medieval Norwich 1370–1532* (Toronto, 1984).

Tugwell, Simon, *Ways of Imperfection: An Exploration of Christian Spirituality* (Springfield, Illinois, 1985).

Watson, *Richard Rolle and the Invention of Authority* (Cambridge, 1991).

Williams, Rowan, *The Wound of Knowledge*, second edition (London, 1990).

INDEX